KESTER ASPDEN

The Hounding of David Oluwale

VINTAGE BOOKS
London

Published by Vintage 2008

2 4 6 8 10 9 7 5 3 1

Copyright © Kester Aspden, 2007

Kester Aspden has asserted his right under the Copyright, Designs and Patents Act 1988 to be identified as the author of this work

This book is a work of non-fiction. The author has stated to the publishers that the contents of this book are true.

First published in Great Britain in 2007 by Jonathan Cape

Vintage
Random House, 20 Vauxhall Bridge Road,
London SW1V 2SA

www.vintage-books.co.uk

Addresses for companies within The Random House Group Limited can be found at: www.randomhouse.co.uk/offices.htm

The Random House Group Limited Reg. No. 954009

A CIP catalogue record for this book
is available from the British Library

ISBN 9780099506171

The Random House Group Limited supports The Forest Stewardship Council (FSC), the leading international forest certification organisation. All our titles that are printed on Greenpeace approved FSC certified paper carry the FSC logo. Our paper procurement policy can be found at www.rbooks.co.uk/environment

Typeset in Sabon by Palimpsest Book Production Limited, Grangemouth, Stirlingshire

Printed and bound in Great Britain by
CPI Cox & Wyman, Reading RG1 8EX

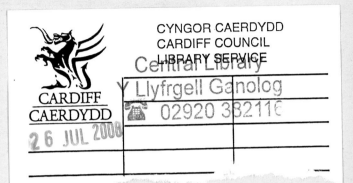

THE HOUNDING OF
DAVID OLUWALE

Kester Aspden was born in Toronto in 1968, and brought up in Todmorden, West Yorkshire, and York. He has a doctorate in history from Cambridge University, and taught history of crime at Leeds University whilst researching this book. He now lives in Istanbul

To Sarah Rainsford

David Oluwale, September 1968

Question 2: Which is the quickest way of reaching England from your town? Which route would you follow? How long would you take?

Questions for the reader, from T. R. Batten,
The British Empire and the Modern World
[Textbook used in Lagos grammar schools in the 1940s]

The Ibuza women who lived in Lagos were preparing for the arrival of the town's first lawyer from the United Kingdom. The title 'United Kingdom' when pronounced by Adah's father sounded so heavy, like the type of noise one associated with bombs. It was so deep, so mysterious, that Adah's father always voiced it in hushed tones, wearing such a respectful expression as if he were speaking of God's Holiest of Holies. Going to the United Kingdom must surely be like paying God a visit. The United Kingdom, then, must be like heaven.

Buchi Emecheta, *Second Class Citizen*

The first and most constant problem with the City of Leeds is to find it. There was never a more faceless city or a more deceptive one. It hasn't a face because it has too many faces, all of them different.

Patrick Nuttgens,
Leeds: The Back to front Inside out Upside down City

'Heard about the Pakistani who wanted converting? So they took him to Leeds rugby ground and kicked him over the goalposts.'

Bernard Manning, *Parkinson*, 1972

CONTENTS

Leeds City Centre – 1968/9

Key

1. Leeds Town Hall
2. Millgarth Police Station
3. Griffin Hotel
4. City Police Headquarters
5. St Anne's Cathedral
6. St George's Church & Crypt
7. Trinity Church
8. Merrion Centre
9. Church Army Hostel
10. Civic Hall
11. The Bridal House
12. John Peters
13. Kirkgate Market
14. King Edward PH
15. St Peter's Church
16. Quarry Hill Flats
17. Pitfall Street
18. Warehouse Hill

INTRODUCTION

Knostrop

Almost the whole of the City can be drained by gravity to the main sewage disposal works at Knostrop.

City of Leeds,
First Review of City Development Programme (1967)

I

Leeds, Sunday 4 May 1969. Nothing could live in this river. You'd hear stories of folk dropping dead from swallowing one accidental mouthful. After heavy rain you'd see foam from all the synthetic detergents rising twenty feet in the air. Fish haven't lived here for over a century, not since the time when the Aire became both reservoir and sewer for the city, since the time when Leeds throbbed with industry and its waterfront teemed with life. Now the waterfront is moribund, and the industries which made this city, and strangled the life out of its river, are either dead or dying.

This river flows north-west to south-east through the city. At one point it disappears under the Dark Arches, a labyrinth of brick vaults built a century ago to provide a platform for the railway station. It flows away from the city, flanked by warehouses, viaducts and tangled towpaths. All to the right of the Aire, so that it seems like a crude class barrier, are foundries, chemical works, textile factories – what remains of them – and swathes of back-to-backs which Leeds Corporation are pulling down with evangelical single-mindedness. Two and a half miles downstream the heavy industry recedes, the landscape becomes bleak and vacant, and the Aire winds by Knostrop.

Between the weir at Knostrop and the Skelton Grange power-station footbridge a few hundred yards downstream, where the river bends abruptly, is the place where they pull him out.

It's a sunny early-afternoon, Leeds pastoral but for the smell from the nearby sewerage works. A group of boys are exploring the fields and tracks around Knostrop, talking about Leeds United and roast dinners. They walk down Black Road, past the old army camp, down to the stretch of banking on the north side. The day is still and nobody is about. They're dragging their way home when they see something strange stuck in the middle of the river. 'We all thought at first it was a sack or a Guy Fawkes but then it rolled over slightly with the current and I realised it was a black man,' Wayne Batley would recall many months later in a statement to detectives. They find a spot where they can scramble down to the edge of the river for a closer look. The man is face down, spreadeagle, head pointing downstream. The body is swollen and straining against the clothing. The boys are fixed to the sight for several minutes.

They see a couple of men over at the rifle range and run over to tell them. The riflemen inform the technician in charge of Knostrop sewerage works, who calls the police. The boys are sent home when the police arrive ten minutes later. After their dinners, though Martin Thorpe couldn't stomach his, the gang rush to a friend's to tell him about the 'nigger in the river'.

A couple of hundred yards further downstream and it would have been West Riding's problem, but since it stuck here it was Gipton's. Two bobbies from Gipton police station, PCs Steve Hall and Albert Sedman, struggle up the bank with the body and lay it on its back on a tarpaulin sheet. It's extremely bloated. They see a face pink and decomposing, skin flaked off in parts, a nasty-looking bruise on the right of the forehead. PC Sedman lights his pipe to disguise the smell.

PC Ian Haste, the frogman who's waded out and freed the body from the debris, thinks it might be David Oluwale. He's one of Leeds's 'characters'. PC Haste moved him on from shop doorways during his time at Millgarth station. But so swollen is his face the frogman can't be certain.

The top man at Gipton, Superintendent Michael Wilson, and Inspector Len Bradley are present when the dead man's pockets are searched. Inside his pockets there are two plastic wallets, mushy and rotten. The items found on his body are:

NHS medical card
two photographs
income tax form
P45
two Leeds City Magistrates' receipts
two aftercare forms
details of Irish Information Centres
11s 10d cash
post office savings book issued by Menston Post Office, balance of 1s
three pens
toothbrush
comb
blue rosary beads
red prayer book inside which are six Leeds City Police charge sheets (known as forms 103)

Inspector Bradley turns the property over to PC Sedman.

Two ambulance men arrive. It is 3.30 p.m. Straight away they see an obvious wound to the man's head. The superintendent and inspector fix on the 103s. Never out of court from the look of it; might well cling to prayer book and rosary beads. The ambulance men speculate whether he took the crack on the head when he came over the weir. Superintendent Wilson records in his duty book that there are no apparent suspicious circumstances. The bobbies return to their station, the frogman gets showered. The power station and sewerage works grind on.

A mortuary van takes the body away to St James's Hospital. The Accident and Emergency Unit Medical Register records that 'Oluwale, David. From Knostrop Sewage Works' was certified dead by Dr Wahba at 4.25 p.m. Then to the mortuary where it is stripped by the assistant, the clothing searched again and bagged.

No record was taken of Oluwale's clothing. Some witnesses would recall a dark denim jacket and jeans, others a boiler suit. Martin Thorpe thought that he had on 'a pair of those yellow boots that builders wear'.

Gipton bobbies arrive at the mortuary. Inspector, sergeant, PC look down at the horrible object on the slab. The bloated genitals attract comment. One of the bobbies says he's jealous of what he's got.

The body's labelled, '451' on the legs, 'Oluwale' on the body, and slotted into the refrigeration unit.

That clutch of 103s says he'll be no great loss to society. Drunk dossers falling into the Aire aren't so rare. PC Sedman prepares a sudden-death report: notes the large lump on the forehead, lips cut, bleeding from right eye, large bruise on right arm. By contrast, when asked to recall the events of 4 May 1969, Superintendent Wilson claimed to have looked closely into the dead man's face and seen no bruise on the forehead, nothing. Wilson would later insist that the marks on Oluwale's face noted in the sudden-death report were consistent with the condition of a man who had been in the water for some time. He would explain that he thought that the pathologist would establish the relevance of the marks, so decided against involving CID.

A message goes out to a detective constable at the Scenes of Crime Department for the body to be photographed. The request lies on the detective's table until it becomes buried under more messages and forgotten.

Monday 5 May: pathologist Dr David Gee conducts the post-mortem. Shortly before he begins, he is told by a bobby that the deceased man had a record of violence, that he'd once bitten a policeman. Herbert Bullock, mortuary superintendent, hears someone say that he had been a violent man, 'a bit of a character'. The body's weighed and measured: ten stone and 5'5". There is a faded tattoo on the left forearm. Gee estimates that the deceased has been in the water for a period of one to two weeks, though it is impossible to be precise. There's moderate putrefaction changes to the body, slight separation of skin on the hand and trunk and some greenish coloration; a small purple-coloured swelling on the right side of the forehead. He carries out a full internal examination: considerable putrefaction change, but no signs of injury. The head is examined and the swelling is found to be a bruise an inch and a half in diameter. Gee believes that this was sustained one or two days before death or a similar period after. The skull is intact; no blood clot or signs of bleeding inside it.

Blood samples are taken to determine alcohol content. The tests will show that Oluwale had consumed the equivalent of half a pint of beer. Samples are taken from the lungs and liver and tests carried out to determine whether any diatoms are present – diatoms being the microscopic plants found in rivers and streams whose presence in the internal organs of a body could help to establish whether a person was alive when he entered the water. For Oluwale, the tests prove inconclusive, but in the absence of any gross injuries or natural disease, Dr Gee forms the opinion that death was due to drowning.

Senior officers at Gipton are satisfied with the outcome. The coroner records a verdict of 'Found drowned' at the inquest held on 14 May 1969. A brief notice in the *Yorkshire Evening Post*.

His death is registered on 3 June. His name is given as 'David Oluwale otherwise known as Alliwala'. Nobody is really sure of his name. His date and place of birth are given as 30.08.30, Lagos. Occupation: tailor, though it's years since he's worked. Usual address: no fixed abode.

The body remains in the mortuary until 4 June when undertakers from W. Roberts on York Road remove it for a 'welfare funeral' at the expense of the city. The 11s 10d found in Oluwale's wallet is put towards the costs. A plate is fixed to the coffin lid: '*David Oluwale Alliwala, 4th May, 1969, Aged 38 years. R.I.P.*' The next morning Oluwale is stacked into a hearse with another welfare case and taken to the Roman Catholic section of Killingbeck cemetery.

A short service is conducted by Fr Martin Carroll from St Anne's Cathedral. A congregation is formed by the cemetery superintendent and undertakers; no family, no friends. The body's committed to the pauper's grave.

It is customary to retain the clothing of the deceased for three months. But since Oluwale's are rotten, full of water bugs and contaminated with filth they are incinerated straight away.

II

It was the book of photographs which drew me in. At first just Leeds street scenes – no people. They must have been taken at first light. The police photographer was interested in two shop doorways: a bridal clothing shop on The Headrow and the wider front of John Peters' furniture shop on Lands Lane. Next came various moody views of Warehouse Hill, a stretch of open ground on the north bank of the River Aire close to Leeds Bridge. Then out-of-town scenes: woodland; a country pub called the Fox & Hounds; shots of the River Aire at Knostrop.

The next group of photographs came from a cemetery. They were of an exhumation carried out on a December morning in 1970. They showed the exposed coffin, remains laid out on the slab looked over by a pathologist, shots of the skull, a close-up of teeth. I think it was those morbid moments which pulled me into the story. What was the connection between a bridal outfitters and an exhumation?

I came across the story of David Oluwale by chance. I was in the National Archives at Kew researching some arid piece of higher-education history for my day job. It was late in the afternoon, my spirits were lagging, and I was looking for a distraction. I'd toyed with the idea of writing something on the nightlife and criminal underworld of 1920s Soho and so I began searching the archive catalogue for source material. It was when trawling through the Metropolitan Police entries that I came across references to something entirely unexpected – the David Oluwale case files. I'd heard the name. It was a Leeds case, the city where I worked, the city I'd grown tired of. But until then I knew only vague details of a black tramp found dead in a canal or river.

The files had recently been released under the thirty-year rule. I was intrigued and the next day began the trawl through several boxes of police statements and legal opinion and learned about the Nigerian who had stowed away to England in 1949. Over half of David Oluwale's troubled life here was spent in mental asylums and prisons. Towards the end he was reduced to sleeping in shop doorways. His mental and physical condition had deteriorated and he was picking up convictions, mostly for disorderly conduct. In October 1970, nearly eighteen months after he was found drowned in the Aire, a police cadet set off the criminal investigation into his death.

I tracked down everything that had been written about the case. There was an article by Ron Phillips in the journal *Race Today*, and a poem in Linton Kwesi Johnson's landmark *Dread, Beat and Blood* collection (1975); Oluwale also inspired music and art. The basic details of the case have appeared in a number of books and articles on the subject of racism. The most substantial thing written was a radio play by Jeremy Sandford, *Oluwale*, aired at the end of 1972 and published as *Smiling David* (1974). The author of the famous BBC TV dramas *Cathy Come Home* (1966) and *Edna, the Inebriate Woman* (1971), Sandford, an Old Etonian, was a brilliant teller of the stories of society's marginal figures – Gypsies, prostitutes and down-and-outs; he had less success when he tried to get the citizens of Leeds to open up to him about David Oluwale. It was still too raw, he concluded. Whereas *Cathy Come Home* was a sensation, forcing the issue of homelessness into public consciousness and effecting social change, his *Oluwale* barely caused a ripple.

Subsequent delving into the archive told me that there was much about Oluwale's troubled life and much about his treatment on the streets which never surfaced at the time. I also saw that the story, though emblematic – and regarded as a defining moment in urban racism – only occupies a small place in history. Whereas the name Stephen Lawrence is seared into the public memory, the Oluwale case has been largely forgotten outside the city of Leeds and the ranks of those tuned in to the history of English racism. I thought it was time to retell the story of David Oluwale to those who have never before heard his name.

Oluwale was an intangible subject. Those who dealt with him in an official capacity knew and cared little about him; he was a problem to be sorted as they saw fit. He appeared to the world mainly through the lens of public authorities: as prisoner, patient or welfare claimant, rarely as someone with feelings or human needs beyond the most basic. Because of this void he has proved a serviceable vessel into which people have poured their anxieties, fears, prejudices, ideals. To some he became an icon, to others he was worthless.

On the one hand, Sandford's play portrayed a popular young man from a pious Catholic background, an innocent who came to the 'mother country' with hopes of being an engineer; a gentle soul who buried himself in the better sort of newspapers during tea breaks at the brickworks where he worked; the student manqué who simply wanted to contribute to society.

But, on the other hand, to those who encountered him in Leeds city centre at the fag end of the 1960s he was at best a pitiful, probably mentally deficient nuisance, unwilling and unable to receive help. To most he was the local idiot who lived in a dream; obnoxious and dirty, snot all down the front of his coat; a deranged excitable nigger; the mucky-faced monkey who'd squeal and run around the city and frighten the shoppers; someone who'd spring up like a wild animal and bite your hand for no reason, who'd drop his trousers and shit all the way down shop windows, who'd piss through the letter box of Brill's on Bond Street; someone with sunken eyes, deep anthropoid features with the dirtiest set of yellow teeth you'd ever seen. Someone with no civilisation, who looked like he might be found up a tree, pouncing on missionaries. Someone who was wholly lacking in positive qualities.

This book isn't an attempt to get to the 'real' David Oluwale behind the rival narratives. Nor is it a probing of Oluwale's inner life or his personality. I don't pretend to identify with him. It's not looking to 'make a difference'. It's an attempt to get to the truth of what happened to one unimportant man on the streets of Leeds, and to understand the crimes against him. It's about the city which Oluwale came to with hopes of a better life, the city in which he died.

My story of David Oluwale has a public context – I believe that it says something about Britain, then and now. This book is a social and political history of these crimes. Oluwale came to this country from Lagos, whose inhabitants had been British subjects ever since it was designated a Crown Colony in 1861 (Lagos Colony was administratively joined to the Protectorate of Southern Nigeria in 1886; the Protectorate of Southern Nigeria was amalgamated with the Northern Protectorate in 1914 to form the Colony and Protectorate of Nigeria under Governor General Lord Lugard). He came at a time when the United Kingdom maintained an open entry immigration policy towards its colonial subjects; they could enter the country without restriction, and as citizens they had the same civil rights, in theory, as an indigenous Briton. This status was entrenched in the British Nationality Act 1948. By this Act, citizenship was granted to millions of British subjects across the world (around 600 million according to Randall Hansen, a leading authority). David Oluwale came to this country, then, as a British subject and citizen, at the start of what can fairly be described as a laissez-faire period in immigration policy. Yet during the course of his twenty years in Britain, these liberal assumptions were reversed by politicians increasingly attuned and responsive to public hostility to mass black immigration. The last months of Oluwale's beleaguered life were played out against a hardening political backdrop. I thought that the study of an individual life might serve as a mirror to public history, illuminating Britain's belligerent adaptation to the reality that black people were part of the national story.

Oluwale's death throws a harsh light on British society as it came out of the 'Swinging Sixties'. Conventionally, that decade is portrayed as a time of immense liberation, as if the windows of some stuffy Victorian parlour had suddenly been thrown open. This revised history shows the back end of that decade as a more unsympathetic time and a harder place: student radicals and flower-wielding hippies giving way to Enoch Powell and his 'Rivers of Blood'; the Paki-bashing craze and Selsdon Man; clergymen urging the return of birch and noose and Mary Whitehouse turning back the tide of immoral filth – expressions of a waning faith in the post-war 'New Jerusalem'. This is the setting for the death of David Oluwale.

The book is my personal take on the case, another story, though one which is grounded in real happenings. It draws on the archival traces that have been left; not just the documentary traces but the living archive of popular memory, the recollections of those who were close to the case.

Part One tries to give a sense of the contours of David Oluwale's life, so as to understand why he ended up on those streets as an isolated individual. For the early years, I draw on the stories of other Africans who came to Leeds at the same time and who knew the young man they called 'Olu', but who would lose touch with him as he progressed through prisons and mental hospitals. This leads on to the key questions which are dealt with explicitly in Part Two, when Leeds City Police is put under the spotlight. Why did Oluwale come to be seen as dirt which needed removing from the streets? Why was he on the receiving end of such violence? Why wasn't it stopped? How did he come to end up in the River Aire? Who was responsible?

This book doesn't promise a tidy outcome. David Oluwale will continue to haunt and trouble and pose awkward questions. He will keep on returning.

One of Oluwale's old Nigerian friends told detectives investigating his death that no matter where he roamed he would always return to Leeds. In fact, Oluwale did very little roaming. Even though the nature of his life was inherently unsettled, even though he slept out in shop doorways, even though by the end of his life he talked of returning to Nigeria, this city was his home. Though he was looked on as an alien presence, he was a citizen of Leeds. And it was his very rootedness in the city which brought him so much grief.

This is, then, a Leeds story as well as a national story, though Leeds might be viewed as Britain in microcosm. Trying to make sense of Oluwale's death became tied up with trying to make sense of a city I thought I knew, but didn't.

Leeds, a Yorkshire city. There was, still is, a strength of county pride in this large chunk of northern England. Yorkshire people make by far and away the best locals, its renowned chauvinism taking extraordinary forms. 'When the Queen takes the salute tomorrow at the ceremony of the Trooping of the Colour,' the *Yorkshire Evening Post* once proudly noted, 'she will be riding a police horse born in Yorkshire.' Within that overarching Yorkshire chauvinism, a hundred little chauvinisms. Bradford, an industrial city just ten miles to the west of Leeds, completely different: different accent, a more radical political tradition (the cradle of the Independent Labour Party), different industry, and no way inferior to its larger neighbour – its massive St George's Hall was the reason why mid-Victorian Leeds had felt the need to go even bigger with its own town hall. Five miles from Leeds is Morley, a fiercely independent small town with its own magisterial town hall – modelled on Leeds's – to prove it. And it has been said that the city of Leeds itself is really no more than a collection of villages, each with its distinctive histories and traditions and chauvinisms. For instance, Hunslet, south of the Aire, had been a separate township until its absorption into Leeds, but its strong and enduring sense of independence was symbolised by its famous rugby league team and whenever Leeds RL club made the short journey to Parkside it was a guaranteed dog fight. Localism and civic pride were very intense when Oluwale came to Leeds in the immediate post-war years.

As its traditional industries collapsed in the 1970s and early 80s, Leeds became associated in the public mind with the darker, more primitive side of life – the Yorkshire Ripper (initially he was the 'Leeds Ripper'), goths, the Leeds United Service Crew. But the city's image began to improve in the 1990s, so much so that Leeds came to epitomise the so-called 'Urban Renaissance'. It now fancies itself über fashionable – 'the Knightsbridge of the North' according to a *Lonely Planet* guide. When a Harvey Nichols store opened in the city in 1996 – 'the first outside London' – it was an emblem of the booming economy which had developed during the 1990s, when Leeds became the most prosperous legal and financial centre outside the capital, and when its cutting-edge nightlife acted as a magnet for a burgeoning young professional and student population. Rough-and-ready pubs made way for branded corporate bars and the new vision of a 'twenty-four-hour' cosmopolitan, Continental café culture. Leeds aspired to a prominent place in the European urban hierarchy. Tetley Bitterman, RIP.

Oluwale belonged to a Leeds of filthy rivers, back-to-backs and pea-souper fogs. So much of his Leeds has gone. His first lodgings went during the slum-clearance programmes of the 1960s and 70s, a time when Leeds was first attempting to reverse the image of a declining industrial city. His last proper address, a Church Army hostel for the homeless close to the River Aire, now houses IT and design consultancies. Another waterfront symbol of social failure, the Dark Arches, was transformed in the late 1980s into Granary Wharf, with cafés and craft shops. The waterfront is no longer the dark and neglected haunt of the homeless and hopeless. Flour mills have become hotels, warehouses have become restaurants, bars and apartments for the recent influx of high-spending young keen to live near to the buzzing centre of one of Britain's economic success stories. Warehouse Hill, the point at which Oluwale is said to have entered the river, has evaded regeneration, but even this melancholy heart of the old port of Leeds has been sold off to developers. It is now fenced off and in a limbo state.

In the time of Oluwale, the three-mile city-centre stretch of the Aire was badly polluted. Occasionally there would be some excited announcement in the local press from the Pollution Prevention Officer that a fish had been sighted, and then a sad report a couple of days later saying that it had washed up dead. Now trout and salmon and even otter have returned.

In 2005 a campaign was launched to remember Oluwale with a plaque. As far as I could tell, the early signs from mainstream Leeds did not suggest any great desire to revisit and memorialise one of the city's shameful episodes. Leeds wants uplifting, historically solid stories of great achievement and civic virtue. 'The last thing I think is appropriate is to start putting little blue plaques on walls saying "Oluwale shat in this doorway",' one eminent lawyer remarked to me. Oluwale is 'the past', a distant memory which has nothing to do with the corporate city of conspicuous consumption. 'As far as we're concerned it's gone and buried,' one retired Leeds City Police officer commented to me. 'It were just an episode that happened thirty years ago.'

The amnesia is understandable. After all, what happened to Oluwale isn't the sort of story a progressive city wants to tell about itself. In the new Leeds there's a high investment in the narrative of the prosperous city and with that an indifference to and intolerance of that which offends the glossy facade. There seems to be no place in the new Leeds for those who disturb the rhythms of the consumer-orientated society. Street homeless and beggars who 'exploit the compassion of the people of Leeds' are pushed out of public sight these days by the issuing of ASBOs, curfews and dispersal orders, rather than by the administering of a copper's boot to the backside as in Oluwale's day; even the skaters and goths are being evicted. Shopping in this consumer city is increasingly geared away from the poor. It's not surprising that Leeds has no interest in histories of failure.

Yet failure is all around the edges. Some of the most crime-ridden and deprived council wards in the country are within a mile or two of Harvey Nichols. And though it prides itself on being a vibrant multicultural city, it was young Muslim men from Beeston, south Leeds, not illegal immigrants or asylum seekers but men born here, who, on the morning of 7 July 2005, strapped bombs to themselves and murdered their fellow British citizens on London Tubes and buses.

The City Council was mortified, desperate as it was for Leeds to be associated with stylish European cities like Bilbao, Barcelona and Milan, not benighted northern places like Oldham, Burnley, Bradford. After the bombings I didn't want to hear any more about 'the UK's Favourite City', 'the Barcelona of the North', 'the UK's Sexiest City', 'the Twenty-Four-Hour City', 'the Shopping Capital of the North', 'the Leeds Initiative' and the 'Vision for Leeds'. I wanted narratives of shame and social failure. It's in that spirit that I offer the story of David Oluwale. I want to show that he isn't 'past', a distant piece of social history, but is still very much part of us, part of Leeds.

To dig into Leeds's history is to become aware that the proud and shameful have always been mixed up together. In the nineteenth century, when it developed into a major industrial town (Leeds was granted city status in 1893), civic pride and business energy went together with civic shame and terrible poverty. While industrialists and businessmen sang hymns to progress, the inhabitants of the crowded streets of central Leeds gagged 'in a midden atmosphere'. Charles Dickens sensed this mixing of pride and shame when he declared that Leeds was both a 'great town' but also the 'beastliest place, one of the nastiest I know'. Did he catch a sight of the River Aire, described in 1843 as that 'reservoir of poison, carefully kept for the purpose of breeding a pestilence in the town', into which was discharged the drainage and contents of about two hundred water closets, cesspools and privies, spent blue and black dye, pig manure, old urine wash and drainings from the infirmary (dead leeches, poultices for patients)? It took the publication of Leeds's medical officer Robert Baker's evidence in the 1842 Blue Book on municipal sanitation to shame the town into action on clean water, a process which culminated in the building of Leeds's first sewage purification works at Knostrop. It seems grimly fitting that this late twentieth-century story of civic shame should have ended at the River Aire at Knostrop.

PART ONE

THE PARTRIDGE-LIKE PERSON

Eniyan bi apãrò ni aiye fe (The world loves a partridge-like person)

Yoruba proverb

To say that somebody is like a patridge means that the person is dirty, poor and incapable of looking after themselves ... The comparison with the partridge is based on its speckled body and the fact that its feathers often appear dirty.

This gloomy maxim assumes that, due to both the malicious nature of men ... and the competitive nature of the world, people cannot but dislike whoever appears to be rising or devoid of distress. On the other hand, the sight of a miserable person will make people feel luckier and give them the chance to portray themselves as charitable.

A. A. Kila, *Òwe Yoruba in Proverbs*

1

'United Kingdom 1949'

I

Lagos, Tuesday 16 August 1949. It was a day to put aside the country's troubles – strikes and rumours of strikes.

Apapa Wharf was heaving with beaming dignitaries and well-wishers who'd come over from Lagos Island on the ferry boat they called *Kathleen*. Shouts of 'Good luck, Nigeria' aimed at the young heroes about to board the Elder Dempster liner *M. V. Apapa* for the two-week sail to Liverpool. A great day for Nigerian sport: the first time its national football team, the first time a black African team, had toured overseas. And where better to make an impact, where better to demonstrate what that day's Lagos *Daily Times* described as 'the traditionally cheerful spirit of the African in victory and defeat', than in the very heart of the British Empire.

Eighteen of the finest products of Nigeria's best schools, green blazers, badges with 'United Kingdom 1949' woven below them, grey flannels, were looking like they shouldn't be travelling, as they were, on third-class tickets. Professional men, skilled men in their daily lives – teachers, clerks, electricians – now 'Golden Boy', 'Thunderbolt', 'Black Magnet'. Just like those comic-book legends of empire.

They were not just footballers but polished young gentlemen, hand-picked by the white colonial administrators who ran the sport to demonstrate the civilising effects of the imperial project. They were the kind of men who could be relied upon not to drop a clanger at a Football Association or Colonial Office tea party.

They called the *M. V. Apapa* the 'scholars' ship', but on this occasion the cream of Lagos's schools, the future doctors and lawyers, were overshadowed by the men in the green blazers. Giving his blessing, Bishop Vining of Lagos was pumped full of pride as the ship swung out of the marina into the lagoon: 'Fare ye well on the voyage . . . Fare ye well in a strange land . . . Fare ye well on the field. Boots or no boots.'

It was a good day for stowaways to try their luck. They always had a chance at Apapa Wharf. Port security was notoriously lax and though the Colonial Office urged ship managers to be extra vigilant, the stowaways were slipping into Britain at an alarming rate. On a day full of distractions like this one, the odds were even better.

First, the stowaway would tap up someone in a position of trust on the wharves and docks. A tally clerk responsible for labouring jobs was a good target. The stowaway would slip him a few pounds to secure a job on board a ship, and with no central tally of dock workers nobody would know if he went missing at the end of a day's work. He would still need to enlist the help of crew members, and it might take £5 to persuade stevedores to conceal him among the cargo. Searches on ships were usually superficial, and even if the stowaway was discovered the maximum £5 fine handed out by the courts was no deterrent.

A stowaway needed paperwork at the other end if he didn't want to find himself on the first ship home. Most stowaways from the West African colonies came armed with a British Travel Certificate. This document was really intended only for travel between British and French colonies in West Africa, but as it included a statement of nationality it was being used by stowaways at British ports to demonstrate their status as British citizens. Since the British Nationality Act 1948, British subjects from the West African colonies, no matter how they arrived, were entitled to the same rights and privileges accorded to any other British citizen. Providing that this certificate appeared genuine there was nothing an immigration officer could do but allow the stowaway to land. The stowaway would receive a short prison sentence for an offence under the Merchant Shipping Act but would then be free to go on his way. In the Colonial Office it was noted that twenty-eight-day prison sentences were a 'small price to pay when compared with the cost of the fare which they have avoided'.

David Oluwale was hanging round the wharf as the footballers waved at well-wishers. He'd decided to take his chances on the *Temple Bar*, which was bound for Hull with a cargo of groundnuts, one of Nigeria's main exports. Six stowaways were turned off the ship before it set sail. Oluwale was one of the lucky three who evaded detection.

Shipping companies like Lambert Brothers who owned the *Temple Bar* had been warned by the Colonial Office to be more alert to the stowaway problem. The captain was taking no chances: the day after the ship set out from Lagos, he suspected that there were still stowaways on board and ordered that smoke be pumped into the hold to drive them out. Two of the unwelcome guests – Victor Lapido Oyewole and Johnny Omaghomi – came spluttering out. Oluwale, the youngest of them at nineteen, survived the fumes but crawled out from the boxes the next day. The three were put to work for the remainder of the voyage. They disembarked at Hull, on the north-east coast of England, on Saturday 3 September 1949, where they were delivered into police custody.

Any illusions about a warm embrace from the mother country were dispelled with one withering look from the chair of the magistrates. Bedraggled and bewildered, the three Nigerians appeared in front of J. H. Tarbitten at Hull Police Court almost as soon as they'd landed. The contrast in the respective sizes of the men must have struck Tarbitten: Omaghomi at over six feet tall; Oyewole in the middle at five nine; David Oluwale then barely five four. Tarbitten was unsympathetic: he believed that England was a soft touch for stowaways; he demanded explanations from the prisoners, though he was powerless to send them back home. Oyewole told him that he thought the government would find them work. Omaghomi said that he hoped to depend on the government when he reached England, to which Tarbitten barked, 'Is there anyone on yonder side who suggests you come to this country?' 'No,' said Omaghomi. Oluwale's words, if he spoke at all, are not recorded. Would have been better off staying at home digging up groundnuts, Tarbitten said, before giving them each twenty-eight days.

The three stowaways were not in Hull long enough to be tainted by the smell from its many fish processing plants, especially obnoxious on sweltering days like this one. Instead, they were moved on to Leeds, about sixty miles west, to Armley prison, a forbidding mid-Victorian building in an industrial part of the city. Oluwale would become very familiar with the place during the course of his life.

As the stowaways served their time, the Nigerian footballers delighted English spectators. The press had wondered whether conditions in England would suit their barefoot playing style. 'Eighteen pairs of eyes are anxiously scanning the grey clouds suspended over Liverpool,' the Lagos *Daily Times* reported. But the summer of 1949 was the hottest in England since records began and the boots remained off.

The month-long tour saw them pitted against some of Britain's leading amateur clubs. A large crowd turned up to the first game against Marine, numbers boosted by many from Liverpool's and Manchester's sizeable Nigerian communities. Marine took a quick lead but it was wiped out within minutes. The power that 'Baby' Anieke packed into his shots astonished the spectators. Shouts of 'Take your boots off' were directed at the bemused Marine players. When the final whistle blew children swarmed the pitch and carried the victors off on their shoulders, touching their skin and pulling on their hair.

'The wizards in bare feet' drew curious crowds wherever they played. Their comportment off the field was also winning them admirers: the technical inquisitiveness they showed on their visits to a Blackburn weaving mill and a Bury printing works; the gentlemanly manner in which the team captain Henshaw, a strapping six-footer, presented that bouquet of flowers to the mayoress before kick-off at Leytonstone. At a civic reception at Leytonstone Town Hall on 8 September, a minister from the Colonial Office commented on the huge interest in the bare feet and the kindness of local Nigerian ladies who ensured the young men got appetising home cooking. 'I am told their only complaint is that the English weather is too hot,' he remarked, to much laughter.

The British press followed their progress. Edgar Kail of the *Daily Graphic* reported on the Leytonstone game and was full of praise for the 'eleven curly-haired chunks of ebony'. But the results started to go against them. The Isthmian League hammered them 5–1: the experts' verdict was that though the Africans had speed and skill, they flagged in the latter stages of games and tactically they were as children. Against the Athenian League the good weather finally broke, the Nigerians couldn't stay on their feet on the skiddy surface, and centre half Anyiam's habit of venturing upfield to make a sixth forward gave the opposing attackers just too much room. They were thrashed 8–0. The Lagos *Daily Times* issued a sharp reprimand to those who were suggesting that the team captain had brought bad juju on the team. Just when it was getting embarrassing they had their best result, dominating Amateur Cup holders Bromley, which stopped the talk of juju.

The final match before their return to Lagos was against South Liverpool. It was the first floodlit match ever played at the ground. A cartoon in the local press was accompanied by the caption: 'Floodlight was necessary because it's always difficult to find a black man in the dark.' At the end of the match children spilled on to the pitch and formed a guard of honour for goalkeeper 'Black Magnet'. The Nigerian tourists, it was observed, had a special bond with children.

The tour was acclaimed a success. Sports writer 'Pangloss' praised the sporting way the Nigerians had received referees' decisions, and the gentlemanly way they fetched the ball for their opponents whenever they conceded a corner. 'Hibernicus' said that the tour gave the lie to the idea held by many of the British public that 'the

Africans are just woolly-headed nebulous sort of people'. *The Times* opined that the disappearance of tribal warfare and 'other inconvenient forms of self-expression has left a gap there. Too often, while exempt from terror and famine, the African peoples are nowadays powerfully afflicted with boredom. They need new interests, cultural and sporting. Given a chance the African is a voracious reader and an avid sportsman. The Nigerian visit has a sociological significance.' If the example of 'Golden Boy', 'Thunder', 'Rock of Gibraltar' were followed by other young Africans, then Nigerians might indeed be ready for self-government.

The team's fortunes had been followed keenly back home. Results and match reports appeared in the Lagos press alongside notices of honours degrees achieved by her brightest sons in the mother country's universities, and alongside the terse report that three of her shameful sons had been smoked out of the hold of the *Temple Bar*.

While Oluwale served his twenty-eight-day sentence in Armley, in another part of Leeds, another young Nigerian, Gabriel Adams – 'Gayb' to his friends – was making a living driving a mobile crane at the railway goods depot on Wellington Street. Gayb's workmates wanted to know whether he would be going to watch his countrymen and asked him how they managed to play in bare feet. Gayb told them that's how they played back home: if you gave them boots, he said, they'd break your legs.

Gayb had been in Leeds six months or so. Life was getting a little easier. It had never been a problem to find work in the city: no questions asked, no references or certificates, no bribes to pay as in Lagos, though he only lasted three days at his first job on a building site at Moor Grange (his hands froze). How different Leeds seemed in that long hot summer of 1949.

It still pained Gayb when he thought of his mother. On the morning of 18 March 1948, when he left Lagos, she'd walked him up their avenue. As he moved off she called after him, 'Turn round and look at me because this is the last time you will see me. Remember me this way.' He never did see his mother again.

Gayb was one of that small number of young men who left Nigeria in the late 1940s and settled in Leeds. He's one of the few remaining links to David Oluwale. Gayb, like Oluwale, belonged to the Yoruba tribe, one of the largest ethnic groups in Nigeria; the great majority of Lagos's inhabitants are Yoruba. Gayb and Oluwale were Christian and had both been educated by the missions which had established themselves in south-west Nigeria in the mid-nineteenth century. Oluwale, it appears, received more of an education, which meant that his family were probably better off, but after their respective schooling both struggled to make a living. And so they made the same long hard journey. Gayb's story helped me to understand something about the society which he and other young Lagosians like David Oluwale felt impelled to leave in the late 1940s, and something of the adventure of stowing away and making a fresh start in a strange new country, in a northern industrial city.

Gayb was born Bababunmi Oluwole Hanidu (his childhood friends called him 'Bumi') in Ijora, Lagos, on 3 November 1929. His mother, Marian, came from the ancient town of Abeokuta, about sixty miles north of Lagos. Abeokuta was the first Yoruba town to receive Christian missionaries, but it was a multi-faith society in which Christianity coexisted peacefully with Islam and traditional Yoruba beliefs. Marian was a devout Christian.

Gayb's father was a carpenter, making furniture and floors for European houses. Like most Lagosians he was a passionate believer in education, and up until the age of eleven Gayb attended Ijora Baptist School where he learned his English through Bible stories. There were British flags everywhere and on Empire Day, 24 May, songs were sung in praise of Queen Victoria for setting slaves free.

Gayb was taught very little about England, but he knew that the King of England was his king. In Lagos, as in London, 'God Save the King' was played at the beginning and end of any show at the picture house. Newsreels began with the striking of Big Ben, and Big Ben seemed to Gayb like the centre of the world. Big Ben and dark mysterious forests – that was his image of England.

Gayb remembers his father sitting on the veranda passing on

news from the mother country to his neighbours. 'Better the devil you know than the devil you don't,' he'd say whenever one of them slighted the British. He never showed any bitterness towards white men, quite the opposite in fact: Europeans were always in and out of their house; the family's pet dog was a gift from his boss, Mr Douglas.

One morning Gayb's father set off for the tax office and didn't return. He was found three days later up to his neck in quicksand. He'd suffered a severe stroke and was left paralysed, unable to recognise his wife and children. He lived in this state for some years and died when Gayb was eleven. After his death his brothers laid claim to his land and property and sold it off. Gayb's mother was left to bring up her son the best she could. Gayb's education, so important to his father, was cut short through lack of money for school fees. They upped sticks, crossing the Carter Bridge to live at Oke Suna on Lagos Island, close to the famous Sandgrouse Market, with Gayb's sister, Molara, and her husband.

Women had to be strong in Lagos; the great majority worked, mainly on the many bustling markets in this city of traders. Gayb's mother was very much in the mould – a robust, independent woman. She made a living taking in washing from the RAF camp at Obalende, getting up at 3 a.m. to start, so that it would be dry by 9 a.m. Gayb helped with the folding and ironing.

The early 1940s were a time of great hardship in Lagos. Food prices rocketed during the war years and there were severe shortages of common foodstuffs like *gari* (a grain from the cassava plant). In response to the food crisis, a price control scheme on selected foodstuffs was implemented – the hated 'Pullen scheme'. The government bought foodstuffs directly from the producer and distributed these to traders who had to sell them at fixed, low prices. The scheme angered Lagos market traders whose livelihood was threatened, and it did little to relieve the food shortage since many farmers diverted their produce to the more profitable black market. Gayb remembers his mother queuing overnight in the long lines which formed behind the barbed wire for supplies from one of these 'Pullen markets', and on one occasion being arrested by whip-wielding officials following the chaos which always accompanied its opening. The administration blamed the breakdown of order at the Pullen markets on African women, suggesting that they might try to behave with the sort of dignity and restraint which British ladies displayed on their ration lines.

For all that food was scarce, his mother never left him without. Like all good Yoruba boys, Gayb idealised his mother. She knew her Bible inside out, and the two of them used to kneel down and pray together at bedtime. He remembers particularly the time she walked all the way to Broad Street, about seven miles there and back, to buy him a pair of white 'Runner can' shoes which were popular at the time. She had saved the 12s 6d for them; she knew how much they meant to Gayb.

Growing up in the war years, youngsters not much older than Gayb went to fight for the mother country and never came back. Troop ships would come every Wednesday to take African Rifles to Burma. Gayb's home was close to the American cemetery: he remembers long trucks delivering dead American servicemen. He remembers running on Lagos racecourse near the tent where Italian POWs were held. On one occasion he saw a prisoner put his hand into his mouth and pull out his teeth, and since Gayb had never seen or heard of false teeth before, he ran and kept on running.

Gayb went out to work as soon as his schooling finished. He found a succession of jobs at the Ikoyi Club, a favourite spot for the European elite. He started out as a tennis ball boy, then, when he was fourteen or fifteen, he became a golf caddy. Each caddy was assigned a number; if Gayb did a good job for a European he might hear them say to the manager, 'I'm coming back on this date, will number 9 be there?' He was paid by the hole: nine holes, nine pence; twelve holes, a shilling; eighteen holes and he might even get half a crown. He caddied for important people like Governor Sir Arthur Richards and his wife. Sometimes they'd pick him up from his mother's to take him to the Ikoyi – of course they never got out of the car, just called out 'Boy'. Lady Richards took a shine to Gayb and tried to help him out. He told her he wanted to be an apprentice motor mechanic; she gave him a letter in an official envelope which he took to the Ministry of Labour, but when he got there the man wanted a massive fee just to deliver it. He couldn't tell Lady Richards in case it was mistaken for begging.

Some of the Europeans were good to Gayb, paying him a little over the odds. One of the regulars at the club, Mr Butterfly, also knew of the boy's ambitions to become a motor mechanic and tried to get him set on at J. Allen & Co. on Broad Street. They couldn't offer him an apprenticeship, but took him on as a messenger boy at £1 15s a month. He ran around collecting groceries and sending cables for the Europeans.

There were few prospects for a boy without much education in Lagos. Bribes were paid to secure even the lowest kinds of jobs. With little hope of an apprenticeship, Gayb took casual work at Apapa Wharf. The contractor, Mr Cole, set him on, taking £1 off his £4 10s wages every month for the favour. Gayb had a variety of jobs: painting; driving the winch; cleaning the scale off the ships with a wire brush in one hand and a hammer in the other.

His friends had often talked of stowing away. One of his fellow caddies from the golf course, Lucky Ackindere, passed on fantastic stories about England from his father – the money you could make, the girls. Another of his caddy friends, Johnny Omaghomi, resolved to make it to England. The first friend to leave the swampy city was Steve Oke, followed by Alfred Young. Since there was nothing for Gayb in Lagos and he didn't want to become a strain on his mother he decided to follow them. His mother didn't try to stop him: if he could make good in another country then he had her blessing.

The first time he attempted to leave he failed. He was only a few miles out of Lagos when he was discovered in the ship's hold. A pilot boat was sent to take him back to shore. But on the second occasion, 18 March 1948, he was successful.

The SS *Duke of Sparta* was bound for Liverpool with a cargo of groundnuts. There were six of them, including his best friend Johnny Otse, known as Slim. Since they were working on the ships it was not so difficult. They hid themselves in a hatch, lying on top of bags of groundnuts, still and silent. A search of the ship missed them. They had torches but they didn't dare flash them around. They made sure they had enough water for the journey; their food consisted of bags of *gari*, which they mixed with the water to form a dough-like substance. Their makeshift toilet was at the opposite end of the hold, and they'd crawl across the bags to get there.

'SIX STOWAWAYS POPPED OUT OF HATCH' was the headline in the *Liverpool Echo*. 'When a Liverpool bound ship was delayed by bad weather the crew had to go on short rations to feed six West African stowaways, discovered when the vessel was fifteen days out from Lagos.' They'd run out of *gari* after twelve days and had gone hungry for three. That's when they decided to come out.

Sailors threatened that they were going to throw them overboard. The stowaways couldn't tell whether they were joking or not, but they'd heard such stories. Thinking quickly, one of them said that Dr Nnamdi Azikiwe knew they were on the ship. 'Zik' was an important man in Nigeria;* they remained on board and were set to work. Gayb was made to scrub the funnel of the ship but he wasn't wearing gloves and the caustic soda blistered his hands.

It was nothing like the arrival of the *Empire Windrush* a few months later, which gave us those iconic images of smiling, smartly dressed Jamaican men and women filing down the gangplank. But they'd made it, this determined, ragged bunch of young men. In his blistered hand, Gayb clutched the certificate which said he was a British subject. They couldn't send him back.

Liverpool, 23 April 1948. Gayb trudged the streets of the war-battered city and gazed up at those magnificent civic edifices built on slave-trade wealth. He knew that he'd find Africans in Liverpool, but he was surprised at just how many there were. For the first time in his life he saw white men swinging pickaxes and carrying heavy sacks. It made him wonder what was in store for a black man.

Most West African stowaways stayed in Liverpool in the hope

* Azikiwe became Governor General of independent Nigeria in October 1960; in 1963 he became its first president.

of finding work on the docks. But the employment situation was poor in 1948. West African seamen and dock workers were blamed for taking white men's jobs (in August of that year tensions blew up into full-scale mob violence). The last thing Liverpool wanted was a further influx of stowaways hanging around on street corners, living off National Assistance.

Waiting to register at Colsea House (or 'Cosie House', as these digs for seamen run by the Elder Dempster shipping firm were known) on Upper Stanhope Street, Gayb and his friend from Lagos, Johnny Slim, were so hungry they saw off three large loaves of bread. When it came to his turn, Gayb told Mr Thompson that he wanted to be a motor mechanic; Mr Thompson, the warden, who worked on the docks in the daytime, said he wouldn't get a job in Liverpool if he lived to be a hundred. Try Birmingham, Coventry, Leeds, Bradford – anywhere but Liverpool.

Gayb and Slim stayed in Liverpool for several months and Mr Thompson was right – they never did find work. They walked the streets, watched the occasional film at the Rialto, went to George Wilkie's dance hall and the African church in Hill Street, Liverpool 8. The highlight of the week were the Friday-night dances at Cosie House where they met local girls.

They tried other cities. Work was plentiful in Birmingham and Sheffield but it was even harder to find digs. They always ended up back in Liverpool, though there was nothing for them but good company. One day they went to the bus station and saw a bus with 'LEEDS' on it. So they jumped aboard.

Muck. Long into the twentieth century, even as the heavy industry declined, even as clean air legislation began to work its influence, the filth is what struck newcomers to Leeds. 'Mucky Leeds' they called it. In 1949, the medical officer for the city would cite statistics of the tons of soot and grit falling annually on each square mile, and calculated that there was enough to form a huge block even taller than the town hall.

Muck and mile after mile of decaying back-to-backs. As many as 90,000 of Leeds's 154,000 houses were classed as slums. There were chimneys as far as the eye could see. Leeds: the once vigorous youth now a decrepit great-uncle with bronchial problems.

Yet this choked city retained a sense of grandeur. It had escaped the heavy bombing which other northern cities experienced, and post-war Leeds, in Pevsner's estimation, showed 'the blessings of civic pride and a certain orderliness'. Its Victorian town hall was 'one of the most convincing buildings of its date in the country'. Its 1930s civic hall, a white Portland-stone building striking against the surrounding black, was a rejoinder to those who dismissed Leeds as just 'a nasty dirty old money box'. Alan Bennett has written evocatively of the 'powerful sense of the city' he felt in the post-war years, 'a sense of belonging ... that can't have been unlike the feelings of someone growing up in a fifteenth-century Italian city-state'. Everywhere, Bennett recalled, 'one was confronted with the owls and the lamb in the sling and the motto "*Pro Rege et Lege*". One could not escape those [city] arms. They were on my schoolbooks and they were at the tram stop; they were on the market; they were over the entrance to the Central Library (where, rather battered, they still survive). At every turn there was this reminder that you were a son or daughter of the city.'

Leeds: a place at the crossing. Medieval Leeds grew from a small settlement at a major crossing point on the River Aire. From the twelfth century it was a regular trading place for wool producers and merchants, a natural market area and distribution centre. When the Aire became navigable at the end of the seventeenth century, goods could be transported more easily to Hull and on to Holland, Germany and beyond. Around the same time many skilled Continental textile craftsmen were heading to Leeds, a place where they could practise freely their trade and their religion, arriving by barge at Warehouse Hill. There's a tradition of liberty running through the waters of the Aire. Centuries later, Leeds would stand at the crossroads of the nation's motorway system, equidistant between London and Edinburgh, at the centre of Britain. Leeds has always been a place of exchange, a place of 'comers and goers'.

Leeds: a town shaped by outsiders. British migrants pulled towards the commercial, administrative and managerial centre, and immigrants from all parts of the world escaping poverty, starvation, religious and racial persecution. The major shaping, though there is a longer history, took place in the nineteenth century as Leeds grew from being a large market town of just over 53,000 in 1801 into a major industrial powerhouse of 428,000 by the end of the century. First came the Irish in the 1830s and 40s. They worked in the booming textile industries and packed themselves into insanitary back-to-backs in the Bank area. Then, in the 1880s, came Polish and Russian Jews escaping the pogroms which swept their homelands after the murder of Tsar Alexander II. By the end of the century Leeds had the largest proportion of Jews in its population in the country. They mostly congregated in the Leylands, a slum as benighted as the Bank. Yet Leeds Jewry produced entrepreneurs like Montague Burton and Michael Marks, whose humble Penny Bazaar stall in the open section of Kirkgate Market ('Don't ask the price, it's a penny!') was the basis for one of the biggest names in retail. Leeds Jews like Burton and Marks exemplified the Victorian values of self-reliance, hard graft and sobriety, values given their most famous expression by Samuel Smiles, in the best-selling *Self-Help* (1859), which was based on a series of improving talks given by the Leeds-based writer to a hundred young Leeds artisans. Smiles's doctrine held out a hope for the immigrant: any man, no matter how humble his rank, could achieve prosperity and a kind of godliness. Even a tailor, Smiles insisted, could rise to the top.

Leeds: an excluding town. The Leeds Irish were looked on as a savage, superstitious race and were made scapegoats for all manner of social ills: the cholera epidemic, driving down wages, immorality and crime. The Leeds Jews similarly were seen as an alien presence inhabiting a twilight part of the city. In time the Jews moved upwards economically and outwards geographically, but it was no smooth path to social acceptance, and they met with much hostility on the way: from rampaging mobs in adjacent ghettos (ironically, Irish areas) in 1917, and later, as the second and third generation attempted to advance, from professions hidebound by social snobbery and anti-Semitism. Long after the Second World War, certain leading law firms in the city wouldn't admit Jewish law graduates to articles; notoriously, in a city with many Jewish doctors there were no Jewish consultants at the Leeds General Infirmary. Golf clubs wouldn't have them. The Leeds Club, the social hub of the city's business and professional elite, excluded them.

The first-generation immigrants could never be 'Leeds Loiners'* – that was a birthright – but they were citizens of Leeds by virtue of residence. Often reviled, often received grudgingly, nonetheless they became part of the fabric of Leeds. In time they too became sons and daughters of the city.

Despite this history, Leeds didn't look like a cosmopolitan place. Whereas ports like Liverpool and Cardiff had long-established African communities, it was rare to see a black face in Leeds. Only five Africans were recorded in the 1921 census. Sikh peddlers and hawkers were familiar sights on the streets in the late 1920s, and there were a few dozen Chinese in the city; Indian and Egyptian students added colour to Leeds's workaday red-brick university from the 1920s – but Leeds's public face was barely changed. A black person walking on the streets of the city was an object of crude fascination. Ces Thompson, who came to Leeds from the West Indies just before the outbreak of the Second World War (and became, in the early 1950s, the first black person to represent Great Britain in rugby league), walked curtain-twitching streets with some trepidation. Somebody once shouted after him, 'Hi, nigger boy, did you come out of your mother's arse?'

Leeds citizens might have read about the arrival of the *Windrush* at Tilbury and the British Nationality Act – those foundational moments in the making of modern multiracial Britain – but a decade after Ces first walked the streets of Hunslet a black face in the city was still rare enough to excite comment. In Leeds the first settlers from the Caribbean were ex-servicemen, mainly from the RAF, who'd been demobilised in 1947 and 1948 and stayed to find work. Young single males, they lodged together in those few houses which would have them. In Woodhouse, 20 Clarendon Road was

* There are many theories as to why Leeds people are known as 'Loiners', the most attractive being that it derives from 'Loidis', the earliest written form of the name 'Leeds'.

the house where the locals said the darkies lived. This is how it stayed until the early 1950s when an increasing number of West Indians began to find a ready supply of rented accommodation in the Chapeltown area as the last remnants of the Jewish community withdrew from their 'Little Israel' for leafier suburbs further up the Harrogate Road. A 1953 government working party on 'Coloured People seeking Employment' reported that Leeds had a black population of recent growth numbering between five and six hundred. Even then the black newcomers were well outnumbered by displaced Poles, Latvians, Lithuanians and Estonians, whose presence in the city aroused far less comment and animosity.

Leeds prided itself on its diversity of employment. It called itself 'the city of a thousand trades' – textiles and clothing, leather trades, engineering, but also a large variety of service industries. But these first black immigrants, many holding professional and technical skills and qualifications, found themselves in low-paid, unskilled jobs, mainly in engineering, textiles, transport and the NHS.

Around the same time as the first Jamaicans settled, a small number of West Africans from the British colonies – Nigeria, the Gold Coast, Sierra Leone, Gambia – came to Leeds: a mixed bag of ex-sailors, ship stewards, stowaways and scholars. Gayb was among them.

Accommodation was the main problem for blacks in Leeds, just as in other cities. Gayb and his friend Slim ended up at the Salvation Army hostel on Lisbon Street. By 1949 electric street lighting was starting to appear on more and more streets in the centre of the city, but Lisbon Street, a fifteen-minute walk from town, was still in the gaslight age. Gayb stayed there for about nine months; 1s 3d a night, paid a week in advance. It was a filthy place; Gayb caught lice. He was surprised to see men who'd been working in the foundry all day going out to the pub wearing the same shirt, albeit with a different collar attached to it, a cardigan over the top, and a tie. It seemed that nobody liked to bathe in England. A good night's sleep was difficult with the background noise of hacking coughs from the hundred or so residents.

Gayb was interested in becoming a soldier, but on the morning he had set himself to signing up, Slim told him he'd be the only black person in the British Army and warned him about the terrible things they'd do to him. Heeding Slim's warning, Gayb stayed at the railway on Wellington Street. When the winter came he found more congenial work in a foundry in south Leeds, stayed there for a few months, before he went on to the copper works, Yorkshire Imperial Metals. It was heavy, hot work, which he stuck at for over forty years, the rest of his working life.

The usual response to black people seeking rented accommodation in Leeds was the slammed door. Sensing an opportunity, a canny Irishwoman who had worked as a cleaner at the university, Helen McCrum, began to buy up houses and let rooms to the small number of blacks in the city. She grandly advertised her properties as 'Private Hotels', charging around £2 a week for bed and board, which took care of a good chunk of a foundry labourer's wages.

One of Mrs McCrum's properties was 12 Grove Terrace, a three-storey red-brick terrace in the Little London area of the city, at the bottom end of Camp Road. Most of the Leeds Africans passed through this house at some point. Camp Road was a part of the city with a notorious reputation. In 1949 a special report in the *Yorkshire Evening Post* attributed the area's decline to the 'foreign element, a floating population inhabiting single carpetless rooms in the once handsome houses of Victorian gentry'; these new arrivals were responsible for nightly brawls, prostitution, assaults on women and 'un-British attacks with knives, pepper and ginger'. Scattered among Camp Road's indigenous population and the descendants of nineteenth-century Irish immigration were a few Sikh hawkers and peddlers; a few Pakistanis; poor Jews who'd never made it to Chapeltown, never mind the suburbs; 'displaced persons' from Central and Eastern Europe; small numbers of Jamaicans and Africans. It was an unlovely setting of clothing factories, printing works, stone and timber yards, rough pubs, army barracks; the only greenery the residents of 12 Grove Terrace could see was the North Street recreation ground, known locally as the 'Jews' Park' (or, more derogatorily, as 'Sheeny Park').

There was a jostling mix of nationalities and tribes at 12 Grove Terrace, each claiming superiority over the other, getting by with pidgin English if they didn't know the other's language. Since Gayb did a few jobs around the place for the landlady he earned himself the luxury of a single room. He'd get letters from his mother; she'd tell him to draw strength from the psalms if he ever felt troubled – 23, 27 and 121 were her favourites. Back in Lagos she'd taken in lodgers from another tribe, and since these people worked on the ships she'd send them over to ration-book England with packages of *gari* and yams, the kinds of food her son missed, and Gayb would pick them up at Liverpool.

English food in those early years never seemed to satisfy Gayb, but he'd go to the Public Abattoir and Wholesale Meat Market on New York Street to pick up chicken necks, fish heads and, even better, sheep's head which he'd cook slowly until the meat fell off the bone and turned into a stew. Then he'd mix in an Oxo cube and serve it with rice – proper rice sent from home, not the 'mock rice' they sold in England. It was beautiful.

More than sheep's head, it was dancing which lifted Gayb's spirits. At one of his first lodgings on Sholebroke Avenue there was a gramophone player, so on Saturday nights the boys would roll back the carpet and jive to the Glenn Miller sound – always Gayb's favourite – until their German Jewish landlord Mr White put a stop to it. Another great dancer was Speedy Acquaye, a small larger-than-life ball of energy. Speedy came to England from the Gold Coast as a sixteen-year-old in 1947 and made his living in a travelling circus: dancing, fire-eating, playing congas. At the Mecca ballroom in the County Arcade, Speedy delighted the girls by pulling up his trousers and setting fire to his legs.

In this drab city where the pubs shut at 10 p.m. the dance halls were a splash of glamour and excitement. The Africans went to dances at Armley Baths and the town hall, but the highlight was those Saturday nights at the Mecca where Jimmy Savile was establishing his reputation as DJ and general manager. Sometimes they'd be joined by West Indian RAF men who'd stay on in Leeds. Though there was a 'colour bar' in some Leeds pubs, the welcome at the Mecca was friendly. There wasn't an ounce of prejudice in Jimmy Savile.

Downstairs was 'strictly ballroom', polite and pre-war in atmosphere; upstairs, where the Africans would go, it was jiving. The exuberant sounds coming from upstairs soon sucked in the people from downstairs, emptying that floor.

At first Gayb found that the women didn't want to dance with him, though he could tell they loved his jiving, and there was occasional name-calling from sullen men. Gayb and his friends thought they could do with a chance, so persuaded the MC to announce a 'general excuse me'; in this way the dance floor was stirred and mixed up. In time, Gayb became friendly with the Mecca regulars, and even the men dropped their guard and got him tickets for dances in the area. Gayb and the boys didn't limit themselves to Leeds. The Batley Gaiety was popular. And they'd go to George Adamson's Galleon dance hall in Dewsbury, where Johnny Dankworth's Big Band regularly played, catching the last train back to Leeds just before midnight.

The warmth of those dance halls contrasted with the chilly, often hostile reception the Africans received elsewhere. Joe Okogba came from Nigeria and would eventually find a job at the same copper works as Gayb, meet a girl, marry, buy a house. But in those early years, Okogba told me, Leeds could be a cruel city. Doors were closed roughly in his face whenever he sought out lodgings and he'd be sent on his way with a 'black bastard'. Worse, the vicar at one frigid church told him that he wasn't welcome since his presence disturbed his flock.

White people had bizarre ideas about blacks. Some of the landladies refused to allow them to use their baths in case their skin came off and stained the tub. They had to go to the public baths to bathe, but Cookridge Street refused them towels because of similar concerns. After one such humiliation there was a bit of a rumpus and the police were called. The police sergeant told the manager that he'd served alongside the African Rifles in Burma and that these people were no different, their skin wouldn't ruin anything. The manager grudgingly gave them towels.

Daniel Okpovie, a Nigerian who came to Leeds around the same time as Gayb, told me that white people would move to another seat if he tried to sit down next to them, and of how a barman in one pub smashed the glass he had been drinking from after he had finished with it. He was once in a cinema queue when a woman grabbed his backside and asked, 'Have you got a tail?' Fellow workers asked Okpovie if he lived in a mud hut back home. Such experiences were common. In his autobiography, Ces Thompson, the former Hunslet rugby player, tells the story of how he found a job at a south Leeds engineering works and on his first day some of the roughnecks taunted him with 'Cecil, is your prick black?' Five of them then crowded round him, ripped off his boiler suit and poured oil over his testicles.

Gayb had two Nigerian friends who were crippled by terrible feelings of self-consciousness whenever they ventured out alone. Lapido had Yoruba tribal markings and was always getting asked, 'What's the matter with your face?' He lived in Birmingham but travelled frequently to Leeds, and whenever he got on the train he drank himself into a stupor so that the stares and comments would wash over him. Another friend with markings, Theo, was asked whether a tiger had been at him. Theo didn't last long in England: Gayb heard that he jumped into the path of a London Underground train.

The streets could be dangerous. A black man out on his own at night was a target for the thugs and for the police. A white woman with a black man was looked on as soiled goods. The wise couples learned to keep away from the well-lit roads, slipping down the ginnels, as though they were breaking apartheid laws. 'Oh, it was shocking after the war,' one Leeds woman told the *Yorkshire Post* in 1955. 'One man in Leeds came up to me and spat in my face. He said it was shameful for English girls to go about with niggers.' England, to the stranger, could be as hard and cold as a knife.

The Africans tended to move frequently between addresses. In 1950, Gayb was living at 175 Belle Vue Road in the Little Woodhouse/Hyde Park area, where most of the Leeds Africans ended up. His landlord was a one-armed boozer with the strength of three men. His place became a dive. There were a couple of Irish navvies living there, who, rather than bothering with the outside toilet, would dump on to a piece of newspaper and chuck the parcel on to the fire. *Oh man*, Gayb thought, *what have I come to?*

The Leeds African community, non-existent before the war, was still very small. In this city of just over half a million there were, according to the 1951 census, only eighty-two West Africans, of whom forty-five (thirty-nine men, six women) came from Nigeria. In the whole of the West Riding of Yorkshire there were less than a hundred Nigerians. It wasn't surprising that they all knew one another and stuck close together. Gayb had several childhood friends around him: Alfred Young, Steve Oke, Sunday Daniel – who he got to know when he was delivering messages – Lucky Ackindere. They'd kicked footballs together on Lagos racecourse and now found themselves looking out for one another on the factory floors, foundries, dance halls of northern England.

It was some time in the autumn of 1949, around the time that he was driving a crane at Wellington Road station and getting asked how his people could play football in bare feet, that Gayb met another man from Lagos, who was known as 'Yankee'. He had come over on the same ship as Gayb's friend from home, Johnny Omaghomi.

II

Even the most basic details about David Oluwale are hard to get at. He provided different dates of birth on different occasions to the authorities in Britain: 8 August 1926, 8 August 1929, 30 August 1930 and 8 September 1931. A consensus formed that he was thirty-eight when he died; this is the age shown on the pauper's headstone.

The most fundamental fact, his name, is also uncertain. I follow the conventional 'David Oluwale' which appears on his death certificate. However, when he was arrested at Hull in September

1949 his name was recorded as 'Oluwole'. Oluwole is the more common Yoruba name, meaning 'God enters my home'; Oluwale means 'God comes home'. The authorities always struggled with his name. Several variations or misspellings appeared in official papers: Oolle, Allowala, Alliwala, Oluwuala, Olewala, Oluwuale. When living in Sheffield he even adopted the alias David Llewelyn.

He was short. According to prison records, as a nineteen-year-old he stood at 5'3½", although he was to grow another inch or so. He was medium build, nine to ten stone, with a muscular physique, though after his death he would be described in exaggerated terms as a 'miniature Mr Universe'. His face was oval-shaped, his eyes brown. His hair began to recede in his twenties.

Details of his family are scant. His mother was called Alice; he had one younger sister. His father, who worked in the fishing trade, is said to have died in 1937. His mother may have been the only breadwinner until Oluwale left school in 1944 at the age of fourteen. The family lived at 4 Tokunbo Street, an expansive thoroughfare in Lagos in the heart of what was known as 'the Brazilian quarter'. An uncle was said to own the Ilojo bar in Tinubu Square, in the commercial centre of Lagos Island, which had been built by a former slave owner returning from Brazil with his fortune.

Though the rosary beads found on his body led the police to assume that Oluwale was Roman Catholic, it is not certain that he was brought up in that faith. Oluwale gave his denomination as Church of England in 1953; police records in later years had him down as Baptist, Methodist and even Muslim.

Yet police investigation into his early life established that he been educated in Christian mission schools up to the age of fourteen. Lagos Grammar School was the place where he was believed to have received his secondary education. There were a number of grammar schools in Lagos he might have attended, for instance St Gregory's College for Catholics and the Wesleyan Boys' High School, but 'Lagos Grammar School' usually referred to the Church Missionary Society (CMS) Grammar School, which opened its doors to pupils in 1859 and was Nigeria's oldest Christian (Anglican) school. Even if Oluwale was brought up as a Roman Catholic it would have been no bar to his entering the CMS school: like other mission schools at this time, it admitted pupils of any religion or belief. (Unfortunately, pupil lists for the period when Oluwale would have been there, according to the current school principal, cannot be traced.)

Since there was no free education in Nigeria and a dearth of scholarships, grammar school involved a major commitment for families. Yoruba families in particular were prepared to make great sacrifices for the education of their children, but a heavy burden was placed on a boy from such a family – it was invariably a boy – to pass his exams and gain entry to the professions, a reliable income and security.

These schools may have been the products of intense interdenominational rivalry, but the distinctions between them were far less apparent than the commonalities. And this means we can be reasonably confident about the kind of education Oluwale received.

The schools orientated themselves towards England, taught its charges to think of her as the mother country, even as 'home'. The mother country was a place of decency and liberty and law. A grammar-school pupil like Oluwale would have had a more developed understanding of England than someone like Gayb, who left school with only vague notions of the land of Shakespeare and Robin Hood. He would have learned about British history, its institutions, industries, weather, its place in the world and its empire. For the colonial authorities, reluctant to invest in the educational development of the natives, the mission grammar schools offered British civilisation on the cheap.

Lagos's premier schools modelled themselves on English grammar schools and tended to provide a literary and classical education suitable for aspiring professional gentlemen, not the technical and industrial skills Nigeria sorely needed. European clothes and anglicised names were the norm, English manners and standards of discipline were regarded as exemplary. The famous English sense of fair play was instilled on the school playing fields (or on the bumpy communal sports pitches on Lagos racecourse if the pupil happened to be at the modestly appointed CMS school). Lagos's grammar schools were bound together not only by shared values but by a common curriculum and the hard currency of certificates awarded by the Cambridge University Local Examinations Syndicate. The School Certificate was the passport, it was hoped, to a comfortable life.

This was the ideal; the reality fell some way short. The late 1930s and early 40s were a time of growing disaffection with the whole imperial project. Ironically, many leaders of nascent anti-British nationalist opinion in Nigeria were themselves products of the very educational system which was one of its key props. Long criticised for encouraging a slavish imitation of European ways and a condescending disdain towards their own communities, the mission schools became a particular target of nationalist contempt.

The mission schools had once exemplified a 'muscular' brand of Christianity, the glorification of God going hand in hand with the glorification of Britain. But the archives of one school, the CMS grammar school, hint at the more downbeat reality.

In the early 1940s, the time when Oluwale was in secondary education, the CMS school, with its predominantly African staff, was teaching around 320 boys. Not all was well at the most exemplary of mission schools. The teachers were notorious for moonlighting and a number of them had been sacked for 'immorality'. The English principal who had been brought in to bring stability and a firm standard of discipline to the school had left for a new post, leaving governors to ponder whether they might risk replacing him with an African. Despite the problems, the education officer for Lagos inspected the school in 1942 and found a cheerful body of pupils with good manners, well-decorated classrooms and a library, though short on books, where pupils could read the 'better newspapers from England'. Pupils could involve themselves in a range of societies: the Yoruba Society flourished, but the Scout Troop, that great British institution, was failing because of low recruitment. Team sports were offered, though cricket had been dropped since there was nobody qualified to teach it. There was a wide range of subjects taught, from Latin to handicrafts, but it was Yoruba language which was singled out as a success. The inspection found that while pupils in history were fascinated by the Industrial Revolution, the lesson on the British Empire was stale and uninspiring. He found that many teachers had a poor grasp of English. The education officer observed: 'It was not surprising that pupils in Class IV were unable to get the spirit of Elroy Flecker's poem "Thoughts on England" . . . both teacher and class read the poem in a monotonous manner with no expression whatever.' Zeal for Britain, if - not for God, had dampened.

A common problem for the grammar schools was ensuring that their pupils went on to secure, well-paid careers. It was a frequent criticism that they turned out a socially useless product with an exaggerated sense of its own worth. Since educated Nigerians were excluded from the upper echelons of government and had limited opportunities in the bureaucracy, the reality was that the schools churned out the many 'writing clerks' who filled the lower posts in the civil service and mercantile establishment.

It appears that Oluwale left school in 1944 at the age of fourteen, probably because his family could no longer afford the fees. It's likely that he was unqualified even for one of those humble clerk positions. His name does not feature in the pass lists of those Lagos grammar-school pupils taking the Cambridge University Local Examinations Syndicate Junior School Certificate.

Times were tough even for the well qualified. In the 1940s and 50s their number was growing much faster than the number of appropriate jobs. The aspirations of the best were frustrated. This was brought home by the tragic story of A. T. B. Ottun. Ottun, the 'Rock of Gibraltar', a defender in that proud Nigerian football team which left for England on the same day as Oluwale in 1949, took his own life after plunging into despair at his inability to find a job to match his skills. Ottun's frustrations were those of a generation of young educated Nigerians.

Out of school, Oluwale was thrust into a fast-changing urban society. The population of Lagos had risen sharply during the course of his lifetime: 126,000 at the beginning of the 1930s to

230,000 by 1950. Social tensions were everywhere evident: food shortages, rising prices, industrial militancy and nationalist defiance of the colonial regime. In 1945, there was a general strike of public workers; the following year nationalist leaders were humiliated and angered by the Richards Constitution (named after the colonial governor), since it was enacted without the consultation of the people and denied them meaningful participation in the running of their country. Unemployment was high and pressures on the labour market were increased by an influx of migrants from the country and demobilised soldiers (an estimated 100,000 Nigerians had been recruited to military service).

Oluwale was well educated by the standards of his Lagosian contemporaries and he was far from being among the poorest. But without qualifications that counted for little. He became an apprentice tailor but found work hard to come by. Perhaps a desire to prove something to himself and his family was the reason he decided to take his chances on the *Temple Bar* on that August day in 1949.

What became of the family he left behind isn't known. Following the opening of the investigation into his death the police searched in vain for relatives. Tenuous leads were pursued. Telephone directories were trawled for anyone with similar-sounding names. There was mention of a brother working in the legal profession in London, a Solomon Oluwale. But no brother was found. There was mention of a next of kin, David Sature Oluwuala from Elekela. Again, the search was unsuccessful. Searches by the Interpol bureau in Nigeria in January 1971 into the background of David Oluwale proved futile. No trace of his family. No sign of Alice Oluwale at 4 Tokunbo Street. 'Subject is not recorded in this country' was the bureau's final word on Oluwale.

Oluwale was part of the last stream of West African stowaways. The Home Office had become alarmed at the rising number coming from this part of the British Empire. The figures seem modest from any perspective – eight hundred West African stowaways between 1946 and 1949 – but it was felt that their presence in the poorer areas of seaports had led to pressures on accommodation and employment, which had aggravated racial tension. Questions were asked in Parliament after violent disturbances erupted at Deptford in July 1949 when a hostel accommodating black seamen and stowaways came under attack from a white mob. Faced with calls for the repatriation of those who came as stowaways, the Home Secretary regretted that he had no power to deport a British subject whether he was a stowaway or otherwise.

But measures were soon taken to stem the tide. The British Travel Certificate, which most stowaways came armed with, was rendered invalid for the purpose of entering Britain. These administrative adjustments were made in September 1949 and resulted in a sharp decline in the number of stowaways gaining entry. Those who arrived in Britain without a proper passport were now turned away. Official figures stated that in 1955 just thirteen stowaways from West Africa made it into Britain. Oluwale had only just squeezed in.

His first sight of Leeds was from the window of a prison van. His short stay at Armley must have been uncomfortable. According to prison records, he received medical treatment for gonorrhoea. During the course of his sentence he was transferred to Northallerton prison in north Yorkshire. Prior to release the Discharged Prisoners' Aid Society advised Oluwale that he'd be best off going to Manchester of Liverpool where he'd find many of his kind, hostels and welfare officers. But when he was released from prison on 3 October 1949 he made for Leeds, possibly because Johnny Omaghomi, his fellow stowaway, had friends there – Gayb, Lucky and Slim. Oluwale had just a few shillings from the National Assistance Board to go towards clothing.

By midday the thick fog had lifted. September had been the warmest since records began; October looked like breaking records also. All the talk in Leeds was of the imminent water crisis.

If David Oluwale had looked at T. R. Batten's history books – set texts in Lagos grammar schools in the 1940s – he might have had some idea of Leeds. He would have read that in the first thirty years of the nineteenth century, as it became an industrial centre, its population grew from 53,000 to 123,000. He would have learned that the life of the poorest classes was lived out in dark places crowded with houses dirtied with smoke from factories; that many families lived in underground rooms without fresh air or sunlight; of the pale, sickly children. He would also have been told a story of civic improvement, of how the terrible sanitation problem had been defeated by enlightened local authorities who had ensured good water, sanitary inspectors, sewerage plants.

For someone trained in tailoring as Oluwale was, Leeds made sense. It was an industry with deep roots in the city. John Leland, Henry VIII's scholarly chaplain, described Leeds as a town which 'standeth most by clothing'; four centuries later the city was famous the world over as the centre of the ready-made clothing industry, principally because of Montague Burton, whose Hudson Road factory, the largest in Europe, employed just over 10,000 at its peak in the 1930s (a quarter of those employed in the Leeds clothing industry). Clothing was an industry which immigrants had traditionally gravitated towards. Many of the Jews who came in the late nineteenth century had been tailors in their homelands and targeted the city precisely in order to participate in an expanded ready-made clothing industry, disembarking at Hull or Grimsby with no words of English except 'Leeds'. Around 70 per cent of Leeds's Jews, mainly young men, worked in the industry. Oluwale was part of a long tradition, then, and though there were signs by the end of the 1940s that the golden age of the industry had passed, he had become a member of a great army of workers (still one in five of Leeds's working population) engaged in the clothing trade. His first few months in Leeds were spent in various small tailoring workshops clustered around North Street.

Oluwale's first address in Leeds was 2 Well Close Place in the Little London area, half a mile to the north of the city centre. Possibly this had been organised by prison welfare (he would find himself at this address again many years later when it was Faith Lodge, a Christian home for alcoholics, ex-prisoners and mental-hospital patients). He didn't stay there long.

His next address appears to have been 12 Grove Terrace, the address at which Gayb had lived. That is where Abbey Sowe, a Gambian who became important to Oluwale later in his life, first remembered meeting him. He seemed content living among other West Africans: Steve Oke, Speedy, Frank Morgan, 'Widey' Williams, Ademola Johnston and Sheia (sometimes Sheba) Savage.

One of Oluwale's closest friends around this time was Lucky Akanidere. Lucky had also arrived in Britain as a stowaway, just a few weeks after Oluwale, on board the *Junecrest*. He also appeared before J. H. Tarbitten at Hull, part of a shoeless, pyjama-clad group of young men, armed only with a letter addressed 'To the Magistrate in London or Hull' declaring their good character, their eagerness to work or be educated, and their earnest desire not to return to their former jobless, good-for-nothing lives. Lucky was small, stocky, a ball of energy. He would go on to father nine children, making his living selling African foodstuffs around the markets of the West Riding. In 1950, when he first met Oluwale, he was, like the others, struggling to find his feet.

A number of the Africans, including Oluwale and Lucky, found digs and work in Bradford, at Croft Engineering. One of its Nigerian employees was Vincent Enyori. When I met him, in 2005, Enyori told me that it was a tough place to work, that blacks were handed the jobs no white man would touch, sweeping up or punishing hand-grinding work where the stones and dust would get into the skin. 'They didn't allow you to touch machines so that you might have made some money,' Enyori told me. During this time Oluwale and Lucky became friendly with another Nigerian, Christmas Ogbonson, who came to England in 1948. Ogbonson lived in a hostel during his time at Bradford; he was a quiet man, painfully so, very different from Lucky and Oluwale. They'd meet in Bradford dance halls or get together with the Leeds boys on Saturday nights at the Dewsbury Galleon.

Oluwale stayed in Bradford only six months before returning to Leeds; Lucky and Christmas would soon follow. He was a hod carrier for a time and then found a regular job at the Public Abattoir and Wholesale Meat Market ('the yard') next to Kirkgate Market.

Alan Bennett, growing up in Leeds in the 1940s, remembers this as the disreputable part of town, with its 'less orthodox retail establishments: herbalists, shops selling surgical appliances, rubber goods, remedies for haemorrhoids and hair, wanted or unwanted, and remedies for babies too, wanted and unwanted'.

Oluwale flitted between two addresses: 175 and 209 Belle Vue Road. But he was soon on the move again. On 3 March 1951 he was in Sheffield, the steel city thirty-five miles south of Leeds, then rougher and even uglier than its Yorkshire rival. He took a room at 15 Oxford Street, a back-to-back in the Crookesmoor area. The landlord was known to be tolerant of blacks, so Oluwale found himself with other Africans, mostly from the Gold Coast. Victor Cole was one of them. In a statement given to the police in 1970, Cole said that Oluwale was an unsociable man with few contacts other than residents of the house, that he was a frequent drug user who would regularly travel back to Leeds to get hold of opium and marijuana.

Oluwale found labouring work for the Sheffield Gas Company but managed just three days before being laid off. He was not in the city long before he ran into trouble.

He had taken on the alias 'David Llewelyn', presumably because he wanted a name more familiar to the English ear. This was the name which appeared in the report in the Sheffield *Star* of Saturday 17 March 1951 under the heading 'WEST AFRICAN BIT P.C. IN BLACK MARIA'. The report stated that on the previous night twenty-year-old West African David Llewelyn was ordered to leave a snack bar in West Bar when the proprietor decided he was drunk. When he refused, the proprietor called the police and PC Richardson came on the scene and arrested him. As he was being taken to a police station in a Black Maria there was a fight. Richardson received a bite and was treated at the Royal Infirmary. David Llewelyn was found guilty and fined £2 for the assault and a further ten shillings for being drunk and disorderly.

After a brief period working in a foundry, Oluwale returned to Leeds in the autumn of 1951, and was back at the slaughterhouse. His social life revolved around the Mecca and the King Edward

Hotel, a raucous city-centre pub with live music. Moses Owens, a Gambian, saw Oluwale in the King Edward regularly around this time, and many years later would tell the Oluwale investigation that the Nigerian was a heavy cannabis smoker who was 'always by himself'. Several African sources who came forward to detectives in 1970–1 to throw a light on this part of his life would also point to his drug use, and there was a suggestion from more than one that he dealt in a small way in marijuana, then readily available in Leeds.

In 1952 Oluwale was living at 209 Belle Vue Road. There is a rare appearance in the electoral register which had him down as 'Olu Davies'. He was living with several Africans, including Widey, fellow Lagosian Isiaka Harding, whom they nicknamed 'Tex' because he loved Westerns and gangster films, and Sunday Daniel, who had played with Oluwale as a boy in Lagos.

Around this time Oluwale is said to have met a white woman from Sheffield, thought to be called Gladys. She was a similar age to Oluwale, five feet tall, slim with long dark hair. It is thought that he lived with her at several addresses in Leeds, including 209 Belle Vue Road and 4 Springfield Place. A 'Gladys' is mentioned in Jeremy Sandford's play. She was said to have had two children by Oluwale. Since Gladys, according to Sandford, wished to remain anonymous, this part of Oluwale's life is a mystery. It was certainly a mystery to his friends, who would tell detectives that Oluwale had little to do with women, who remembered no particular girlfriend, no wife, no children. The main source for the existence of Gladys was the wife of Christmas Ogbonson, Ann. She saw a lot of the couple around 1952. She would tell the press in 1971 that Gladys had been Oluwale's common-law wife, that she was a nice quiet woman and that the two of them were very happy together. She did not, however, mention children. She said that Gladys left Oluwale and returned to Sheffield after he was sent to the mental hospital in 1953.

Oluwale was well known among his fellow Africans and, it appears, well liked. 'A quiet man and he was always happy and smiling,' according to Christmas Ogbonson. 'He was not aggressive and would not harm anybody.' Abbey Sowe remembered him as 'a very happy individual, and a good conversationalist, he was always making jokes and could be the life of the party'. But some thought of him as a solitary personality, even as a young man.

Gayb remembered a lively soul who always wanted to be where the action was, a high-spirited joker who could get a bit out of control, argumentative. He couldn't stay still, one day in Leeds, the next in Bradford, sometimes as far as Sunderland and Sheffield. He was a good talker, their favourite topics of conversation being the Mecca ballroom and food. He wasn't a particularly big drinker, but he enjoyed cannabis.

He had two convictions, one for stowing away and one for the Sheffield assault, but he couldn't be described as a criminal. He couldn't stand to be pushed around or ordered about. When provoked he was capable of violence, but those who knew him also testified to his eagerness to avoid trouble, even his gentleness.

His nickname was 'Yankee', sometimes 'Yankee Doodle' – it was the way he carried himself, a bit of a swagger. 'He was always wanting to be like a Yank,' Gayb told me. Joe Okobga told me that Oluwale always wore a sharp suit and trilby hat. In this city of cloth there were so many tailors, and every young man, whether it was to go to the cinema or the dance hall, wore a suit. For the Leeds Africans it could only be Henry Price's Fifty Shilling Tailor on Briggate where they could select a suit length and have it made to measure. Rather than have one back pocket on his trousers in the traditional English way, Oluwale, one of the more clothes-conscious, insisted on two. It was the Yankee style, he explained.

Gayb wanted to settle down. He met a girl at the Mecca, Joyce Winter, and fell in love. Her parents didn't approve. They told Gayb that they would send their daughter to her relatives in Middlesbrough if he persisted in courting her; Gayb said they could send her to Australia – he'd still find her. He wrote and told his mother of his intentions, and she wrote back and asked how he was going to afford an English girl, that he could have two wives in Lagos for what Joyce would cost. But the couple were married in January 1951 at Blenheim Baptist Church on Blackman Lane. Revd Howard Williams, a liberal-minded Welshman, wished the couple well and warned them that a lot of ignorant people wouldn't tolerate the mixing of the races. Joyce's family came to terms with the marriage and grew to love their son-in-law.

Gayb and Joyce put three weeks' rent down on a house and ordered a new fireplace, but when he went to the landlord's office to sign he said he wouldn't let it to a black. Shortly after, a local newspaper went to the copper works to see how blacks were getting on with whites, so Gayb told them about the landlord and the rent and the fireplace; he told them about a black workmate who had fought for the British in Burma and said, 'You call us British subjects, but we are only British objects.' The landlord was furious and went round to Gayb's mother-in-law's to complain about the slight on his reputation. She put him in his place. Very soon after, he called round to say he had a house going.

It had been a hard journey. Some of the Africans who came to Leeds at this time would reflect later that if it hadn't been for the girls who'd made them welcome they would have returned home.

More than anything, Gayb wanted to bring his mother over to England. He tried to send money back home but he barely had enough to live on after he'd paid his rent. A few months after his wedding he received a telegram from Lagos which informed him of his mother's death.

The memory of what she did for him, and of how little he could give her back, pains Gayb to this day. That day he left her in Lagos is still vivid. 'It's always with me, that moment in time – I can see her, as she stood.' A photograph of her, an elegant woman holding the book she knew by heart, hangs on the wall of his neat Beeston home: it makes him think of those 'Runner can' shoes which, over sixty years ago, she walked all the way to Broad Street to buy.

2

Menston

These were his lost years; they should have been his best. Between 1953 and 1969, David Oluwale spent almost a decade in a mental asylum. The rest of the time he was mostly on the streets or in prison. He hardly worked, rarely slept in a normal bed in a normal house. Most of his friends appear to have either lost touch with him or deserted him. There were no more nights at the Mecca – his dancing days were over.

These were the years in which he fell off the map – the social, physical and moral map. Because of the nature of his life he left few traces. There's the occasional terse press report: 'NIGERIAN BIT MAN'S FINGER, COURT TOLD,' was the story in the *Yorkshire Evening Post* on 4 October 1962. There are few humanising anecdotes.

Yet making sense of this bleak period of Oluwale's life is crucial. Though it is hard to imagine anyone more isolated, he didn't live a completely atomised existence. The racial politics of the period, colonial psychiatry, mental health care, even housing policy, formed the context in which he lived out his life. It's also vital to place Oluwale within the story of a city. By getting to know Leeds I thought I might get closer to understanding his death.

What happened to Oluwale shouldn't have happened. This after all was the 'golden age' of the welfare state, when society was becoming more closely knit, when British people were, to borrow the words of Leeds United's signature song, 'marching on together'.

* * *

In law David Oluwale was a Citizen of the United Kingdom and Colonies, the status bestowed by the British Nationality Act 1948. But even before that, the moment he was born, thousands of miles away in Lagos, he became part of us. Because there was this long tradition captured in the phrase *civis Brittanicus sum* ('I am a British citizen') which said that every individual born within the sovereign's empire was a British subject.

To understand why Oluwale ended up in the River Aire I needed to look further back than April 1968 when two Leeds policemen came together and set about clearing him from the city centre. I wanted to know how an apparently happy-go-lucky livewire ended up a pitiful character important to nobody, somebody 'Other', 'Nigerian vagrant' rather than 'British citizen'.

Like Gayb, Oluwale might have joined the humdrum stream of industrial labour, become factory-disciplined, met his wife, found his own home, quietly got on with his life. By 1953 most of his friends were moving on in this way. Lucky and Johnny Omaghomi married Dewsbury girls; Slim married a nice Batley lass. Christmas Ogbonson had met his wife at the Mecca. Families were started. They were beginning to make their separate lives. Speedy, who could never be contained, headed for Soho's jazz clubs and ended up playing congas for Georgie Fame's band, having a number-one record in the 1960s with 'Yeh Yeh'. A few returned to Africa with tall stories and no money; others just left Leeds, its warm girls, pigeons, chimneys and chilly faithless churches, for similar towns and cities.

Perhaps Oluwale would never have settled – he was Yankee after all. He wanted more than just a slaughterhouse job and a tiny room in one of Mrs McCrum's 'Private Hotels'. But restless black men in 1950s Leeds were more likely to find trouble than the pot of gold.

Maybe Oluwale was always an unwelcome part of us: a British subject, but one we never wanted. Boasts of our long tradition of hospitality to British subjects from all parts of the empire were punctured every day as black citizens met a grudging, often hostile, reception on the streets, in pubs, in the workplace. The story is well known.

Less well known is the full depth of official antipathy. The year 1953 brought the first rumblings of disquiet about the growing number of black migrants. This might seem strange given that the British Nationality Act 1948 secured the theoretical right of 600 million British subjects to enter the United Kingdom. Yet the Act was never intended as an encouragement to immigration; it was a sorting-out of a vexed constitutional problem, an attempt to secure a uniform status for British subjects throughout the empire. At a time of expensive transportation, large-scale migration from the New Commonwealth was not envisaged.

But in 1953, 3,000 people entering Britain from the New Commonwealth was enough for the government to appoint a working party on 'Coloured People seeking Employment in the United Kingdom', with a remit to consider whether black immigration should be halted. When that figure leapt to 43,000 in 1955 there was a clamour for controls; that Britain didn't go down that path until the 1960s was not out of any enthusiasm for a multicultural society – that great defender of empire Sir Winston Churchill said he didn't want Britain becoming a 'magpie society' – rather, to have embarked on a restrictive policy which embraced all overseas British subjects would have threatened the deeply felt link to the 'Old Commonwealth'. And if the government could not contemplate a policy which extended restrictions to Canada, Australia and New Zealand, then the alternative – restricting those from Africa, the West Indies and the Indian subcontinent – risked alienating a large part of the British Empire and exposing *civis Brittanicus sum*, an ideal which still had its defenders, as a sham.

In the official mind, David Oluwale was the worst kind of black. The West African seaman or stowaway was at the bottom of Britain's racial hierarchy. That same working party took evidence from urban police forces on the law and order problems that black people presented, and though the information gathered showed that blacks were no more given to theft or robbery than the indigenous population ('Although he tends to be unstable the coloured worker is more law-abiding than generally supposed,' Hammersmith police reported), West Africans were identified as threats to social order. 'Arrogant and violent . . . and have little regard for law and order and other people's property'; 'dirty and lazy ways'; 'standard of living is low'; 'work-shy and content to live on national assistance' – these were the kind of observations the Home Office was receiving about men like Oluwale. They were the zoot-suited pimps defiling British womanhood and staining the nation, the ill-disciplined chancers who wanted the quick route to the high life. They were from the most backward sections of their communities, incapable of assimilating into advanced societies. 'Little more than savages,' as one immigration official put it.

There's an important story to tell about the openness and hospitality, not just the small-mindedness of this small island in the post-war years. But this isn't one of those stories. The gap which separated Oluwale from 'us' grew and ossified.

In June 1953, just under four years after his arrival in Britain, Oluwale was committed to Menston Asylum. He didn't re-emerge until almost eight years later. He was sectioned a second time in 1965 (by which time the asylum had been renamed High Royds Hospital). Taken together, he spent just short of half of his twenty years in this country locked up in an asylum.

Many of the places associated with Oluwale's life in and around Leeds have disappeared. But High Royds Hospital kept going long into the era of community care. In the hospital's centenary year, 1988, Jimmy Savile led a fancy dress fun run around its expansive grounds and there still appeared to be a future. Yet in 2003 High Royds decanted its last patients into the community. Two years later, GladeDale Homes stepped in and set about turning the site into 'the newest Yorkshire village'. The landmark 129-foot clock tower, surely the first thing Oluwale noticed as the ambulance snaked up the long driveway, is the project logo. The slogan reads: 'High Royds Village: Simply idyllic'. A strong sense of community is offered as part of the package. Residents of the five hundred or more apartments are promised a doctor's surgery, nursery, retail outlets and sports facilities. GladeDale Homes doesn't advertise it like this on its website, but High Royds Village will retain something of the self-sufficient character of the old nineteenth-century asylum, which was a classic 'total institution' with library, bakery, ballroom, farm and railway station.

The new villagers will no doubt be made aware by older Menston folk of the rich social history of their surroundings; on windy nights delicate minds will surely discern the pitiful wails of madmen. Stories will be told. Of the mortuary attendant with the gnarled hand and a passion for glamour photography who picked up willing models at staff socials. (He'd take the girls to his place of work and nod towards the mortuary slab with a 'Get yourself up on there, love'.) And there are the sad stories. Of Eddie Waring, the legendary rugby league commentator, who towards the end failed to recognise his old *It's a Knockout* colleague and pal Stuart Hall. And there's David Oluwale.

To understand why Oluwale died the way he did, the gates of Menston might be the place to start. Prior to the asylum's closure his case records were lost, along with those of many others. This archive – the archive of the obscure and unimportant – had been shoved into a cellar, out of sight, to gather dust, get damp and mouldy. And then a flood obliterated it. So there is no official record of this yawning stretch of Oluwale's life. That his case records should have perished is no doubt just one of those things, but it reminded me of all the other episodes of carelessness and neglect: the photographs which should have been taken of his dead body, but weren't; the indifference to the injury to his head; even the hasty destruction of his clothes. And I was reminded of that terse Interpol statement: 'Subject is not recorded in this country'.

The grim truth is that Oluwale was nobody in life, and he only assumed an importance because of the crimes against him, and because of his death. This is why we can know something of his life. The psychiatrist's statement to detectives, the testimony of a charge nurse, coupled with those institutional records which found their way into the National Archives, give a glimpse of those desolate years in Menston.

The most eloquent piece of detail came in a statement from

Oluwale's psychiatrist. According to Oluwale's hospital record card, in all those years he did not receive a single visitor.

The road to Menston began with a mundane incident. A Saturday-night fight.

The African boys had always had to fight. 'The white man – he want to do you all the time,' Frank Morgan, a big Nigerian, used to warn Joe Okogba. They weren't afraid to retaliate against those who picked fights with them at the Mecca, they even earned respect this way; but they knew it was a fool who took on the Leeds City Police.

On this particular Saturday night, 25 April 1953, there was a fight in the city centre. The Millgarth occurrence book recorded that 'David Ulowale', a twenty-one-year-old West African who resided at 4 Springfield Place, was apprehended at 11.20 p.m. in King Edward Street, and that he was charged with disorderly conduct and assault on police and damage to police uniform. According to the report, PC Maurice Roberts, the arresting officer, was seen by a doctor and received medical treatment for an unspecified injury, while Oluwale was taken to the Bridewell lock-up under the town hall to await a court appearance. Oluwale appeared in front of the magistrate on the Monday and was jailed for two months.

There is no press report to fill in the gaps left by the official record. The story in Jeremy Sandford's *Smiling David* is that Oluwale was arrested during a raid on a black club in connection with the theft of metal; that he brushed against the arm of a policeman and found himself charged with assault. But there was no black club on or anywhere near King Edward Street where the incident occurred; the fact that PC Roberts needed medical treatment also suggests a more violent struggle.

In 1970 detectives questioned Oluwale's old friends about the incident. Their accounts differed on the detail, but all agreed it started with an argument over an unpaid bill at a café or restaurant. One friend, Katsina, placed the incident at the King Edward Hotel, a hang-out of Oluwale's on King Edward Street; the entry in the Millgarth occurrence book supports this. Police were called, the story goes, and a scuffle broke out, during which Oluwale banged his head. The consensus was that he was never the same after that. Certainly, Oluwale's life changed that night.

In Armley jail, serving the short sentence, Oluwale missed the joyous celebrations which marked the Coronation of Queen Elizabeth II. According to the prison's medical officer, he began to act strangely. On 6 June 1953, prisoner 1586 was admitted to St James's Hospital Psychiatric Unit on a fourteen-day court order. He saw psychiatrist Michael Leahy, who recorded that Oluwale appeared 'apprehensive, noisy and frightened without cause'. Leahy saw him again five days later and he was still loud, excitable and appeared terrified. 'Childish and wept when talking of his fears,' Leahy observed. The same day Oluwale was put into an ambulance and driven eleven miles out of the city to Menston Asylum. It was the last Leeds saw of him for eight years. Time passed and his friends stopped asking, 'Where's Yankee?'

David Oluwale was in a long tradition. Since ancient times, deviants, criminals, unwanted people, have been cast out from cities. In Book IX of the *Laws*, Plato describes how, in the model state, incurable criminals who 'pollute the city' were 'cast naked beyond the borders of the land'. Foucault's *Madness and Civilisation* records a medieval German ritual where madmen were whipped, chased in a mock race, then driven out of the city by quarterstaff blows.

The 'others' of society – from the lepers of medieval Europe to the various unproductive social failures of modern Europe – have always been kept at the margins of communities or outside the gates of cities. The modern asylum, which dates from the late eighteenth century, recalled the leper house in its physical segregation from the community, and from the seventeenth-century houses of correction it took the rules of forced labour, physical punishments for the recalcitrant and the belief that madness was a moral and social failing.

Menston had contained Yorkshire's mad, turbulent and inconvenient adults since 1888, when it opened as the West Riding Pauper Lunatic Asylum. Like all the great Victorian asylums it soon filled up, becoming a dumping ground for the senile, elderly, epileptics, hypochondriacs, the son of Bismarck, any number of Jesus Christs and, perhaps the most deluded of all, the hawker convinced he was receiving financial support from the ex-mayor of Bradford.

Far from being swept away in the new enthusiasm for social welfare, the asylum proved highly durable in the post-war years, and the numbers held in such institutions soared to record levels, a consequence of the loosening of familial ties and networks which left families less able and willing to cope with disturbed relatives. Menston was typically overcrowded and understaffed. Its average daily population hovered around the 2,500 mark until the end of the 1950s, with a slightly higher number of women to men. Around the time of Oluwale's admission, patients were forced to sleep on mattresses on the floors because of the shortage of beds.

Set in two hundred acres of woodland and built in solid stone, the asylum was gaunt and imposing with its turrets and arched windows. Its interior was stinking and dirty. General Nursing Council inspection reports from the 1950s reveal that on the male wards the pervading smell was of urine: chamber pots made up for the shortage of proper urinals, piled up in bathrooms waiting to be cleaned; the sluicing of foul linen was undertaken by nurses on the wards. The inspector observed that eleven typhoid carriers were kept at one end of a crowded female dormitory.

A lively twenty-two-year-old at the time of his admission, Oluwale, patient number 30643, must have felt starved of air and space at Menston. Patients slept in overcrowded dormitories, beds (or mattresses) inches apart, harsh red blankets. Some toilets had no doors. Clothing was institutional. There was little to lighten life: few pictures on the uniformly mucus-green walls, uncomfortable chairs, barely any cushions or rugs. Even the softening influence of women was absent. Apart from the occasional mixed social event, a rigid division of the sexes was maintained. Most patients spent long days sprawled out on their beds, played desultory card games, joined the interminable quest for tobacco, sat stupefied in front of the television (which appeared on the wards in the late 1950s) oblivious to what was going on in other wards, never mind the outside world. 'The impression in some wards was of custodial care . . . Keys are very much in evidence,' noted the inspector.

Dr Richard Carty was consultant psychiatrist at Menston. In 1970 he gave this statement: 'When Oluwale arrived at the hospital he became my patient and I examined him. I found him to be restless, noisy and restive. He spoke English fairly well but he was so confused he could give no clear account of himself. He did not know his whereabouts, whence he came or the day or date. He was visionally [*sic*] hallucinating seeing imaginary animals which he described as lions with fishes' heads which he believed were going to kill him. He continued like this for a couple of months then he settled down and became quiet and reasonably lucid. At times he was completely withdrawn and mute. At intervals of about two or three months he would relapse and became overactive, impulsive and aggressive. When he was in this state he was prone to bite people, especially on the fingers.' Dr Carty diagnosed schizophrenia.

Physical treatments such as electroconvulsive therapy (ECT) and insulin coma therapy (ICT), first introduced in the 1930s for severely disturbed patients, have since acquired grisly reputations, but Oluwale entered Menston at a time of high optimism in such treatments. ICT fell out of fashion during the course of Oluwale's confinement, superseded by antipsychotic drugs; ECT, however, was in use throughout the period, into the 1960s and beyond. Oluwale would have experienced the range of treatments.

A common theme in the witness of mental health patients of this period (the Mental Health Testimony Archive which is held in the British Library Sound Archive gives a unique insight into their experiences) is a sense of powerlessness in the face of white-coated authority. Patients often felt pressurised to undergo courses of ICT and ECT, told that it was in their 'best interest'. In ICT the patient was given a controlled dose of insulin to induce a hypoglycaemic coma, which could last a couple of hours, before they were brought round by an injection of glucose. The treatment induced feelings of serenity, making the patient more cooperative; it quelled hallucinations and aggressive outbursts. With ECT, Oluwale would have been picked up from his ward first thing in the morning, put in the minibus and driven round to the treatment room. Consent forms may or may not have been produced. He would have been ushered into the treatment room or wheeled in on a trolley, put on to the bed, strapped down, and given something to bite on so that he didn't swallow his tongue. It wasn't unknown for patients to be given ECT without anaesthetic, but since this carried a risk of fractures it was usual practice to put them under. The nurse would inject him with Pentothal sodium in the back of the hand; a muscle relaxant, scoline, was also administered; the balance had to be right since patients had been known to wake up while the relaxant was still doing its work and find themselves unable to move or speak. Electrodes would be attached to his temple and a high voltage current sent to the brain to bring on a seizure. Nobody knew for certain how it worked, but the effect was to calm the patient. In the 1950s professional faith in ECT was high; the testimonies of those who experienced it tell of severe headaches, feelings of confusion and restlessness, short- and long-term memory loss.

Keeping patients subdued by such methods was the signature of daily life in Menston. There was little occupational therapy in the 1950s. Nurses were largely ignorant of psychiatric approaches to mental illness; no counselling or talking therapy then. When antipsychotic drugs such as chlorpromazine (trade name Largactil) came in around 1955, the tempo of life on wards became slow and more soporific. Throughout the period there was a serious shortage of nurses at the asylum and a general atmosphere of neglect. Hard-pressed nurses doled out medicine (often in slapdash fashion, one inspector noted) between bouts of ward cleaning and food serving. Patients could go for weeks without seeing a doctor. The days passed, one much like the other, turning into months, even years. Typically, there were high numbers of elderly patients left to rot.

Oluwale's life in Menston was particularly grim. He was held on Ward 8, which housed around seventy of the worst cases: chronic patients, the violent, the suicidal and persistent absconders. It had single side rooms with thick doors, spyholes and no lights, where troublesome and recalcitrant patients might find themselves. 'Mechanical restraints' were still in use. Ward 8 stank of paraldehyde and old men's piss.

Eric Dent was a staff nurse at Menston. Apart from the psychiatrist's terse report, the statement Dent gave to detectives in November 1971 is the only significant source for Oluwale's time in the asylum. For this reason it is worth quoting at length:

I am a staff nurse in charge of a unit of wards at High Royds Hospital. I have been employed there since 1952.

I know David Oluwale. I have seen his picture recently in the papers and on television.

I remember him as a patient in High Royds Hospital when it was known as Menston. I knew him for eighteen months, though it may have been longer.

He was in Ward 8, which was a refractory ward. That was for disturbed patients. There would be seventy-two patients in that ward. I was on day duty. There would be seven of us on general duties, but sometimes, due to absences and leave, it would be reduced to six or five.

All of the patients were difficult and violent and unmanageable in other wards, and that was the reason they were placed in a refractory ward. It was a security ward because some of the patients could be violent to the public if they escaped. All could be violent without escaping. Oluwale walked round with a grin on his face and a cloth tied round his head. He was small, about nine and a half stone, and built like a miniature Mr Universe. He was well muscled. During the day he would rather lie on the floor than sit in armchairs. He would particularly lie on the floor near a radiator. Cleaning in those days was done by patients under the supervision of the nurses. He would be asked to move. He would be on the floor with the coat over his head. The patients would ask the nurses to move him on. Generally one would get no response. I would nudge him with my feet on the sole of his foot so I could be as far away from him as possible. That was because he was unpredictable. I would never lean over him and shake his shoulder. Sometimes he would move, other times he would attack the person nearest to him.

When he has been asked to move on I have seen him attack the Charge Nurse. One in particular, Leonard Clapham – everything was going: he was flying at him. It took four of us to restrain him. You could never subdue him. I have never seen him subdued by other patients who he has attacked.

On occasions he has been put into a single room and it has taken three or four of us to put him there. A blanket would be thrown over him and the door locked after we had beaten a hasty retreat.

He attacked Tom Jones, a patient weighing 13½ stone. Tom Jones was trying to ward him off with a chair. He bit through Tom Jones' hand. I remember this particularly because Jones had to have a tetanus injection and tetanus had to be brought from Otley General Hospital because we had none in Menston.

On one occasion a patient called Charlie Ben Clegg was reading a newspaper and Oluwale bit Clegg's left cheek. I approached with others and Oluwale let go of the patient.

He bit Sam Graham, a nurse who is now deceased, on the hand, right through to the bone. He was second in command. I remember this because Sam Graham had been bitten previously and the wound had not healed up when Oluwale bit him again.

He attacked a patient called Eugene Lanche who himself could be violent. Lanche was a big man.

From my experience of nursing patients, I would say he had the most unpredictable behaviour I have ever seen. One did not know whether he would be violent when approached or whether he would smile at you. One always had to be on guard, more with him than anyone else. I would try to deal with him myself knowing that assistance was readily available and nearby within a few feet.

I have seen him attacking other patients who have defended

themselves. Oluwale never got the worst of it. He was too quick and too lithe and he was all go. He was very wick. It was frightening to see him attack someone. It was even frightening for me who am [sic] experienced in mental nursing.

Even if he was controlled one day, he might repeat his conduct the following day. I had been moved to another ward by the time Oluwale had left Menston. It has been known for him to urinate in the ward. His violent and unpredictable behaviour was what struck me. He could take more than Cassius Clay and give back far more. I once saw a patient, who I think was Eugene Lanche, strike him in the toilets. Oluwale had his back to the toilet wall. He struck the wall and he must have hit his spine. I got the impression from the crash that even the wall was shuddering. Oluwale came back snarling like an animal before we restrained him.

Many of the incidents I have mentioned would have been recorded in writing, though some may well have been only reported to the Charge Nurse whose duty it was to record unusual occurrences. All the incidents may not have been recorded because they may not have been considered unusual in that ward.

Oluwale had a great mouthful of teeth and all he wanted to do was get your hand into his mouth and bite. Failing that he would bite you anywhere. He would punch and kick at the same time. He was a patient who one would only approach with the greatest care. Trouble inevitably started when he was asked to move on. When he was violent it was not a matter of subduing him, but self-preservation whilst other help came. Then we had to subdue him. There was no chance of restraining him by oneself.

Unintentionally, the statement revealed a bleak state of affairs on the closed ward. Dent saw Oluwale as a primitive being, moronic grin pasted on his face; someone who disdained the markers of civilisation – armchairs, lavatories; an animal with a snarling 'great mouthful of teeth'; someone who refused to bend to the routine of the ward; someone with superhuman physical capabilities, dishing out the violence and soaking it up like Clay. It was a grotesque image – and it was the one presented at the trial of the men held responsible for Oluwale's death at Leeds Assizes. Oluwale was not like the other patients. He was 'Other'.

Menston had little, if any, experience of someone like Oluwale. There were few patients from outside the West Riding of Yorkshire, never mind Britain. Though his religious affiliation in the register of patients places him with the majority – Church of England – the Lagosian stands out among all the Bradfordians and Loiners. He was one of a small but growing number of black patients in British mental hospitals. A survey in 1962 put that number at 164, including twelve Nigerians; in the early 1950s there were perhaps a few dozen at most. Yet it was enough of a problem to register with the authorities. From the late 1940s there was a social welfare interest in 'colonials' suffering from mental distress, part of a wider concern about what society should do with Africans and West Indians who had become 'destitute and incapacitated' in Britain. A scheme was introduced in 1949 to support the voluntary repatriation of such people.

What little psychiatric interest there was in black people in Britain and mental health in the 1950s was focused on students. The pioneering British-trained Nigerian psychiatrist T. A. Lambo was commissioned to explore the worryingly high incidence of mental breakdown among Nigerian university students in Britain, a problem also addressed by Raymond Prince in an article in the *Journal of Mental Science* (1960), 'The "Brain Fag" Syndrome in Nigerian Students'. Lambo gave weight to the social and cultural factors which were causing mental distress: loneliness, language difficulties, cold lodgings and frugal meals, neglect and social isolation, discrimination in housing, the racism of other students, financial insecurity. Raymond Prince, like Lambo, noted that going overseas and taking something back had become a growing obsession in the better-off Nigerian (and particularly Yoruba) homes, and that the pressures to succeed bore down heavily and unhealthily on the student. But he reached very different conclusions to Lambo. His patients typically complained of a burning sensation in the head and an inability to read – the 'Brain Fag Syndrome' – and he located its causes in the inherent unsuitability of the Nigerian to Western styles of learning. The European approach, which stressed solitary endeavour and personal responsibility, was alien to the Nigerian personality, which preferred collective endeavour and tended to the blind acceptance of authority. He explained this syndrome as an 'unconscious rejection of the education system', a regression to a childlike state free of personal responsibility. The implication was that the Nigerian was fundamentally unfitted for the rigours of intellectual life.

The concerns of Lambo and Prince did not loom large in mental health at that time. Race relations workers barely noted the presence of blacks in the mental hospitals of Britain. It's different today: research has shown a disproportionate number of Afro-Caribbean people in the psychiatric system, and a disproportionate diagnosis of schizophrenia. There isn't space to enter that debate here, but Oluwale's experiences will resonate: the greater likelihood of being sectioned and of being sent to high-security hospitals or wards; the racial stereotype of the black patient as strong, paranoid and dangerous; the feeling that he is more difficult to subdue and needs higher dosages of drugs. The research has shown that the black experience is more likely to be one of control – and the harder end of control – than assistance, and in this respect there are continuities with the black experience of policing and the criminal justice system.

The highly unpredictable Oluwale described by the Menston staff nurse confirmed the racial stereotypes all too predictably. The African as a troublesome child outside rationality, slave to his passions, given to violence, was part of the psychiatric orthodoxy of the 1950s. Respected figures in psychiatry such as J. C. Carothers, whose main research was conducted in British-ruled Kenya, developed a theory of 'The African Mind'. The African was distinguished sharply from the civilised man since he was 'given to phantasy and fabrication ... unstable, impulsive, unreliable, irresponsible, and living in the present without reflection or ambition'. He lived, Carothers wrote, in 'that strange no-man's land 'twixt sleep and wakening where fact and fancy meet on equal terms'. Older prejudices lurked beneath the surface of this so-called ethnopsychiatry: that the African was so dominated by his instincts and emotions that it was dangerous to allow him emancipation; that his brain was less developed than that of a European; that he was unequipped for the serious business of life.

The Oluwale presented in the statements of the psychiatrist and the staff nurse looks like the classic pathological African: aggressive, excitable, childish, prone to aggressive outbursts and persecution anxieties. He is less a real man than an abstraction, an archetype.

Psychiatry, in what was the late autumn of colonialism, was no more enlightened than the rest of society, reflecting its prejudices no less than, say, policing. British popular culture, saturated in empire, had never recognised 'real' African people – just types. Africans were somewhere down the evolutionary scale, somewhere between man and monkey. It was a time of the BBC show the *Coloured Coons Carnival* and Enid Blyton's golliwog stories which every British child was reared on. Every British child knew from his comic books that there were good coons and bad coons: the good coons were the childlike, credulous cretins who laughed at the simplest thing, just passing through the country with the circus, clownish characters; the bad coons were quick of temper, sullen and resentful towards their white masters.

Contemporary politics also had its African bogey figures. Around the time Oluwale was sent to Menston, the British newspapers were full of lurid reports of the atrocities of the Mau Mau, a movement formed from Kenya's largest ethnic group that staged an armed uprising against their British colonial rulers. Ironically, it wasn't a political scientist or a historian who was called on to help the colonial government understand the Mau Mau, but J. C. Carothers. His short report *Psychology of Mau Mau* (1954) presented those resisting colonial rule not as real people with political and economic grievances, but as pathological. It provided a prop for a Manichaean view of the insurgency which ranged beneficent British rule against 'bestial' savagery and terrorism, and which viewed the enemy as a force to be subdued by greater force, greater violence. Since the Mau Mau was classified as subhuman, the rule of law was irrelevant and brutal measures to subdue it justified. Nothing could disrupt Britain's civilising mission.

Perhaps, then, there is something archetypal about Oluwale's violent experiences on Menston's chronic ward. Certain hoary prejudices are present in the staff nurse's story. Oluwale's apparent capacity to soak up physical violence recalls an idea with roots in the Atlantic slave trade that African people were immune to physical suffering. The impossibility of subduing Oluwale other than by great force was another – though one with contemporary colonial resonances also. It's possible to see in Oluwale's life the shadows of a long and violent colonial history in which the bodies of native people were worthless and expendable.

Eric Dent's statement is interesting for another, more mundane, reason. The statement was given to detectives in November 1971 as the trial at Leeds Assizes was under way. Dent came forward with his testimony because he wanted to help the police out: he was worried that the deceased man, Oluwale, was being presented in court as a harmless, Chaplinesque tramp. In the statement, which after all was given over a decade after the events described, Dent's fragmentary memories are shaped into a coherent narrative. The police appear to have suggested words and phrases to him – 'he was asked to move on', 'violent when approached', 'only approach with the greatest care'. This in itself isn't surprising – it was common practice at the time for officers to write up statements back at the station, and police terminology often crept in. But what is so striking is how Dent's statement echoes the testimony of police officers at the trial that was under way – Ward 8 of Menston could almost be the shop doorways and streets of Leeds. The police narrative had Oluwale lying in deep shop doorways; he would be 'moved on' in response to the complaints of shopkeepers; he was 'tickled by the boot' when he didn't respond; and he was so unpredictable and violent – a biter – that it would take several officers to restrain and subdue him. Eric Dent had Oluwale lying on the floor trying to keep warm by the radiator; he would attempt to 'move him on' only after the nurses received complaints from patients; he nudged him with his feet if he didn't respond; trouble started when he was asked to 'move on'; he was so unpredictable – a biter – that it would take several nurses to restrain and subdue him.

This isn't to suggest that Dent's statement was a fabrication. It does suggest that Oluwale's life in Menston had been a violent one, and that in resisting violence he brought further violence on himself. Oluwale's experiences on Ward 8 were a depressing anticipation of those on the streets and in the shop doorways of Leeds city centre.

By the end of the 1950s the tide of opinion had turned against long periods of incarceration in brooding asylums far from anywhere. One reason was cost; another was that antipsychotic tranquillisers opened up the possibility for those suffering from mental illnesses to live as normal a life as possible outside the hospital gates. In March 1961 Enoch Powell, then Minister of Health, gave his famous 'Water Tower' speech, in which he declared that the mentally ill should not be held in 'great isolated institutions', but that the future lay in 'care in the community'.

Just a month after Enoch Powell's speech, on 19 April 1961, Oluwale was discharged from Menston. It was his first taste of freedom since March 1953 and that Saturday night out in Leeds with the boys. The best years of his young life had gone. Ambition had gone, zest for adventure had gone. The sharp clothes had gone, the swagger had gone, Yankee had gone.

3

The Best and the Worst

The pace of change was fast in 1960s Leeds. Not the sort of changes to get nostalgic about. Liverpool had the Beatles, Leeds got an inner ring road, 'Britain's first urban motorway'. No summer of love here: Leeds was, as Bagchi and Rogerson drolly put it, 'a city still more enthralled by Harry Ramsden than Hare Krishna'. The only thing swinging in Leeds was the demolition ball. In 1968, a heady year of liberation and rebellion, student protests at Leeds University were led by a man in a tweed jacket. His name was Jack Straw. Civic pride found its expression, not in monumental buildings, but in motorways, pedestrian precincts, shopping centres, multi-storey car parks, high-rise flats. These were the emblems of Leeds's hurry to embrace the future; mills and back-to-backs, soot and hard toil, were history. And the trams went too.

Much of what the city valued as new and exciting in the 1960s now seems crass and materialistic. To read the memoirs of Alan Bennett is to get a sense that the moral core of Leeds resided within those tightly knit communities killed by overzealous slum clearance programmes. The 1960s was when the city 'fell to greed and mediocrity' and 'avarice and stupidity got to the wheel of the bulldozer'. Walk around Leeds, see the soulless legacy, and it's easy to side with Alan Bennett; but it's also easy to forget the sense of civic pride which was invested in those shopping centres, car parks and precincts. Making Leeds modern, shaking off the image of a dirty Victorian city, was the ambition of the 1960s.

The Leeds David Oluwale returned to was in the demolition stages of this modernising period. His life story from April 1961 was one of struggle to establish his place again in a fast-changing city where the old and the redundant were swept away without sentiment.

Oluwale wasn't the only African having to come to terms with a strange city in April 1961. The same month a young South African called Albert Johanneson signed for Leeds United, a struggling second-division football club. Leeds United was a joke team then, but would end the decade as the best in the country. It was the kind of success that a forward-looking city like Leeds could be proud of. The story of Leeds in the 1960s was the story of Leeds United.

Albert – they struggled with Johanneson in Leeds – would play a big part in that story. He would also become the most famous of that handful of black footballers who played the game at a professional level in 1960s England. In 1965 he made history when he became the first black player to play in an FA Cup Final at Wembley. That match heralded Leeds United's arrival as a serious team, and proved to be the pinnacle of Albert's career.

In 1961 there were around 450 Africans in Leeds. Two of them, Albert and Oluwale, couldn't have been further apart. They were the best and the worst.

Britain presented a hard, cold face to black people, and if anything it was becoming more inhospitable. The public mood was turning sharply against black immigration and the laissez-faire assumptions which had underpinned its immigration policy. In 1961 the Conservative government introduced the Commonwealth Immigrants Bill which proposed ending the unlimited right of all British subjects to enter the United Kingdom. The bill became law and an employment voucher scheme was introduced with quotas favouring those with useful skills. The liberal ideal that its black Commonwealth subjects could think of Britain as their own was being eroded.

The irony was that the legislation, against its intentions, acted as a catalyst for black migration. News of the impending clampdown only prompted a massive surge of immigration: in 1961, 136,000 Commonwealth immigrants arrived in Britain. That number was halved in 1962 as the bill became law, but since the Act had guaranteed the right of spouses, children and grandparents (aged over sixty-five) to enter, there was still substantial immigration throughout the 1960s.

Popular antipathy to immigrants was running high in this period and was not placated by these controls. In every poll conducted, ordinary white British people came out overwhelmingly against black immigration. The 1962 Act was in itself partly a reaction to a hardening public mood after the violent disturbances in Nottingham and Notting Hill four years previously, when white mobs went 'nigger hunting' and blacks fought back determined to show that they were here to stay. The riots were seized on by those who believed that blacks had disturbed the social order. Popular racism had deadly consequences. When Kelso Cochrane, an Antiguan carpenter, was stabbed to death in Notting Hill in May 1959 by a gang of white youths, the murder sickened the same public who didn't want him in this country.

Racism was in a very overt phase. Politicians who stood out against further controls were punished by voters; those who demanded 'Keep Britain White' were rewarded. Albert had left apartheid behind, but in 1960s Britain a colour bar operated in many areas of social life. Dance halls were still refusing entry to blacks. Building societies routinely turned down mortgages to blacks. In 1963, Albert might have heard about the protest against the Bristol Omnibus Company's policy of refusing to hire black workers on the grounds that it would put white women off becoming conductresses (the idea of blacks as sexual threat was the subtext). Legislation was eventually introduced by the Labour government to end such public expressions of discrimination, though it would be powerless against the racial prejudice which still thrived in private establishments, in places such as Woodhouse Recreation Club and Social Institute in Leeds, which passed a resolution in 1964 that 'no coloured personnel should be allowed membership or to frequent the club'. Working men's clubs were at the very heart of northern male working-class culture, a symbol of fraternity, but this particular club would go on excluding blacks right through until the end of the 1970s.

Albert

It was an awkward, soft-spoken shy young man who arrived from Johannesburg early in 1961 to begin a three-month trial with Leeds United. Many years later, towards the end of his life, Albert recalled his complete ignorance of life beyond his township: 'I didn't know there was an England. Or even a Queen.'

Blacks under South Africa's apartheid system were not told about England or the Queen or anything else other than the fact of their complete subjection. They had their assigned place, useful for the dirty work – servants in white homes, shovelling rocks in mines. Born in 1942 in Germiston, the industrial powerhouse of the East Rand, Albert reached adulthood as apartheid was entering its hardest period, a time when black opposition to the pass laws – the symbol of their daily humiliation – was crushed mercilessly. Gang fights and lawlessness, alcoholism and drug addiction, were rife in the townships. Football, hugely popular among young urban blacks, offered the cleanest of the temporary releases from appalling poverty and brutal policemen demanding 'Where's your pass, Kaffir?' In football you were judged not by the colour of your skin but by how skilful and how fast you were. Albert was both. Playing barefooted for Germiston Coloured School they called him 'Hurry Hurry' Johanneson. At the highest level, however, sport, reflecting society, was divided on colour lines, Albert's local professional team, Germiston Callies, playing in the whites-only National League.

But a schoolteacher took Albert under his wing and gave him his lucky break. He had connections with Leeds United: one of his discoveries was Gerry Francis (not to be confused with the QPR and England star of that name), who had been at Leeds since 1957 and was the club's first black player. Between them they managed to secure a trial for Albert. Even to be on the plane to England was an extraordinary achievement. His trial period went well, the fans chanting 'sign him on', though he suffered badly from the northern cold. Leeds's new manager Don Revie took to him and in April 1961 Albert became his first signing.

Leeds United protected him as he found his feet. He soon moved into a club-owned semi-detached in West Lea Gardens, Moortown. Most of the people who lived around there were white-collar types. His neighbour, Gil Greenwood, and Leeds teammate, Willie Bell, took him to a football match at Huddersfield the night he moved in – a wet, cold night under the new 'Denis Law lights'. Albert was slight, a little over 5'6", and seemed very vulnerable, shivering on the terraces in his raincoat.

It was difficult for the South African. He struggled to adjust to the climate and the food, except, and rather worryingly for the manager, he got a taste for fish and chips (Leeds was, after all, the 'intellectual capital of fish and chips'). Not everything was strange and different: his home town was at the centre of South Africa's clothing industry, just as Leeds was at the centre of Britain's. And some of the pain of adjustment was eased by the presence of Gerry Francis. At the end of the 1960–1 season they played in the same side and the media made a huge fuss and called them the 'Johannesburg Twins'. But it was to be a one-off: Francis was transferred at the end of the season.

At the time of Don Revie's appointment, Leeds United was in danger of being relegated, playing to sparse crowds in an indifferent city where the oval ball ruled. They were referred to locally as the 'Clowns' and 'Leeds Urinals' and hadn't won a thing since 1924. Revie pledged to turn his team into the best in the country; in 1961 they weren't even the best in the West Riding. Revie wanted his players to think like winners. One of his first disrespectful acts towards the traditions of Leeds United – such as they were – was to jettison the blue-and-all-gold strip, the colours of the city, for an all-white one. He reasoned that since white was the colour of the best club team in the world, Real Madrid, that was good enough for Leeds. When they ran out in that gleaming pure kit for the first time there were wolf whistles from the Scratching Shed. Revie wanted the club, from chairman to centre forward to laundrywoman, to be as a family; the individual was nothing, the tribe was everything. Though the heart of the team would be Scottish, and though there were Welsh, Irish, Geordie and African players, as a collective Leeds United became the perfect expression of Yorkshireness. In time, as the never overpassionate Leeds public warmed to its team, Revie's creation would become a perfect expression of the character of the city.

Revie's team was full of 'characters', tough lads from tough backgrounds. Into this environment came Albert, an intensely private person. Few had any sense of the society he came from; even to his closest friends he shared little of his early years in Germiston.

To be talked to respectfully by white men, to be called 'Albert' not 'Kaffir', was new. Revie had to insist that Albert let an apprentice clean his boots after he'd refused, unable to get his head round the idea of a white person doing his dirty work. On his debut he crossed the ball which led to a Jack Charlton goal, but froze when his teammates ran over to congratulate him – back in Germiston to have white men running after you was bad news. The Scratching Shed took to him, chanting 'Albert, Albert', but he would never be comfortable with the adulation of the crowd. He always addressed autograph hunters as 'Sir'.

The most traumatic experience for Albert was the team bath. Bathing was strictly segregated under apartheid. The first time he dillied and dallied round the edges. He was told he had to get in the bath to be one of the lads, that he was equal, that God had given every man a cock and two balls. They had to grab him and throw him in.

His speed and stamina astonished his teammates. In cross-country he could slaughter the field. Peter Lorimer recalled that 'Albert would set off like a puma homing in on its prey, with everybody shouting, as he started to disappear from view, "Slow down, Albert. Give us a chance!" That is, everyone except Jack Charlton who'd say, "Look at Albert. Daft bastard. Let him run."' Some of Albert's ball skills seemed uncanny. He got called the

'Black Stanley Matthews'. Everyone remembered the time he slipped the tackles of three Newcastle players who seemed to have boxed him in, then chipped the keeper to score one of the best goals ever seen at Elland Road. The fans loved their 'Black Flash'.

But for all that Leeds was a family, Albert was a distant member. Lorimer told me, 'He never mixed with the guys. He was always invited when we were going in town – but he preferred to keep himself to himself. He didn't invite conversation. Quietly went about his business. Nobody knew nothing about his life in South Africa. After matches he would just get off.'

Oluwale

Nowadays we might refer to someone like Oluwale as a 'care-in-the-community type', by which we would mean someone whose path we'd try to avoid crossing at all costs. Oluwale was discharged from Menston when the idea of community care was first in the air, but for many there was no community to return to. He was like so many other mental hospital patients who, on release, simply drifted into the shadow parts of Britain's cities.

Within days of his release, Oluwale found a room at 209 Belle Vue Road and a labouring job at Storey Evans & Co., but his efforts to adjust back into society failed. He was soon sacked from his job when the foreman – so it was alleged – caught him with his hand in the pocket of another man's coat. Christmas Ogbonson, one of the few old friends to help him, found him work at the West Yorkshire Foundry. He lasted a few months before he was sacked for fighting with a Jamaican worker. The story was that Oluwale pulled a knife. The foreman was to tell detectives many years later that Oluwale 'thought he was better than the other coloured fellers'.

From then on Oluwale found little in the way of employment, which meant that he couldn't get lodgings. In the summer of 1962 he left the city. In June he signed on at a labour exchange in Islington, London; in August he was back up north, signing on in Sheffield, where he'd lived for a short time in 1951. Perhaps he was hoping to get back together with the Sheffield woman said to be called Gladys. If so it must have been a long shot: Oluwale had received no visits from a Gladys, or anyone else for that matter, during his eight years away. He was back in Leeds by September.

So much had changed. There were no friends to whom he could turn. Most were married by then and raising children. They didn't want him around. Tex said that Oluwale could stop just one night when Slim took him round soon after his release. He was a very different person from the exuberant Yankee they'd known: nervous and twitchy, slow, laughing for no reason, shuffling along. They thought that the bang to his head had made him simple. They couldn't know that these were side effects of the kinds of treatments he'd received over a long period.

Oluwale hung around parks. He was seen sleeping in the 'Jews' Park'. He used an executive briefcase for his pillow and covered himself in *The Times*. When he got up in the morning he'd fold his newspapers carefully and put them back in his briefcase.

In a workaday city with unemployment running below 1 per cent, those who wouldn't or couldn't conform to the routine of home, family and job were always likely to fall within the gaze of the police. PC Dave Stanton had not long been a beat constable when he encountered Oluwale. It was September 1962, Stanton was working nights, patrolling the middle section of the city centre. In the doorway of Maple, Denby & Spinks' furniture shop on Albion Street he came across a pile, almost tripped over it, and realised it was a body wrapped up in newspapers. He put a torch on it, gave it a tap, and said, 'Can't sleep here, pal.' Oluwale got up and started to dance round him, shaking a bag which (as he told the Oluwale investigation) 'rattled as if it contained bones'. Stanton thought it some weird voodoo ritual. A few weeks later, the PC saw him on Boar Lane. Stanton asked him how things were going, why he wasn't making his way up to St George's Crypt, the homeless shelter. Oluwale told him he got a hard time there because of his colour. Stanton got a sense that there was no support for him at all. The young bobby saw a lot of Oluwale after that, usually sitting by himself on the bench outside Holy Trinity Church. Oluwale would acknowledge him with a lift of the hand.

More often Oluwale met with incomprehension. Officers who came across him on the streets or sleeping in shop doorways would describe him as 'jabbering away like a witch doctor', or muttering in a strange tongue.

On 21 September 1962, Oluwale was on Woodhouse Moor up near the university and, according to reports, shouting abuse at passers-by. When the park keeper ordered him to leave, Oluwale turned on him. More than forty years on, Harold Robinson, the arresting officer, recalled the incident. 'It was one Saturday morning in midsummer and a call went out for any officer in the vicinity of Woodhouse Moor where an officer was wanting assistance. I was only a couple of minutes away and I told them on the radio I'd be there. And when I arrived, there were three people. A very young police constable (PC 551 Read), clearly not long out of training school. An old park ranger in a state of shock – and he pointed out his, I think it was his left ring finger, which was hanging on with a bit of gristle, covered in blood. And he pointed to a black man who was nearby. He was a shortish, thick-built man with deep anthropoid features. Huge teeth, sunken eyes. He was a black tramp, that's the top and bottom of it, living rough, very poorly educated, unable to express himself. When I arrested him it was as if he was living in a dream. He made no comment.' The report of Oluwale's court appearance in the *Yorkshire Evening Post* stated that the unemployed labourer of no fixed abode had broken the park keeper's finger, which had needed ten stitches. Oluwale was jailed for six months for malicious wounding. He served his sentence in Hull prison during what was England's coldest winter since 1740.

Albert

Frozen pitches meant there was no football for three months. On an icy Wednesday in February 1963 at Blenheim Baptist Church, Albert married a Jamaican woman, Norma, a dispenser at the Leeds General Infirmary. As the wedding party trooped out, schoolboys in the shivering huddle of well-wishers shouted 'Good old Albert'.

As he waited for the thaw, he could look back on his best run of form, five goals in seven games in the autumn. The pile-up of fixtures after the long break damaged Leeds's promotion chances, but Albert had made his mark. The next season, 1963–4, would be his best. United won the second-division championship and Albert scored fifteen league and cup goals, a post-war club record for a winger. A record in the calypso style ('The Leeds United Calypso') was cut to mark the club's success.

Leeds United calypso
Leeds United calypso
I feel so happy I feel so fine
The Elland Road lads are pals of mine

We've got Englishmen and Irishmen and Scotchmen, too
And our goalie called Sprake (from Wales look you)
Albert Johanneson is one of the few
I don't know where he comes from but I think it's Timbuctoo

It's the Leeds United calypso (sing it now)
Leeds United calypso

Albert was glamour and excitement in a dour team. He had skills and tricks that nobody had ever seen before in this direct, no-nonsense part of the country. He was 'our Albert', one of the family.

And he was, as that calypso song pointed out, 'one of the few'. There had been black and African players before him in the English professional game, but at this time he was the only one playing at the highest level. An anomalous presence, he had great curiosity value, and in that pure white kit a real aura. No more Scunthorpe, Rotherham, Northampton, he was now playing in front of crowds of 50–60,000, at Arsenal, Everton, Manchester United, running down the wing just touching distance away from packed terraces.

He was coming up against much tougher opponents and, away from the Elland Road cocoon, tougher crowds. He was in a team infamous for its combative, robust approach to the game, such that they earned the sobriquet 'Dirty Leeds'. Revie's men attracted violence. Albert, slight and skilful, was frequently kicked off the park. He bore many scars. In one particularly notorious game at Everton in 1964, the ball was an irrelevance, the tackling so vicious that the teams were taken off the pitch to cool down (the first time this had happened in an English league game). 'A Z Cars match in Z Cars territory,' the *Yorkshire Evening Post* called it, a reference to the hard-hitting TV police drama. Goodison Park bayed for Leeds blood; Leeds players feared they might be lynched; rubbish and missiles were thrown at the directors' box, a rocket was aimed at Leeds goalkeeper Gary Sprake. For Albert it was a harrowing occasion, with monkey noises and bananas aimed at him. At half-time he complained to Don Revie that an Everton player had called him 'black bastard'; Revie told him he should call him 'white bastard' back. Albert came off the field in tears that day.

It could hardly have been expected for football – that cornerstone of white working-class communality – to have been more sensitive than the wider society. Just weeks before that Everton game, a Conservative candidate for a West Midlands seat at the general election famously campaigned under the slogan 'If you want a nigger neighbour, vote Liberal or Labour'. He bucked the national trend and ousted the sitting candidate.

Albert's former teammates downplay the impact of racism on his career. Peter Lorimer, a young player coming through when Albert was at his peak, told me: 'I was a Scotsman and they give us as much stick. We were "Scottish bastards" and the Welsh were "Welsh bastards" – and you just accepted it. But if you say it to the coloured guy they seem to take exception as if it's against them. I don't think it's against them. I think it's a way a crowd gets on to you. But being a professional is all part of accepting all these things.' Albert, according to Lorimer, 'didn't seem to be able to cope with the bigger stage, the bigger crowds, the better teams. It all seemed a bit too much for him, culminating of course in his FA Cup Final display which was very poor. I think that the occasion was just too much for him.'

I'd heard the stories. Albert's non-performance always gets mentioned. According to Ian St John, who played for Liverpool in that final, Albert looked drawn before the game and vomited. The consensus was that he 'bottled it'. I thought I should see a video of that game. *1 May 1965*: Leeds United's first ever Wembley appearance. It's not a DVD that flies off the shelves in Leeds.

I watch the game with BBC commentary. During the warm-up: 'There's Johanneson, South African, the first coloured player ever to appear at Wembley.' The crowd's songs and chants tell you about the characters of cities. Liverpool: 'You'll never walk alone' – sentimental, tuneful, Celtic. Leeds has no songs, just *Leeds, Leeds, Leeds, Leeds, Leeds* –

Albert starts off brightly enough. 'Looking for all the world like a Brazilian than a South African,' the commentator remarks. Gary Sprake throws a ball out to him on the left, the first time he's had space to run, and there's a din of monkey noises from the Liverpool fans.

Albert hardly gets a touch; the defenders are always on to him. In extra time, chasing an equaliser, he finds yards of space and there's an expectant roar, he loses control of the ball on the rain-sodden surface and it turns into a huge groan. He looks a forlorn figure by the end.

He receives his loser's medal from the Queen. He can barely meet her eyes as she shakes his hand. Commentator: 'Albert Johanneson – first South African, well, the first coloured player rather, to play here.'

Oluwale

This was the ideal. Welfare-state Britain as a family, each individual connected to and taking responsibility for the other. The inclusive society.

The stranger, the immigrant, the deviant, the maladjusted, the criminal – they were part of us too. The marginal would be brought in from the margins; assimilated, reintegrated, socialised, cured, corrected by experts, social workers, counsellors, enlightened penal policies, probation officers, therapeutic drugs – until they became like us. One of the family.

Another ideal: economic citizenship. A society which would incorporate ever greater numbers of its population into the social dream of full employment, good health care and home ownership. The 'better Britain' would be the 'home-centred society', a dream which, with full employment and rising incomes, was coming within the grasp of an ever larger part of the population.

One of Oluwale's few permanent addresses after his discharge from Menston was 15 Mexborough Avenue, Chapeltown. He stayed there for several months in 1963. Many years later, the landlord, John James Mills, would tell detectives that they exchanged few words 'because he was an African and we are West Indian'. Oluwale's 'home' for the middle chunk of the 1960s was a derelict house, 12 St Alban's Place. He was there, squatting, on and off, between 1964 and 1967.

There was optimism in the post-war years that homelessness and vagrancy would be consigned to history. If homelessness was thought about at all it was regarded as a problem of incurable late-middle-aged alcoholic men, less a societal problem than one of individual failing. Yet Leeds had large numbers of homeless in the 1960s. At the centre of Britain's transport network, it was a natural stopping-off place for itinerant labourers on the new motorways and the office developments. Most of the homeless still had a roof over their heads at night. There were nine hundred hostel beds in Leeds and they were always occupied. The largest, Shaftesbury House, only took those who were working. Going down the scale, there were two church-run hostels in the city centre, the Church Army and the Salvation Army, which together accommodated around two hundred men. Lower still in the hierarchy was the Grove Common Lodging House on Wharf Street, a desolate hole with rows of ex-army beds and chamber pots. Finally there was St George's Crypt. It had been started in the 'hungry thirties' by an energetic vicar who cleared the church crypt of decaying coffins and turned it into a place where the destitute could shelter and get a hot meal. Over a hundred men a night were accommodated free of charge. It was said that the Crypt refused nobody.

At the very bottom were the rough sleepers or 'dossers'. A few dozen at most slept on the streets of Leeds, under railway arches, in derelict buildings, church grounds and at the brickyards. Oluwale was one of these. An anomalous presence: younger than most, the only black man. Among the dosser community, he was the lowest of the low.

During this bleak period of his life, Oluwale only had one experience of something resembling normal home life. In June 1964, shortly after serving a month in prison for disorderly conduct, he was admitted to Faith Lodge. An annexe of St George's Crypt opened in 1953, Faith Lodge gave a home to alcoholics, ex-prisoners and ex-mental hospital patients. Faith Lodge was at 2 Well Close Place, the terraced house he'd stayed at fifteen years earlier after serving his sentence for stowing away. Though it was still the same gas-lit street, many houses had been divided up into bedsits. Two houses were crammed with Africans studying at Leeds Commerce College. It might have reminded Oluwale of those early years with the boys at Belle Vue Road and Grove Terrace. The students may have wondered how a fellow African had come to find himself in a home for middle-aged derelicts.

Faith Lodge was one step above the streets, but it was a community for those who had nothing. Residents were usually middle-aged men who'd shown commitment to change. Oluwale's name appears on the electoral register alongside eight other men, some who'd been there two or three years. It wasn't a hostel for the transient. They shared spartan rooms, privacy barely protected by flimsy partitions. The warden, Donald Paterson, lived in a one-room flat on the ground floor. He tried to inculcate a Christian family ethos. Oluwale stayed there until October 1964 when he was jailed again for being drunk and disorderly. 'A timid little man who had language difficulties and was simple-minded,' is how Paterson remembered him. He guessed he may have been Nigerian – he wasn't sure, he hadn't asked. They weren't interested in pasts at Faith Lodge.

On his release from prison he was back on the streets and at the same derelict house. It was there, a year later, that he got involved in a violent struggle with two policemen who caught him entering the premises, as a result of which he was charged with malicious wounding.

While on remand in Armley, a report was prepared by the senior medical officer, Dr Power. Dr Carty, who knew Oluwale well, was called in from High Royds Hospital, and found Oluwale garrulous, overactive and aggressive in manner, 'very paranoid about the police who he accused of ill-treating him, stealing his money and persecuting him' and 'paranoid about the National Health Insurance authorities'. To Carty, Oluwale admitted attacking a police officer and being sacked from his job for fighting, that he'd lived a vagrant life and was a heavy drinker of rum and sherry. Carty reported that Oluwale claimed to hear threatening voices (sometimes in English, sometimes Yoruba). He concluded that Oluwale was a 'dullard'. Dr Power recommended that he be detained in a psychiatric hospital under section 60 of the Mental Health Act 1959 – an indefinite period. He was sent to High Royds Hospital on 11 November 1965.

Menston Asylum had been renamed High Royds in 1963. Part of the rebranding involved naming the old numbered wards after places in the Yorkshire Dales – rolling allusions for the psychotropic age. Some of the hardness had gone. Standards of sanitation and hygiene had improved, but there were still too many beds and too much communal clothing. Some wards had an 'open door' policy, but Ward 8, now called Hazelwood, did not.

Oluwale became Dr Carty's patient again. When he was admitted he told Carty he was a single man, of no fixed abode, and had no idea who his next of kin was. He slowly settled down, becoming less 'aggressive' and 'overactive', but according to Carty he remained elated, garrulous and 'somewhat childish'.

Because of his history of violence he was held in Hazelwood. Now a senior probation officer in Leeds, Leroy Phillips was a psychiatric nurse at High Royds in 1970 and worked on Hazelwood. He didn't know Oluwale, but when the former patient's name was all over the newspapers he heard the stories. Phillips got the sense that while Oluwale could be a handful at times, if he was dealt with in the right manner he was fine. There were far worse than him on Hazelwood. Most felt pity for the young man, apparently without family or friends, who'd spent so many years of his life in such a dismal place. When Eric Dent went into the witness box with his story, there was a feeling that he had exaggerated the danger Oluwale posed to staff and other patients. Phillips remembered Dent as an 'old-school charge nurse'.

It was unfortunate that the only testimony Leeds Assizes heard from High Royds should have been so completely damning of Oluwale. Care, concern and sympathy for his plight seemed to be absent. It was a pity that the court never heard from David Odamo. In November 1971, just after the trial began, Odamo wrote a letter to the Chief Constable of Leeds City Police. Odamo, Nigerian and Yoruba like Oluwale, came to England in the mid-1960s to train as a psychiatric nurse. He had been surprised to see no mention of Oluwale's stay at High Royds in the press coverage of the case, and he was aggrieved by the one-sided portrayal of Oluwale as a violent man. This was Odamo's brief testimony: 'Though he was a victim of circumstances, he was not a violent person. He was one of the unlucky ones among us immigrants that accepted his fate . . . It was in the hospital where I was a staff nurse that I came across David. I helped him two times to write letters to his father whom he said was a Chief at Ikole-Ekiti in Western Nigeria . . . He was then expressing his wish to go back to Nigeria if they could send the fare back to him.' (A number of Oluwale's old friends would confirm that he was expressing a desire to go 'home'.) We don't know what happened to the letters, whether they reached the man Oluwale referred to as 'father' and what response there was, if any. David Odamo, perhaps one of the few people to show Oluwale care and sympathy, was not called to Leeds Assizes to tell his story.

Oluwale left High Royds on 27 April 1967 and returned to Leeds. According to Dr Carty, he was quiet and 'cooperative', his hallucinations had faded and he had lost most of his 'persecutory ideas'.

Leeds 1967

Political leaders in Leeds had either to be endowed with a big personality or, failing that, rapidly acquire one. It was an obsession of the local constituency machines to have parliamentary candidates of front-bench potential. Keith Joseph, Merlyn Rees and Denis Healey were MPs for Leeds seats at this time. The message: Westminster, keep your nose out of the affairs of our city, we are important, we are Leeds, we have to be treated with respect. Even purely local leaders acquired national reputations, Karl Cohen in the 1950s and 60s for his pioneering work in housing restoration (though he was an even more enthusiastic demolisher) being the best example.

If decline was not to become an irreversible fact, Leeds in the 1960s needed big men with big visions, a fresh injection of that Victorian self-confidence. Frank Marshall, who became leader of Leeds City Council in May 1967, the first Conservative leader since 1953, was the man to deliver it. 'No doubt many people will put themselves forward as the saviour of Yorkshire,' he declared, 'well, I intend to get my blow in first for Leeds.'

It wasn't that Leeds hadn't been modernising – Labour leaders were always urging the electorate to remember how grim the city was before the war, and how far it had progressed – but to the outside world it retained an image of muck and misery. Under its new saviour, Leeds began to tell a different story about itself – of dynamism and the embrace of the modern. If the motorway was the icon of modernity, then Leeds would identify itself wholeheartedly with motorways. Early in 1967 the first stage of the inner ring road was opened; by October of that year the M1 had reached Stourton on the edge of Leeds – the obsession over the next few years was to bring it right into the city centre. Marshall's vision, packaged as 'Project Leeds', was of 'exciting flyovers and splendid roads' twisting and spiralling their course round the city. Leeds, 'a city magnificently placed at the civilised centre of Britain', would surge forward into the next decade. Someone dreamed up the phrase 'Leeds: Motorway City of the Seventies' and it stuck:

when the new decade came, letters posted from Leeds were franked with the slogan.

Despite its sooty image, the post-war years saw Leeds's manufacturing industries contract and service industries – health and education, hotels, shops, insurance and banking, law and accountancy – expand. By 1968 more people worked in offices than in the clothing industry. It was becoming a different kind of city. Yet the population of Leeds was declining, with young people leaving in droves for better opportunities down south. To reverse this trend the city geared all its efforts to attracting more investment in the burgeoning service sector. Changing the image of the city was vital.

The Conservatives under Frank Marshall positioned themselves as a force for all that was progressive, dynamic and modern. Its manifesto, 'Let's get Leeds moving', said that the country's third largest city (in area) should be in its 'right place of importance and influence', 'good to live in, good to work in, good to look at, in short, a city to be proud of'. Leeds had been gloomy under the socialists; Tories would brighten up the city centre and abolish 'dereliction and decay'. Its narrow traffic-choked streets would be paved over to form spacious tree-lined pedestrian precincts 'to the delight of retailers and shoppers alike'.

'Project Leeds' gave the city a vigorous push in a direction it was already heading: motorways and shopping centres were already a part of Leeds's landscape; the war against dereliction and decay was well under way. The city had lost its seedy wartime reputation but with that much of its rough-and-ready energy. 'A curiously deserted place,' that's how one writer saw Leeds. 'Project Leeds' was in no way a celebration of urban living – the city was a place to work in, shop in, and then leave.

The large numbers of homeless – those who could never be part of the 'Shopper's Paradise' – were an embarrassment to the city. That there were fewer hotel beds in the city than hostel beds was an uncomfortable fact for those trying to present a vision of social success. Would that the homeless problem could be cleaned away like the Gypsy problem. In 1967 the council appointed an enforcement officer whose job was to tow Gypsy caravans away and drop them on the other side of the city boundary. An ex-policeman was given the job, the son of the Revd Charles Jenkinson, visionary chairman of the Leeds housing committee in the 1930s. Revd Jenkinson's legacy was the revolutionary Quarry Hill flat complex, which became the largest municipal housing estate in England and replaced some of the city's most terrible slums. Every time Jenkinson Jr towed a caravan off Holbeck Moor I imagine he might have dignified his task by thinking of the great family tradition of removing eyesores from the city.

Albert

Leeds United was hungry for success. Anxious his team was doomed to be perpetual runners-up, Don Revie believed Leeds United's poor fortunes were down to a curse placed on the club when scrubland was cleared of Gypsies to make room for Elland Road Stadium. Revie was an intensely superstitious man who always wore a lucky blue suit, always took a rabbit's foot with him to the dugout, and so nobody was too surprised when he brought in a Romany Gypsy from Scarborough to exorcise the curse.

Under his leadership a new team was in the making, and it was attracting a vociferous, more youthful following. The aura of violence still clung to Leeds, but there was a new professionalism to their cynicism, a move, as Bagchi and Rogerson put it in their history of the Revie years, from 'brute force to gamesmanship, white-collar sharp practice instead of blue-collar barbarity'.

Talented youths were coming through. One of the strongest of the younger generation was Eddie Gray who played in Albert's position on the left wing. Gray was confident, sure of his abilities and cocky – everything Albert wasn't. And he was hungry for Albert's place.

Peter Lorimer thought that the first time the club became aware of Albert's drink problem was after a game against Nottingham Forest: 'Albert was having a bit of a stinker and Don took him off at half-time. Les Cocker always had a bottle of whisky in the dressing room. Some lads liked a quick shot to clear the pipes before they went out. And when we came in he was sat in the corner and it was obvious he was drunk and the bottle of whisky was empty.' Eddie Gray tells a similar story, dating it at some time during the 1966–7 season, though placing it at Stoke.

The more upset Albert was at not getting selected the more he drank, and the more he drank the more his fitness suffered and his play deteriorated. He began to miss training or turn up the worse for drink. He showed up for reserve games smelling of booze, giggly. Relations with his manager became strained: Revie felt let down by an ungrateful son; Albert felt rejected by the father figure.

Albert still made twenty-two league starts in the 1966–7 season, scoring a creditable seven goals. He even got a hat-trick in a European game. And when he wasn't training at the club he would be seen running around Moortown. He was holding it together, but only just.

The following season he made only eight league starts, though again he got goals. The fans still loved him, still sang 'Albert's better than Eusebio', but he was drifting to the margins of the Leeds United family.

When Leeds beat Arsenal 1–0 in the 1968 League Cup Final at Wembley it was their first major trophy and a watershed moment for the club. Albert wasn't part of that team. Greater successes would come, but Albert wouldn't share in them. Later in that season Leeds went on to lift the UEFA Fairs Cup. Some said that the Gypsy's curse had been lifted.

Oluwale

Every policeman in the city centre, every shop cleaner, every nightwatchman, knew him. Some gave him nicknames. 'George' was one. 'Lame Darkie', because he walked with a limp, was another.

He was faithful to the same shop doorways: John Peters on Lands Lane, the Bridal House on The Headrow, Eve Brown's on Kirkgate, Peter's 'Sew and Save' button and cotton shop in Thornton's Arcade (this Victorian arcade connected Lands Lane and Briggate and was built along the line of a medieval burgage plot). He liked deep doorways where he'd be less exposed to the northern nights.

Some saw a passive thing who would talk to himself in a 'sing-song voice'. Harry Franks, an optician who had a business next to Peter's 'Sew and Save', used to have the odd word with Oluwale when making late visits to his shop on Tuesday nights. 'He never gave me any trouble . . . He always appeared to me to be an inoffensive sort of man,' he told a detective on the investigation. A traffic warden, Harry Henderson, once saw Oluwale outside Lewis's department store with a baby's dummy in his mouth.

'[He] just seemed to walk around and have nowhere to go,' Costas Athinodorou, proprietor of the Riviera restaurant on New Briggate, would tell detectives. 'He seemed to be a harmless type of person although I formed the opinion that he was a bit mental. He used to wear dark clothing but sometimes I saw him wearing a red woollen cap or sometimes a cap with a peak and sometimes a coloured scarf, thin, like a woman's. He used to wear boots, black like a soldier's. He never carried on a proper conversation, just something like "Hello, pal, how are you keeping, all right?" and then he would walk away towards Chapeltown. Every time I saw him he looked miserable and scruffy.'

Oluwale was living a solitary existence. He wasn't part of the rough-arsed bonhomie of the city's rough sleepers – he was too different. When the investigation opened into his death, detectives were frustrated by the elusiveness of the man. Hostels and lodging houses didn't appear to know him. The Crypt said there was no record of him ever coming to them for help. The manager of the Grove hostel said: 'Our hostel does not take in coloured men and never have [*sic*] done.'

Policemen tried to move him from their patch. Typically, he would grumble, gather up his belongings in his duffel bag and 'shuffle off', 'chuntering' under his breath. Sleeping out was not an arrestable offence and Leeds City Police standing orders stated that officers were to direct vagrants to the nearest reception centre; only if they persisted in sleeping out would they be arrested and charged with an offence. Since the nearest reception centre was in Bradford, vagrants were usually pointed in the direction of the Crypt. But Oluwale wouldn't go to the Crypt.

In 1967, the vagrancy laws were used against Oluwale on four occasions, and on three occasions the arresting officer was PC Thorne, just out of training school and no doubt keen to impress his superiors. When questioned by detectives, he told them he'd moved Oluwale on and directed him to the Bradford reception centre, but that he kept returning to the same spots, leaving him with no option but to arrest him.

Oluwale was in Armley again in September 1967. He was interviewed by the prison welfare officer, F. Hartley, prior to his release. Hartley recorded that the prisoner had been out of work since 1961 and that work was unlikely in the future; that he wasn't worried about accommodation and intended to move into Faith Lodge; that he had no clothes of his own; that he wouldn't be contacting aftercare. The prisoner gave his next of kin as David Sature Oluwuala – perhaps this was the father the High Royds nurse had tried to contact. In his physical description of the prisoner, the prison welfare officer noted that he was of 'slight' build.

Oluwale found trouble again on the afternoon of Boxing Day 1967. Two women complained to PC Simpson that a black man had exposed himself to them on Lands Lane. Oluwale admitted the offence when Simpson caught up with him in Queen's Arcade (one of the arcades linking Lands Lane and Briggate). He was charged with indecent exposure and given a three-month prison sentence, most of which was served in Preston.

There are two sources which give us a glimpse of Oluwale at this time. One, who came forward at the time of the investigation of Oluwale's death, was Leslie Shepherd. He had known Oluwale from Sheffield and met him again in Preston prison in early 1968. He found a 'vastly different' Oluwale from the man he'd known. He managed a brief word with him in the exercise yard but found it impossible to communicate with him – he'd just laugh or shrug his shoulders. Shepherd thought 'that he had gone a bit mental' and remembered him walking round the exercise yard and spitting into his jacket pockets.

The second source is a report from A. T. Elliot, the prison welfare officer at Preston. He met Oluwale on 13 March 1968 to discuss his 'discharge plan'. Oluwale told him that he had a wife and children in Sheffield but that he didn't want to see them again. He told him that he had served a number of 'wandering abroad' sentences, and that he'd be back on the streets since he had no home to go to. Elliot observed that he was 'a man of very low IQ' with an 'extremely shaky' command of English. Oluwale was released from prison on 29 March with a small discharge grant.

His old friends bumped into him around Leeds from time to time, to mutual embarrassment. Steve Oke saw him at a bookmaker's on North Street and thought that he had gone 'a little bit mental'. The last time Tex saw him was on North Street sometime in 1968; Oluwale told him he was fed up and thinking of returning to Nigeria. Oluwale took Tex round to see the derelict house he was stopping at; Tex gave him a few shillings for something to eat. Christmas Ogbonson saw him for the last time – he thought it was early 1968 – from a bus window as he made his way home. He was sitting with a couple of tramps on a bench outside the Holy Trinity Church.

Nobody had more contact with Oluwale in 1967–8 than Abbey Sowe. He knew him from those carefree nights at the Mecca. Since then much had changed. Sowe had moved to the suburbs, he had children, he was building up his wholesale crockery business, Northern Pottery.

They met again sometime after Oluwale's release from High Royds. Sowe's warehouse was near to the squat and Oluwale more or less landed on the doorstep, looking thin and weak. This is how Sowe remembered their meeting: 'I noticed that Olu was in a very bad way, he was shabbily dressed in a very old raincoat and a flat cap and was carrying an old duffel bag with all sorts of things in it. I invited him to my premises for a warm because he looked terrible. I could see that Olu had fallen on hard times but I didn't want to embarrass him so I did not remark about it to him. I asked him where he was living and I think he told me he was living up Woodhouse Lane somewhere, but due to his appearance I formed the impression he was sleeping rough. At this time Olu only talked "small talk" mainly about my business and did not talk about himself. Olu was a very proud person and would not ask for help. I took pity on him and he realised this. I gave him some clothes and some money. I could see by talking to Olu that he was a completely different man. He was not the man I used to know. He didn't talk sense and I thought he was a bit simple in the head. After I had given him the money and clothes he left.'

Oluwale called round frequently after this. Sowe discovered that he was sleeping in a derelict house and that his duffel bag contained all he owned. He let Oluwale help around his warehouse, keeping him away from the heavy jobs because he appeared physically weak. Sometimes Sowe's children would be around the place and Oluwale would enjoy their company and took pleasure in giving them bits of loose change. Despite his troubles, Oluwale 'remained happy in himself and was always laughing'.

Sowe remembered Oluwale disappearing for short periods – presumably to prison. It was when he reappeared after one of these regular absences that Oluwale opened up to him about the treatment he'd been receiving from the police. Sowe had asked him where he'd been, to which Oluwale replied: 'I've been to London, they always hit me on the head when they take me to London.' Sowe realised later that when Oluwale used the word 'London' he really meant prison.

Once Oluwale saw a policeman coming and he said to Sowe, 'Better go inside, O brother, if he see me he take me to London and go beat my head.' Sowe couldn't believe the police did that sort of thing, particularly to someone so obviously weak. But Oluwale's fear was genuine. One day Oluwale was standing outside the premises and he ran inside looking terrified saying, 'They come.' 'He go take me to London and he go beat my head up . . . That man bad, O brother,' he said when he eventually came out of hiding.

Sowe, who more than anyone held together the interests of the West Africans in Leeds, began to put feelers out to see whether money could be found to help send Oluwale back 'home'. But nobody was interested.

In April 1968 Sowe's business premises burned down. Northern Pottery moved to a new address in south Leeds. The last time he saw Oluwale he gave him £2 for something to eat. Oluwale later returned and tried to give him the change.

When the investigation into Oluwale's death was opened in November 1970 detectives tried to trace anyone who had contact with him in 1968–9. Only a handful responded. Their number, and their tales, gave police a sorry impression.

Ibrahim Swarray came to Leeds from Sierra Leone in 1953. In the early 1960s he occasionally saw Oluwale in the Hyde Park area or up the Roundhay Road. Swarray didn't speak to him 'but took notice because he was coloured'. The first time he talked to Oluwale was in 1968 at Jack Ash's betting shop on North Street. Oluwale was looking at the racing paper on the wall. Swarray asked him which horse he fancied and they got talking. Swarray wanted to be friendly to a fellow African and asked Oluwale back to his house for a meal. He noticed that Oluwale's top lip was unusual in that it 'seemed to turn up at the bottom'. Back at his house, Swarray asked him about this; Oluwale said, 'Police beat me so.' He talked quickly as he told the story of the trouble at the derelict house, moving his hands nervously and laughing a lot. Swarray thought that he was 'a bit simple-minded'. As they ate Oluwale told him that he had had some trouble with a white woman he was living with and went to prison for it. Swarray asked him about this but Oluwale laughed in an odd, distracted way. He told Swarray that he was living in digs up Blackman Lane, but in truth he was homeless and probably said this to save face. Oluwale stayed with him that day for two hours and Swarray told him to visit again. He never saw Oluwale again.

He could just about make do on his dole and whatever money he was given on the streets. His health was poor. He was a shuffling, jerking witness to the power of Largactil and ECT. Day-care centres for the mentally ill had been slow to develop and Oluwale appears not to have had access to what limited provision there was in Leeds. His last contact with the mental welfare section of St James's Hospital was in 1967. He was alone. There seemed no way back to society.

April 1968

There was no escaping the subject of race in April 1968. Martin Luther King's assassination on 4 April provoked riots across America. In Britain anti-immigrant feeling was running high. The Labour government had just forced through a Commonwealth Immigrants Bill which deprived Kenyan Asians who held British passports of the right of unrestricted entry. Critics said the bill was a blatantly racist piece of legislation, a yielding to populist hysteria; yet Labour's tough stance was welcomed by a public that didn't want a flood of Asian immigrants, even if they were British citizens. There was never a lower moment for the idea of Commonwealth. The tradition of *civis Brittanicus sum* was well and truly dead.

Eager to exploit the hardening public mood and stake his claim to be the next Conservative leader, Enoch Powell gave his notorious 'Rivers of Blood' speech. That speech, delivered to a small gathering of Tories in an upstairs room in Birmingham on 20 April 1968, sent shock waves throughout society. Liberal Britain said he shouldn't have talked of rivers foaming with blood, of wide-grinning piccaninnies shouting 'Racialist' through the old woman's door, of excreta pushed through letter boxes; said it was the language of a fascist brute, not a Cambridge classical scholar of international repute. But the great majority of ordinary British people believed that Enoch had spoken the truth, that we were a 'nation busily engaged in heaping up its own funeral pyre', that in time 'the black man will have the whip-hand over the white man'. A year later, a Gallup poll found that Powell was the most admired man in Britain.

One Leeds African, Gayb, could see Enoch's point: he believed there were too many immigrants getting in and that they had everything presented on a plate for them, council flats, benefits. There had been nothing like that for him when he arrived in Britain twenty years previously to the month.

Gayb was the kind of black Enoch Powell didn't talk about: a hard-working, God-fearing, home-building not home-threatening family man. And a loyal British subject. Every day after finishing his shift at the copper works, Gayb would make his way to the army barracks at Woodhouse Lane. His old friend Slim had once tried to warn him about what they'd do to a black man in the British Army. But as he became settled the old desire came back and Gayb joined the Territorial Army. He competed in athletics meetings, winning sprinting competitions, and the press reported that he was the first African to represent the regiment. Once, when someone insulted him, he challenged the man to a race and destroyed him; after that the taunts stopped. Gayb believed that if you could run faster than the other man you could never feel inferior.

Gayb followed closely the terrible news that was coming out of Nigeria. He was appalled by the Biafran War which broke out in 1967; his daughters would collect jumble and sent what money they made to help those suffering. He thought back to his own father, sitting on the veranda at home in Lagos, warning his neighbours: 'Better the devil you know.' The break with the country he still called 'home' was almost complete. Gayb's passport said he was a British citizen; in his heart he was a Loiner.

He kept in touch with a few of his African friends from the old days but they were making their separate lives. Once – it would have been in 1967 or 1968 – he bumped into Oluwale in Park Square. Oluwale was nervous and twitchy, couldn't make conversation, looked at the floor, over Gayb's shoulder, anywhere but his face. Gayb watched him walk off and that was the last time he saw him.

On 17 April 1968 Oluwale was arrested inside the doorway of the Queen's Hotel by PC Greenwood and Sergeant Kitching. He was charged with disorderly conduct and received a conditional discharge. It was Sergeant Kitching's first known contact with Oluwale.

Later that day he met his probationer officer, John Sugden. Oluwale told him that he'd been sleeping in John Peters for the last few weeks. Sugden made a call and secured him a place at the Church Army hostel. Sugden remembered Oluwale as 'a very backward sort of person, with a very poor knowledge of the English language'. This would be Oluwale's last permanent address – a forbidding four-storey Edwardian corner building on The Calls looking over the River Aire. The motto of the Church Army was *Go for the Worst*.

Oluwale had one year to live.

Albert: postscript

28 April 1969. On the greatest night in the team's history and one of the greatest moments in the city's history, Oluwale's body was drifting down the River Aire away from Leeds and Albert was getting steadily out of it. In Liverpool that night a dogged Leeds United secured the point it needed for its first ever league title. Billy Bremner, the captain, hesitated when Revie said he should lead his team up to the Kop end, but he did and 20,000 Scousers joined with the Leeds fans chanting 'Champions, Champions'. Leeds United was the best in England.

Albert played only one league game in that championship season, coming on as substitute and scoring as if to say *I'm still here, boss*. And so Revie's first signing didn't feature in the champions' photograph. Towards the end of the next season Albert played twice in meaningless games in teams stuffed with reserves, one of these games earning Leeds United a heavy fine for fielding an uncompetitive team. In what turned out to be Albert's last game, 4 April 1970, in front of the lowest crowd of the season, Eddie Gray, the talented teenager who had taken Albert's first-team place, was also playing, scoring what many said was the greatest goal ever seen at Elland Road. As Gray twisted and turned around five Burnley players, Albert was flat out injured in the penalty area.

And that was it. The club let him go on a free transfer and he ended his playing days soon after at humble York City.

A few months after his transfer, *Forward with Leeds* by his former teammate Johnny Giles came out, and delivered the verdict that Albert was a great second-division player who could have been 'one of the game's outstanding personalities', but that he was overawed and out of his depth on the bigger stage. Through some flaw, some defect of character, Giles (and others) believed that Albert never became the player or indeed the man that he might have been.

The verdict of posterity would be more generous. Like the Bermudan Clyde Best who made his West Ham debut in 1969, Albert would go down in football history as someone who braved the racist taunts and served as a trailblazer for the next generation of great black players. Clyde Best was awarded an MBE in 2006. Albert didn't live long enough to receive any such reward.

In 1974 Norma left him, making a new start in Jamaica with the two kids, Alicia and Yvonne (Lisa and Vonnie, Albert called them). That's when his drinking got worse. He seemed to lose interest in everything except his record collection. His neighbours would hear him playing Jim Reeves's 'Please Release Me' over and over again.

He eventually lost the house. For a while he ended up on the streets, taking refuge in derelict houses. He dossed down in the TV lounge of the Griffin Hotel (the hotel which had hosted his wedding reception in 1963). He tried to get admitted to St George's Crypt but the warden turned him away saying it was no place for someone who'd been a hero.

There was still a vestigial affection for Albert in Leeds, always someone who'd stand him a pint, and he wasn't shy of tapping into it. When his old teammate Eddie Gray was manager of Leeds in the 1980s, Albert turned up at Elland Road and asked for money for new football boots – he wanted to get back in training, he said. It seemed everyone had grown weary of his hard-luck tale.

In a feature on the 'forgotten hero' which appeared in the early 1990s, Albert told the *Yorkshire Evening Post* that the pain of not having seen his daughters for so many years was killing him (he saw Vonnie sometime in the mid-1980s, but never saw Lisa again after 1974). And he opened up about his addiction, tracing it back to his youth in the township when he and his pals sniffed benzine to kill the days.

He did little bits of work here and there, washing up in a Chinese restaurant, sweeping up trimmings in a tailoring factory, but mostly he was jobless, skint and alone. He was seen wandering around derelict parts of the waterfront, ghostly. 'He knew that he was letting himself down and he was very ashamed to face his friends,' his old friend Freddy Apfel recalled. 'He was very dejected. Because apart from football what else did he have?' Not long before the end Albert gave his trophies and medals to Apfel because he was afraid that he would pawn them for beer money.

Albert's old club heard about his state and paid for his stay at a drying-out clinic. They held a fund-raising reception and unwisely sent a car to bring Albert up for the event. He proceeded to get smashed. Leeds did all it could, Peter Lorimer told me: a football club wasn't a benevolent organisation.

Towards the end Albert was living in a tower block in the Gledhow area. His neighbour Barbara Stephenson used to see him about, though they exchanged few words. He looked sad, but always gave a pleasant smile and was well turned out – brown suit, shirt and tie. She'd see him on the bus coming back from town and though it was obvious he had been drinking he was never totally out of it, just a slight stumble as he stepped off on to the pavement.

The police surgeon estimated that he'd lain dead for a week before his body was discovered. He was just fifty-three when the loneliness and the drink killed him in September 1995. Lisa and Vonnie attended the funeral at Lawnswood cemetery. Representatives of Leeds United were also present. It was over quietly, quickly, but hadn't they done all they could for Albert? The club and the Football Association agreed to share the costs of the headstone, and lines from a Maya Angelou poem, chosen by the family, were inscribed on it.

> Out of the huts of history's shame
> I rise
> Up from a past that's rooted in pain
> I rise
> I'm a black ocean, leaping and wide,
> Welling and swelling I bear in the tide . . .
> Bringing the gifts that my ancestors gave,
> I am the dream and hope of the slave.
> I rise
> I rise
> I rise

PART TWO

THE LONG HOURS:
ANATOMY OF A CRIME

I do solemnly and sincerely declare that I will well serve our
Sovereign Lady the Queen in the office of Constable for the
City of Leeds, without fear, favour, affection, malice, or ill-will;
and that I will, to the best of my power, cause the peace to
be kept and preserved, and prevent all offences against the
persons and properties of Her Majesty's subjects; and while
I continue to hold the said office, I will, to the best of my
skill and knowledge, discharge all the duties thereof faithfully
according to law.

Oath sworn by officers of the Leeds City Police

'kúrò ńiléè mi' kì í se 'kúrò layé', ('Get out of my house' is not
'Get out of the world')

Yoruba proverb

1

North

Killingbeck Cemetery, Leeds, Wednesday 9 December 1970. Old Leeds city telephone directories, great thick things, had been stuffed in the coffin around the African's body. As if the undertakers had been having a clear-out.

At 1 p.m. the previous afternoon, under the supervision of Edward Viles, superintendent of the Catholic cemetery at Killingbeck, gravediggers worked down to just above the level of the first coffin, then sheeted it over for the night. At 5 a.m., the usual exhumation hour, under arc light, four men dug round the frost-covered common grave until they were able to tilt the coffins and pull them out one by one on canvas straps. All ten of them. Decaying pauper efforts. John Murtagh was on top of David Oluwale. He'd been found dead at his digs the same day the African was fished out of the Aire.

A small group of men were struggling to keep their feet at plot number BS 85 A: Detective Chief Superintendent John Perkins and Detective Sergeant Basil ('Baz') Haddrell of Scotland Yard; Chief Superintendent Dennis Hoban, Head of Leeds CID and his deputy, Detective Superintendent Jim Fryer; the coroner; a couple of forensic scientists from Harrogate and a number of bobbies. Professor Keith Simpson, world-famous Home Office pathologist, was eager to complete the routine business of taking soil samples from above, below and to the side of the coffin. His Crombie overcoat was soaked; rain bounced off his trademark bowler hat.

He slipped and would have gone in if he hadn't been grabbed by a hefty policeman from the coroner's office. 'Nay, governor, we'll need a Secretary of State's order to get you out again,' he said. On the other side of black polythene screens, press photographers and reporters kept popping out from behind tombstones (there had been talk of an exhumation for weeks).

The coffin nameplate was cleared of soil and Philip Williams of W. Roberts funeral directors solemnly read out: 'David Oluwale Alliwala.' The coffin lid was loosened a little to allow foul gases to escape into the Leeds air – better there than the mortuary. The coffin was put on a stretcher and taken by ambulance to St James's Hospital.

It was DS Haddrell's first exhumation. He was surprised at how well the body was looking. There was pink in the African's flesh, firmness in the ligaments and cartilages. A terrible cheesy-ammonia smell was coming off him – adipocere, the pathologist explained. The autopsy began, Professor Simpson in his white post-mortem gown, rubber apron, rubber gloves, cheery as ever.

Haddrell, detective in Scotland Yard's Murder Squad, had been in the North with his colleague DCS Perkins for just over a month. The call had come at an ungodly hour as he lay in his bed in Orpington. Haddrell was number one in the Murder Squad 'frame' so he was expecting it. He could have been sent anywhere in the world to assist or lead investigations into crimes of 'special importance' – to any British protectorate, any colony, any British ship on the high sea, any other police force in England which required Yard help. He'd been looking forward to a decent murder abroad, somewhere warm and sunny, Bermuda perhaps. Not Leeds; not an exhumation.

In this investigation, Haddrell would be assisting Perkins. Perkins had been selected by the Assistant Commissioner of the Metropolitan Police in response to a request for assistance from the Chief Constable of Leeds City Police on 29 October 1970. Where serious criminal allegations had been levelled at police officers – as they had been – it was necessary to bring in an outside force.

Haddrell only knew John Perkins by name. At the Yard they called him 'Polly Perkins' after the music-hall song 'Pretty Polly Perkins of Paddington Green'. By all accounts he was a funny fish. Worse still, the suspects were senior police officers. Haddrell wasn't long off an investigation into corruption within his own force, the Met, and knew that it was more likely to break a reputation than make one.

He'd never been to the North. He was sat in the car with Polly and as they passed Sheffield he could see these eerie lights in the darkness from steelwork furnaces.

Yorkshire – 'God's own county'. Haddrell was a sportsman so he had an idea. It was where they played a different kind of rugby. Leeds. Home of the best football team in England, Europe even (it was a rare visiting team who came away from Elland Road with a result). Home of Yorkshire county cricket, Headingley. Sacred ground. Fred Trueman and Geoff Boycott – bloody-mindedness, call a spade a spade. Nobody born outside the county boundary could wear that precious white rose badge. Everyone who cared about English cricket could admire such a rule and envy such purity. When Yorkshire was good, England was good.

Leeds was once completely surrounded by dense woodland. Its very seclusion saved it from marauding attacks. As late as the seventeenth century somebody was employed to direct travellers through obscure woodland between Leeds and nearby Wakefield. It was inscrutable country. No more: a high-speed rail link, London less than three hours away; the M1 driving right to the edge of the city. Signs all the way into Leeds announced that it was the 'Motorway City of the Seventies'.

The Scotland Yard men stopped first at the Great Northern before switching to the Hotel Metropole. Inside, brazen giant columns, a cantilevered bronze-panelled staircase – product of a more optimistic age. Polly didn't relax for one minute in the North. It was so bloody cold and the nights were drawing in. He didn't trust the natives.

Every now and then someone at Millgarth station would mention the dead black tramp. There was a sergeant fixated with Oluwale who'd say, all mock-conspiritorial, 'Did he fall or was he pushed?'

But the months went by, into a shiny new decade, and folk stopped talking about him. The streets where he had slept were paved over to form a smart tree-lined pedestrian precinct (the most extensive in Europe, the boast). Leeds was becoming the cutting-edge shoppers' paradise.

The story of David Oluwale would have remained buried but for a cadet, a youth at the very bottom of Leeds City Police's hierarchy of 1,300 officers.

Gary Galvin – Gazzer – was an eighteen-year-old living with his parents in the Beeston area of the city. They were originally from County Clare, and when they arrived in Leeds they carried on the family tradition by opening up a fruit and veg shop on the Dewsbury Road. Gazzer, south Leeds with a splash of the Irish, attended Cockburn High School whose most famous past pupil was Richard Hoggart, author of the classic Hunslet-inspired book on working-class culture, *The Uses of Literacy* (1957). Hoggart's south Leeds was a tough society where an unsentimental attitude to life was expressed in matter-of-fact language ('policemen don't shit roses,' was one local saying). The traditional industries – engine-making, textiles, engineering – were still alive, just, during Gazzer's youth, as were the native characteristics. *By Industry we Prosper* was the motto the mature Gary Galvin would choose for his family coat of arms. Just like one of those improving maxims dotted around Leeds Town Hall.

Gazzer devoted most of his energies to sport, neglected his studies and left Cockburn High School at fifteen. After a false start at art school and uninspiring work as a gofer and tea-masher in the printing house of the *Yorkshire Post*, he found his direction when he joined Leeds City Police in July 1969.

This was Gary Galvin, without whom the story of David Oluwale would have remained hidden. He had a tough time of it afterwards. Friends within the police were thin on the ground and his car tyres were slashed. Some in Leeds City Police would admire his guts, but many couldn't understand why he did what he did. Some put it down to Gazzer's youth: he was naive, hadn't learned to see the world for what it was.

After the Oluwale case he would throw himself into individualist pursuits. He became a weightlifter and a black belt in judo. Later, he ran marathons. The slight teenager became a stocky and muscular sixteen stone. When he got cancer for the first time in 1983 (which he beat) he decided he needed to make a mark in life that was more than just physical. He chased academic qualifications in the social sciences in the evenings, eventually achieving a PhD for his research into schemes to rehabilitate young offenders. Gazzer Galvin had become Dr Gary Galvin. A forceful personality with a strong sense of justice, that's how Russell Murray, his teacher, remembered him. Someone who looked like a typical bobby, was a proud bobby (his son would follow him into the police), but was unpredictable in his views – sometimes law-and-order, sometimes liberal. He'd just retired from the police (he had risen to the rank of inspector) when he found out that he had a rare muscle cancer. His powerful body wasted away in no time. He had only just turned fifty when he died in March 2002.

Back in October 1970, Gazzer was enthusiastic about 'the Job', enjoying his sports, learning to drive. A proud cadet.

The Galvin family home was large enough to take lodgers and the previous year Brian Topp, a probationer constable, moved in. Though born in Leeds, Topp was brought up in Nottinghamshire, and the arrangement with the Galvins helped him find his feet. Like Gazzer, Topp had left grammar school with few qualifications. He was in a factory knitting socks when he decided to try for the police.

Topp was a beanpole, one of the tallest in the force. Though they weren't close they got on fine and Gazzer would sometimes take the car up the Dales and they'd talk about coppering.

It was the evening of 22 October. Topp was troubled by a looming court case in which he would be giving evidence, and was worried for his job.

The facts were these: on a Friday night in September 1970, as they made their way for last orders at the Palace, a young man (who I'll call Mike) and his girlfriend got involved in a fight with a drunk. While Mike was relieving himself under the railway arches, the drunk offered his girlfriend a fiver for 'a short time'. Seeing this,

Mike bounded over and punches were swapped. The pest ran off, but not before a bus driver who had witnessed the fight called the police. PC Topp arrived on the scene shortly after. He'd just about managed to calm the couple down when the J4 police van, driven by PC Ken Higgins, turned up. This wound the couple up again and Mike was bundled into the back of the van, throwing a few punches at Topp as he went. A sergeant, Ken Kitching, reached over from the front seats and gave Mike a few slaps to shut him up. To Topp, Kitching seemed the worse for drink – more so than the prisoner. Mike was subdued by the time they arrived at the central charge office (commonly known as the 'Bridewell').

PC Higgins remained in the van, leaving three policemen with the prisoner: Sergeant Kitching, PCs Keith Seager and Topp. They were buzzed through the first of the two sets of security doors. When they were in the 'air lock' between the doors, Kitching pushed the prisoner to the floor and stamped repeatedly on his head. Topp had to hold Kitching off. Mike was later charged with disorderly conduct and with assaulting Topp.

Topp was due to give evidence in the impending court case and was worried that Mike might counter with allegations of police brutality. Sergeant Kitching's attitude appeared to Topp to be, 'It's down to you, kid.'

All this was on Topp's mind when he opened up to Gazzer Galvin that evening. Just days before the case was due to be heard,[*] Topp told him a story he'd heard some weeks before.

It was a week or so after the incident at the Bridewell. Topp was patrolling with another probationer constable, Gary Briggs. They were having a moan about Millgarth generally and their shift sergeant Ken Kitching in particular. Topp was telling Briggs how sickened he had been by Kitching's attack on the prisoner. Briggs agreed that Kitching was brutal and told him about an incident

---

[*] On the advice of his solicitor, Mike pleaded guilty to the assault on condition that the disorderly conduct charge was dropped. His solicitor had earlier warned him of the futility of making a complaint of assault against the police, though Topp was unaware of this as the trial loomed.

which had happened early in 1969, some months before Topp had joined the force.

Briggs had been patrolling the city centre in a panda car when he received a call over his radio to return to the station. It was sometime in the middle of the night shift. Waiting for him was his shift inspector, Geoff Ellerker, who told Briggs to drive him over to Lands Lane. On the way, Inspector Ellerker asked Briggs whether he had his stick, Briggs said he had, and Ellerker told him to hand it over. They pulled up at John Peters' furniture shop. Sergeant Kitching was there with PC Keith Seager. Ellerker went into the shop entrance. There was a man in there, a 'coon' who was something of a joke around Millgarth. Briggs, who drove straight off after dropping off Inspector Ellerker, had assumed that Ellerker and Kitching were going to give the coon a good hiding, as they had done on previous occasions, though he didn't actually witness any violence. At the end of the shift Ellerker returned the truncheon to Briggs and said he wouldn't be needing it again. A fortnight later Briggs heard that the same man had been found in the Aire. Briggs told Topp that he had just put it to the back of his mind – it was one thing for Ellerker and Kitching to be involved in giving this coon a beating, quite another to be involved in his death. He told Topp the name of the man, but it was foreign so it didn't stick.

Topp, who had sat on the story for weeks not knowing whether to believe it, now told it to Gazzer. Gazzer didn't need to think it over, he just said that something ought to be done.

Gazzer didn't know any of the individuals personally. But he knew the name Geoff Ellerker. The thirty-seven-year-old inspector, along with three other officers, was currently standing trial at Leeds Assizes on a number of criminal charges, including misconduct as a police officer. The press called it the 'Leeds Police Trial'.

Gazzer's opportunity came after work the next day, Friday 23 October 1970. There was a bus strike in Leeds and Galvin offered one of the sergeants in the Training Department a lift home. Sergeant MacLeod told Gazzer that it was probably just malicious gossip, but the next day checked Scenes of Crimes to see whether there were any photographs of a black man who had been pulled out of the Aire. He didn't find any. On 27 October Gazzer repeated the story in front of Inspector Jim Bass, who appeared shaken by what he heard. That afternoon Jim Fryer, Deputy Head of Leeds CID, instructed DCI Len Shakeshaft to begin enquiries. Later that day, after a two-hour interview, Sergeant Kitching was suspended from duty (Ellerker was already under suspension).

A name was put to the black man. PC Gary Briggs was interviewed, as was the constable who was with Kitching and Ellerker at John Peters, Keith Seager. Just a week after Topp's conversation with Gazzer, Scotland Yard was heading for Leeds.

The Leeds detectives assisting the Yard in the Oluwale investigation had never encountered anyone quite like Polly Perkins. In his mid-forties, tall, dark, painfully slim and pale, he was conventional enough on the surface in his immaculate dark suits. But at a time when the table-banging management style prevailed, Polly was quiet and understated. He had strange habits and an odd way of sitting for a policeman, both feet up on the chair, cross-legged. Once they found him under the table in the incident room at Brotherton House searching for bugging devices. Since the investigation was being conducted from the nerve centre of Leeds City Police he was understandably wary that it might be compromised. Someone pointed out to him that they couldn't even get the personal radios to work properly in Leeds.

Polly had a solitary hobby. Collecting Goss crested china. Village churches, delicate little boots, pretty country cottages. He wasn't a drinker, barely ate, picked at his breakfast like a bird. At Scotland Yard the story was that Polly carried a certificate around with him declaring his sanity and fitness for work – just in case. He would suffer a nervous breakdown soon after the close of the Oluwale investigation. It was said that the case drove him crazy.

His colleague DS Haddrell was very different: thirty-three years old and sporty (he played rugby for the Met XV); a lover of pub life; a handsome man who caused a stir among the typists at Brotherton House. Haddrell tried to convey an impression of normality to the Leeds lads. While Polly was an introvert, Haddrell was emphatically outward.

After a guarded beginning, Haddrell and the Leeds team began to relax. Haddrell made the best of the North. He enjoyed the funny sayings. *Hear all, see all, say nowt.* He became pally with DS Charlie Longhawn, who took him to see some proper, honest rugby at Headingley and at Odsal in Bradford. He loved the smoky intimacy of the Town Hall Tavern (the feisty Irish landlady Kathy Moran kept a gin-loving Green Amazon parrot called Biddy behind the bar until its constant foul language necessitated its removal from public earshot). He drank in the Jubilee and the Victoria where the coppers, lawyers, crooks, court reporters (the devoutly Catholic Hunter brothers and the devoutly Catholic homosexual Jim Wilson, whose prayer every night was that he might go before 'My Lady Mother') swapped gossip over halves. 'The Town Hall Village' they called it. Haddrell took to the warm Leeds people (once they accepted him), the Tetley's mild, the fish and chips – though he never got on with mushy peas. To show him that they weren't heathens, the Leeds boys took him to the most sophisticated fish and chip restaurant in the North, Harry Ramsden's. *Eat all, sup all, pay nowt.*

The investigation was conducted from an incident room on the third floor of Brotherton House. The day-to-day running of operations was down to Haddrell. He worked with a team of Leeds detectives: DCI Len Shakeshaft, DI Eric Bullock, four detective sergeants, two detective constables, as well as a number of detectives who were on the case in its initial stages. A few days in and reinforcements arrived from Scotland Yard: DCI Wilson and DS Grateley. To keep an eye on Polly, Haddrell suspected.

As Scotland Yard detectives (the 'best in the world'), Polly and Haddrell knew that they had a certain aura. When England had many local police forces it was common for the Yard, with its greater technical knowledge and experience, to send a senior detective to assist in murder investigations. He would arrive, in trenchcoat and trilby hat, at some small provincial train station, just a small bag and a detective sergeant in tow. There was a certain glamour about that. But none here, not in Leeds.

Leeds was on the alert for any whiff of arrogance, any sense that they were being patronised by their sophisticated guests. Scotland Yard hadn't been up in Leeds before – not that anyone could remember – and it was a journey into the unknown for both sides. The Yard knew that Leeds City Police would be a tightly knit body of men, and that the code of loyalty and institutional pride would be deeply entrenched. It was a particularly steep learning curve for Polly, who wasn't experienced in murder investigations and who had never been on one outside the Met area. At the first meeting, Polly, a poor communicator, mumbled something along the lines of 'We're not taking this investigation from you – we're helping you with it'. Scotland Yard had its pride and Leeds City Police had its pride.

Much of the early work of the investigation was drudgery. Every pub, every library, anywhere where David Oluwale might have spent his days, was contacted. Cafés favoured by the jobless and homeless were visited: the Exchange Café on Call Lane and the twenty-four-hour café on Kirkstall Lane, the Tomato Dip, so-called because the house speciality was a slice of bread smeared with tomato sauce. But nobody seemed to know him. Park keepers were questioned; 126 dentists and 257 doctors were asked to search their records; 157 vagrants were asked what they knew of him – only a handful claimed knowledge. They appealed to Catholic priests. They tried the hostels. They went to the Deinfestation Centre on Stanley Road to find out if they had any record of Oluwale. The Scabies and Pediculosis Assistant said not.

Digging for the truth about a man's death meant digging for a man. Oluwale, Polly Perkins told his first press conference, was a man who appeared to have 'no real roots'. If anyone had seen him between 10 April 1969, when he was discharged from Armley prison, and 4 May, when he was pulled out of the Aire, they were to call Leeds 22800. But in this city of 506,000 people, only seven came forward with information in the first few days of the investigation. The call was repeated. 'Was not known to have friends or regular acquaintants,' Detective Superintendent Jim Fryer said.

They began to track down Leeds's West Africans, asked them whether their former friend could swim, whether he had any enemies, whether he might have committed suicide. They heard that his family were fishing people so he surely swam, that he had no enemies, that for all his troubles 'Olu' had always been a cheerful man and that suicide was unthinkable.

The 'Leeds Police Trial' which was under way in Courtroom 1 at Leeds Assizes gave Polly a chance to study the dynamics within the force at the time. It also introduced him to Geoff Ellerker, the thirty-seven-year-old inspector now implicated in the death of David Oluwale.

Polly would have learned that Ellerker was well regarded in the force with fourteen years' service under his belt. Most of that had been in CID, and his reputation was that of a highly competent detective. He had been made inspector in April 1968 at the relatively young age of thirty-four, serving for almost twenty months at Millgarth before his transfer to Ireland Wood subdivision.

The man Polly saw didn't quite match the image from the CV. Ellerker had sustained an injury making an arrest a few months before which left him with terrible back pain. He needed sticks to get around. At one point during proceedings, Mr Justice Mocatta gave him permission to lie down on a stretcher in the well of the court. A photograph in the newspaper showed Ellerker being carried down the town hall steps. By the end of a fraught twenty-five-day trial, he had a conviction for falsifying evidence in a road traffic accident involving a fellow officer.

That officer was Superintendent Derek Holmes, known to everyone in the force as 'Big Red'. On Christmas Eve 1969, Big Red was driving the car which knocked over an elderly lady as she crossed the road. She died from the injuries sustained. Big Red was a power in the land, part of a group of hard-working, hard-playing senior officers clustered around the then Head of CID, the maverick Frank Midgley, whose influence over the careers of aspiring detectives was so decisive that they were known in the force as the 'Leeds Mafia'. Ellerker, who had served under these men, had given a false statement to the coroner which had the effect of removing any blame from Big Red. Ellerker stated that the woman smelt of drink (she happened to be a lifelong teetotaller) and that she had been crossing the road at some distance away from the pedestrian crossing. Two traffic policemen at the scene were to testify that they could smell drink on Big Red, and other witnesses said that the woman was hit while on or at least very near to a pedestrian crossing.

During and after the trial the two traffic policemen had a torrid time, so great was the pressure to demonstrate unqualified loyalty to colleagues. Their careers never recovered (one officer was diagnosed with stomach cancer around that time and died in 1973 at the age of forty; the other was injured in a road traffic accident and was forced to retire the same year). Ellerker was found guilty of misconduct as an officer of justice and given nine months. On conviction he was dismissed from Leeds City Police. A very promising career had been ruined through what the judge had called his 'misguided sense of loyalty to another officer'.

The fact that Ellerker was convicted, and therefore to some degree discredited, made it arguably easier for the officers in the Oluwale investigation to break rank. It was possibly for this reason that Polly Perkins was able to begin to build a case against Ellerker and Kitching.

The investigation into Oluwale's death began while the conspiracy trial at Leeds Assizes was in progress. At that stage, Oluwale was still something of a joke – in death as in life. 'The Kitching Sink Drama', that was one of the jokes. At a practice of the Leeds City Police band someone suggested adding 'The Deep River Rhapsody' and 'The Oluwale Chorus' to their repertoire.

The investigation involved wide questioning of officers throughout Leeds City Police, but Polly and Haddrell directed most attention at those on Ellerker and Kitching's shift – 'Ken Kitching's Deep River Boys' as they were now known. Polly and Haddrell didn't run up against the wall of silence they had half expected. Some officers cooperated out of self-interest, fearing disciplinary proceedings and worse if they didn't. PC Keith Seager was formally interviewed ten times – about twenty hours of questioning in total. One of Seager's colleagues recalled seeing him at the magistrates' court: he had lost weight and looked drawn; he was anxious that he was facing disciplinary action and possible criminal charges. PC Gary Briggs gave statements on 28 October, 17 November, 23 November, 24 November, 15 December 1970. His penultimate statement began: 'I now want to tell you the whole truth about what happened in the car when I was taking Mr Ellerker up to John Peters in Lands Lane.' The truth was slowly and painfully wrung from often very reluctant witnesses.

Those who broke the code of loyalty could expect pariah status. Millgarth officers would have had in mind the two traffic policemen who had given evidence in the 'Leeds Police Trial'. Certain officers who were helping the investigation were shipped out of Millgarth to other subdivisions. When Brian Topp was transferred to Dewsbury Road on 6 November nobody would talk to him – it was as if a leper was in their midst, he told me.

The most important task for the Oluwale investigation was to establish when the alleged John Peters incident could have taken place. It was discovered that Oluwale had signed on for his dole on 16 April 1969. This narrowed the time frame of the investigation. The duty books of Millgarth officers were scrutinised. Polly was becoming interested in the night of 17/18 April 1969.

A postman came forward in response to the press appeal with some interesting information. He said that he was on his way home on the bus one early morning when he saw police vehicles by the river at Warehouse Hill. He thought that it was around the time the body of Oluwale was pulled from the Aire. He recalled having a brief conversation with the bus conductor, who told him that he had just seen two policemen chasing someone down Call Lane to the river. The postman didn't think any more about it, he explained to detectives. Detectives examined the postman's rota and established that the incident had probably taken place on the early morning of 18 April 1969. When the bus conductor was eventually traced his statement appeared to confirm what the postman had said.

In the course of the investigation, allegations were made of other assaults on Oluwale going back to August 1968. Polly and Haddrell heard that Ellerker and Kitching had hounded the man.

Cadet Gary Galvin, the youth who'd set the whole investigation off, was an isolated figure. But he was toughing it out.

5 November 1970. Gazzer should have been at one of the great south Leeds bonfires; instead he was up in front of Scotland Yard's Murder Squad at Brotherton House. Polly asked him why he thought Oluwale had ended up in the river. Gazzer replied that he'd possibly been pushed in 'because he was coloured and there is racial prejudice everywhere'. It was just his personal opinion, he said.

While digging into David Oluwale's antecedent history, the investigation team turned up a couple of documents: two innocuous-looking Leeds City Police charge sheets. Oluwale had picked up a number of these during the last few months of his life. These two dated from 23 February 1969 and 11 March 1969. There was space on these forms for various details: name, date of birth, address (by this time Oluwale was always N.F.A.), sex, marital status, etc. There was also a space for the nationality of the prisoner. On the first charge sheet 'BRIT' had been typed in under NAT, but had then been crossed out by hand and 'WOG' scrawled instead. On the second charge sheet, a few weeks later, no alterations had been made. It was simply typed to read 'NAT: WOG'.

The racial politics of David Oluwale ran alongside the criminal investigation. Leeds City Police was fortunate in having an astute politician in its deputy chief constable. It was Austin Haywood who tried to ensure that the Oluwale case did not develop into a catastrophe.

The man responsible for discipline in the force would never be loved. Haywood even looked like a bringer of bad news. His face was narrow, thin and bloodless; a frugal eater, he remained as stick-thin as he was in his younger days. With his dark suits and dark hair his look was funereal. He fancied himself as something of an academic authority on the finer points of police discipline. Nothing mattered to Haywood more than the good name of his force.

Leeds City Police had a proud history going back to 1836, but by the late 1960s it was a threatened institution. Following the amalgamations of other Yorkshire forces in 1968, there was talk of disbanding the Leeds and Bradford City forces and merging them with the West Yorkshire Constabulary. Leeds City Police was trying to persuade the Home Office that it was a large enough city with a large enough policing establishment (1,300 officers) to justify its continued separate existence. However, its case had been undermined by a number of damaging criminal cases involving its officers. The corruption trial at Leeds Assizes came on top of other recent prosecutions of Leeds police officers, some for petty thefts, others more serious. The most serious involved an entire shift in the Ireland Wood subdivision, which led to a sergeant and a number of his officers receiving prison sentences for theft. But Haywood knew that these were nothing compared to the damage Oluwale could cause.

Racism had loomed larger in the public mind since Enoch Powell's speech in April 1968. But there was a happy delusion in Leeds that it was too moderate a city, too phlegmatic in character for race hatred. In the council there was agreement that Leeds didn't need to invest, as other local authorities had done, in a community relations officer, since that would look like an admission that it had a race relations problem – and it didn't. And then came Burley, July 1969.

Violent disturbances broke out in the Burley Lodge area on two successive nights after nineteen-year-old Kenny Horsfall was stabbed in the head and killed by a young Asian man. The attack followed an argument outside an Indian café in which racial abuse was thrown. The night after the stabbing, a sweltering Sunday, between six and eight hundred white locals spilled out on to the streets after closing time. The mob, appalled by the death of one of its own (which had left a young woman widowed), vented their anger on Asian houses and premises. Chants of 'Go home, wogs' and 'Get the Pakis' were heard. Women urged their menfolk on. Without a solid show from seventy Leeds City Police officers there could have been lynchings. There was further trouble on the

Monday night. Far-right activists were in the area hoping to exploit the situation – but Burley's hatred wasn't ideological, it was tribal. For days the local Asian community was under siege; some gathered up their belongings and fled to Bradford.

The national papers were up to find out what had fired the largest outbreak of anti-immigrant violence post-'Rivers of Blood'. Khan Chaudhry of the Pakistani Muslim Association told a *Sunday Times* journalist, 'I can hardly believe this is England; that I cannot walk through this part of Leeds without fear of my life.' Glen English, a West Indian who came to Leeds after the war, said that Enoch Powell's speech had made it worse for black people: 'Ten years ago nobody bothered about coloured people, now you hear white people saying: "Time they were sent home", and "There's too many".' Reporters found deep resentment against the Asian residents. The indigenous inhabitants of Burley were repelled by their poor hygiene, the smells from their cooking, hated to use the shared outside toilets if they were unlucky enough to live next to them. It used to be single men, doing the dirty jobs. Now their wives were over and they were buying up all the houses and having kids. They had disturbed the order of their community.

In the civic hall and beyond it was said that what happened in Burley was nothing more than 'beer riots'. According to Merlyn Rees, MP for South Leeds and Undersecretary of State with special responsibility for race relations, when people had too much ale on summer evenings they did silly things. The Lord Mayor declared: 'There is no racial problem in Leeds.' And the police agreed.

But Leeds now looked like a city where race mattered a lot. Diana Phillips, who became Leeds's first black Justice of the Peace in 1967, was on the bench when a number of the Burley rioters were up to request bail. Gilbert Parr, the chairman of the bench, advised Phillips that she should stand down in the interests of impartiality. Phillips respectfully submitted. Defence solicitor Ronnie Teeman was amazed: he hadn't even suggested that bias might be an issue. The national press picked up on the story. A *Times* editorial deplored Phillips's exclusion. One of the most prominent members of the local West Indian community had been humiliated. Phillips deeply regretted giving in to Parr's request.

Two men were sentenced to life for Kenny Horsfall's murder, and a number of rioters received lengthy prison sentences. Though the activists managed to prise a community relations officer out of the council, there was a reluctance in the city to see what happened in Burley in July 1969 as anything other than criminal thuggery. There was no soul-searching. Burley was ignored.

Austin Haywood was acutely conscious that a racial controversy would be disastrous for the reputation of Leeds City Police. Though the force had been praised for its robust action in Burley (angry white residents taunted the police with comments like 'Why don't you black your faces?'), relations between police and public in areas of black settlement like Chapeltown had deteriorated. It wasn't just Leeds. Nationally, police–black relations had worsened over the course of the last decade and was becoming the subject of political comment, books and TV documentaries.

Leeds City Police wasn't ignorant of racial problems. In 1969 the force appointed four part-time liaison officers to work with immigrants. Probationer constables were lectured on race relations. Pushing this agenda was Leeds's scholarly Assistant Chief Constable, Adrian Clissitt, who had been the recipient of a United Nations Human Rights Fellowship to study the role of the police in the protection of the rights of immigrants in the United States and the Caribbean. And in DC Peter Blakeney, who had been raised and educated in India, it was blessed with somebody who knew Hindi and Urdu and was sensitive to the different cultures – knowledge which, in an increasingly racially mixed Leeds, the force was happy to utilise.

Yet there had been no progress in Leeds City Police in the recruitment of black police officers. In 1969, with an immigrant population of 7,000 Indians and Pakistanis, 6,000 West Indians and 1,000 Africans, Leeds had not one black police officer (the records of other forces were little better). Few police officers had any understanding of, or sympathy with, the black communities they were serving, and black people didn't recognise themselves in the police. Unpredictable, lazy, noisy, brash, untidy, deceitful, aggressive, excitable, arrogant – this was the stereotype of the black person which the average British bobby nursed. Most Leeds bobbies went on calling Chapeltown's International club 'the coon club'.

Haywood had good reason to be anxious about the impact the Oluwale case would have on the police's relations with the black community. It was becoming a more questioning, more radicalised community, with the Black Power movement making its influence felt among the young in Leeds around this time. So Haywood began to cultivate those he saw as the influential, responsible leaders of the community. In November 1970, shortly after the investigation was opened, Haywood summoned Maureen Baker to Brotherton House. A white Irishwoman, Baker had been at the centre of anti-racist campaigns in Leeds and Yorkshire since the days of the Coloured Commonwealth Citizens' Committee in the mid-1950s. Haywood and Baker struck up an understanding. She'd return to the community and make it known that it was policemen themselves who had exposed the story of Oluwale's death, and that Leeds City Police was leaving no stone unturned in the search for the truth. In return, Baker left with a commitment from Haywood to introduce potent measures to improve police–black relations. A few months later, the Chief Constable met representatives of the United Caribbean Association. The Leeds Scheme, as it became known, brought rank-and-file policemen into dialogue with ordinary members of the black community, not the activists or self-appointed leaders. Introduced in 1971, it would be commended by a parliamentary select committee as an innovative contribution to improved race relations, one worthy of imitation.

Haywood appeared to Maureen Baker as a concerned reformer looking to adapt policing to changing times. But running even deeper within Haywood was the instinct for institutional self-preservation. He wasn't just worried about Chapeltown, a marginal black community; he was also worried about how the Oluwale case would be received by the majority society. Even in these racist times the idea of the police going for a man simply because he was black would have been repugnant to Middle England, with its deep conviction that Britain was synonymous with fairness and the rule of law. Even when hostility to immigrants was at its highest pitch – 1969 – a Home Office poll found that Powellite sympathies could coexist with support for anti-discrimination measures. The attitude seems to have been: we don't really want you here but since you are here and British citizens in law, you shouldn't be treated like a dog. Haywood knew that if the alleged crimes against Oluwale were seen to be racially motivated then the case would achieve far greater notoriety. Not just two police officers, but Leeds City Police as an institution would be in the dock. It could spell the force's ruin.

Leeds was in the dark the week they dug David Oluwale up. Electricity workers were on strike; Monday 7 December was 'Black Monday'.

Prince Charles was up in Leeds that week to open the new *Yorkshire Post* building. Fog meant that he had to abandon plans to come up by helicopter. Shivering crowds cheered him. He unveiled a plaque and was presented with a Georgian silver mug. 'That must have cost you a bob or two,' he said, a gentle nod to Yorkshire's famous carefulness. He raised it in the air: 'From one mug to another.' He went on to a gala performance of *Oh Glorious Jubilee* at the new Playhouse, a piece of froth which pleased the City Fathers very much.

It wasn't a secret, the exhumation. All the men of the press had turned up to watch this rare event and to catch a glimpse of the legendary pathologist Keith Simpson.

The African's body was well preserved. Simpson located one area of injury, the bruising on the head which Dr Gee had noted in the original post-mortem examination. No skull, mouth or facial injury. Brain liquefied, no longer suitable for examination. On the question of causes of death, Simpson found no evidence to contradict Gee's assertion that the condition of the body was consistent with immersion and drowning. He noted the small bruise above the right eyebrow. Gee had left open the question of whether or not the injury had been sustained prior to death, but

Simpson concluded that it would have been sustained very shortly before drowning.

Two days later, Oluwale's body was reinterred at Killingbeck cemetery. Fr Carroll from St Anne's was asked to conduct the brief ceremony, just as he had done on a much warmer day in 1969.

Prayers were said for Oluwale's soul. A congregation of gravediggers and a few policemen on the edges. No family, no friends. The same pauper's grave.

DS Haddrell was at the cemetery. Cameras from *Look North* were there. The coffin was of a far better quality than the rotten thing they'd pulled out days before. It had gleaming new brass handles and fittings. There were wreaths from a voluntary society and a religious confraternity; one from Leeds City Police as well. And this great shiny black limousine with an advert conspicuous for the cameras: 'W. Roberts, Funeral Directors, 82 York Road, Leeds, 28114'.

In prison for misconduct as a police officer, Geoff Ellerker didn't feel disposed to assist the Oluwale investigation. Detectives went to see him in HMPs Leeds (Armley), Lincoln and Drake Hall in Staffordshire, and each time he sent them back with nothing. His solicitor, Peter Fingret, remembered him as 'a very cold and unemotional man. He maintained his denial of the offences throughout and was quite immovable on that. He was bitter from day one of the perversion of justice investigation right through to the end. Because he was abandoned.'

Ellerker's children were taunted at school. His wife found the prison visits particularly stressful, and lost a stone in weight. The sheer grimness of Armley, the inhumanity of the staff herding prisoners' families around as though they were the criminals, came as a great shock and led to an involvement with the Howard League for Penal Reform. She wrote to her MP to complain that her husband was being treated like so much human baggage, moved between prisons without any warning to the family. While in prison, Geoff Ellerker's mother died and he attended the funeral under prison escort.

Ellerker's story to other prisoners was that he was a solicitor's clerk. His knowledge of the law, which had helped him to the rank of inspector, gave him status. The prison welfare officer at Lincoln said that he was 'suffering from his misdeeds in ways not obviously shown in other people', 'extremely mixed up', displaying 'some bitterness towards the Leeds police'.

Ellerker told his wife to expect worse, that he was being linked with the suspicious death of a Nigerian. Early on he had waved it away as more malicious gossip, but then a detective superintendent began to sniff around, asking Mrs Ellerker if she knew where her husband's warrant card and duty books were. The family were having to make do with the few pounds a week she brought in as a catering assistant at Leeds Training College.

Around this time Mrs Ellerker contacted Fr Martin Carroll, the priest who had buried David Oluwale. Fr Carroll, now based in Canada, remembers little about the meeting, though he does recall that she was deeply troubled. His main memory of that time is the sadness of those pauper funerals, and with David they weren't even sure of the deceased's name.

Sergeant Ken Kitching was still a Leeds City Police officer throughout the investigation, albeit under suspension. Though the men on his own shift were beginning to turn against him, he was not without friends. Kitching was overheard by PC Seager in the Regent pub just before Christmas 1970 saying that Superintendent Marsden frequently visited him to check that he was still in one piece. He was also heard saying that he was becoming a pretty good snooker player with all that time on his hands.

Questioned by Polly Perkins and Haddrell, Kitching never denied that he'd been violent towards Oluwale on occasions. He said that it was impossible to deal with such a man without employing force. He denied having anything to do with the alleged assault at John Peters in the early hours of 18 April 1969, or having chased Oluwale down to the river. Haddrell's recollection of Kitching is of a crude, unintelligent man with 'scattered eyes'.

After the first interview, Kitching employed Ronnie Teeman as his solicitor. Teeman remembers Kitching turning up at his office one Saturday morning saying that he thought he was going to be charged with murder. He was in an agitated state, picking constantly at his nails. On that morning, 2 January 1971, Kitching went to Brotherton House with Teeman and was questioned about the assault on Mike at the Bridewell on 4 September 1970.* Teeman advised him to say nothing.

The investigation continued into the new year. Tests were carried out to establish how long Oluwale's body had been in the water. Dr Gee's estimate at the first autopsy was between one and two weeks. The Forensic Scientific Laboratory at Harrogate prepared twelve packages of documents similar to those found on Oluwale's body. They were then placed inside a wallet and secured with an elastic band. Twelve dummies were dressed in jackets and the packages placed inside their pockets. The whole lot was then lowered in wire cages into the River Aire a hundred yards downstream from Warehouse Hill. DS Haddrell joked that his new mate DS Charlie Longhawn should take the place of one of the dummies. Instead they tied a Leeds rugby scarf on one – blue and all gold, the colours of the city – and named it 'Charlie'. Over the next few weeks at one- or two-day intervals, 'Charlie' and the other dummies were pulled, one by one, from the Aire. The ink transfers on the documents from the wallets were then compared to the forms 103 found on Oluwale. The scientists concluded from this that the forms had been in the river between fourteen and eighteen days. The date the investigation was most interested in, 18 April 1969, fell within this time bracket.

Yet some doubted whether a body could travel the two and a half miles to Knostrop, the point at which Oluwale was pulled out, as it would need to go over two weirs. But the investigation discovered a recent precedent. On the early morning of 30 January 1968, two police officers had chased Reginald Tisor, who had been acting suspiciously, down Call Lane and down to Warehouse Hill. Tisor ran along the towpath until he came to a wood yard and

---

* Sergeant Kitching would be charged with the assault, though it wouldn't go to court.

could go no further. He jumped into the river. Police officers dived in but lost sight of him. The frogmen were called but couldn't find him. His body was recovered two months later at Allerton Bywater, which was even further down the river from Knostrop. An experienced civil engineer for the Yorkshire Ouse and Hull River Authority, John Tinkler, went back over the records to check the water levels of the Aire in the days following 18 April 1969. He found that the rate of flow of the river was sufficient to carry a body over the two weirs to Knostrop as long as it was floating on or near to the surface.

Polly Perkins became convinced Oluwale was chased down to Warehouse Hill around dawn on 18 April 1969 and that he met his death in the Aire as a result of this chase. A 'most unusual and difficult case', he described it in his 121-page final report submitted to the Director of Public Prosecutions (DPP) on 14 January 1971. He believed that there was evidence to suggest that Ellerker and Kitching were responsible for Oluwale's death and he recommended that the DPP take up the matter.

His colleague Basil Haddrell remembers that report to this day. Polly told him to fetch a pair of scissors and a stapler and then hovered over him saying, 'Cut that paragraph out; put that one there.' They ended up with a twenty-six-foot roll; the typist said that she usually received reports in single pages. 'She couldn't believe it. We tried to fold it,' Haddrell recalls. The writing was unusual as well. He even cited Edmund Burke. It was no clinical, detached exercise. 'These two police officers were the guardians of the law and Oluwale was entitled to its protection and their regard,' Perkins declared. 'By their horrible actions they have brought shame and discredit on an honourable and hardworking Force.' It was evident from his investigations, Perkins stated, that Kitching and Ellerker, whom he referred to as 'despicable individuals', had 'little or no regard for Oluwale as a human being' and that they 'actively desired' to get him out of Leeds.

Perkins was also scathing of the social services. 'Whilst in prison Oluwale was seen by several prison welfare officers and probation officers. They all appear to have come to the conclusion that he was most difficult to communicate with, and was quickly aroused. He was obviously, from their point of view, a hopeless case, unemployable, homeless, unambitious, of low mentality, coloured, un-cooperative and anti-authoritarian. The picture that emerges when one reads the reports is that all Oluwale really received during the last few months of his life from these services was advice, reference to other departments and a few odd pounds social security benefit.'

'He did his duty in a very humane and very professional way,' Basil Haddrell told me when assessing his former colleague. 'He had the strength of character not to allow himself to be tempted or coerced into taking the easier path – which was to say there was no evidence. He knew it would be bad for the police service, not just for Leeds. Polly was very sorry for Oluwale. There were times when I had to remind him, "Are you sorry for the shop keepers who have this mess to deal with?"' It was all of a piece with his thoughtful, sensitive streak, the part of him which took pleasure in little Goss boots and cottages.

In July 1971, the ordeal of the investigation over, Polly Perkins suffered a complete nervous breakdown. His police career never really recovered. He was forced to retire on grounds of ill health a few years later.

2

The Old Law

It didn't look like the sort of place you would go to for help. Millgarth Street station's heavy double doors told you that. They had metal loops on the inside so that a wooden beam could be slotted in whenever the security of the station was threatened. All the windows were fitted with strong iron bars let into stone window frames. The back door, which led out to a yard and garages for police cars, was secured by a heavy hasp and padlock. Millgarth was a place designed to keep you in, or keep you out.

In 1968, the city of Leeds was modernising, not that Millgarth knew it – modernity was just a rumour there. 'The replacement of Millgarth Street station in particular is one of urgency,' the Leeds City Police's Annual Report for 1967 stated; but almost a decade passed before this happened. When the Inspector of Constabulary carried out the annual inspection of the force in April 1969 he reported that he had seldom seen a city of the size and dignity of Leeds with such poor police stations.

Millgarth belonged to the Victorian age, built where cholera houses once stood, opposite a textile mill: a reminder that if factory discipline didn't keep you in place then police discipline would. When it first opened the station housed a barracks and the city mortuary, but they were long gone. In 1968, Millgarth looked out on to a piece of derelict land where the mill had been; beyond that was Quarry Hill Flats, once the largest municipal housing estate in Europe (Adolf Hitler was said to be an admirer).

The outer structure of the building had changed very little over time. With its Gothic arched doors and windows it was somewhere between school and chapel, blackened by time. A gloomy place of correction.

Forget those cosy images of the blue lamp glowing over the station door, of the ruddy-faced, avuncular bobby dispensing homespun wisdom from behind the counter. Leeds City Police, Millgarth, was Old Law coppering.

There was nothing reassuring about Millgarth station. Once through the double doors there was an enquiry office for the public, though it wasn't the sort of place the public cared to linger. Through another set of doors, out of the view of the general public and to the left, was a passage which led to the cells. The smell of sewerage and unwashed bodies was strong here. To the right a twenty-foot-long, L-shaped mahogany counter divided the office area and the public area – the notorious Millgarth counter which had jumped up and hit many a belligerent drunk in the face. Millgarth didn't concern itself with presenting a benevolent front to the public. It was a police force, not a police service. There were no rights down Millgarth.

Straight ahead from the entrance was a staircase leading to the first floor. Until his retirement in 1956, Superintendent Herbert Goult lived up there with his wife Elsie.

Superintendent Goult had been an officer during the First World War and his approach to discipline reflected this experience. Nothing sloppy escaped his notice: Millgarth men were in the city centre and in the public eye and were expected to comport themselves like proper bobbies. Unusually for an officer of that lofty rank, Goult conducted the parades himself and PCs had to salute him as they left the station. Out of his earshot his men called him 'The Führer', but he enjoyed their absolute loyalty and led from the front. On Bonfire Night 1949, when Sheffield Wednesday fans were making their way back to their coaches after a match at Elland Road, a disturbance broke out near Kirkgate Market. Hooligans who'd been happily throwing barrow boys' barrows on to fires turned their attention to a number of plain-clothes officers.

Wednesday then attempted to storm Millgarth to spring the prisoners. And in front of those intransigent doors, arms folded, immovable in the face of the baying mob stood Herbert Goult. After all, it was his and Elsie's home he was protecting.

After Goult retired the top floor of Millgarth was given over to the bobbies – a recreation area with a kitchen and mess room, a bar, a couple of billiards tables. His successor was Bryan Molloy. Though Molloy had never been a military man, as a smart barrel-chested six-footer with a thick neck he had the bearing. Nicknamed 'Bismarck', he was a rigid disciplinarian who came down heavily on the most minor infringements of the code, conspicuous and self-important. 'A gas lamp in an atomic age,' some said. Policing was his life. His father had been a policeman, his brother was a policeman. When he took over at Millgarth he continued to live above a police station in Chapeltown. He even took the *West Riding Crime Report* as his holiday reading. His only interest outside the police was the Yorkshire branch of the Gilbert and Sullivan Society. But for Molloy a policeman's lot was a happy one indeed. He was the top man at Millgarth when Geoff Ellerker and Ken Kitching first came together in 1957.

'If you were warm and you walked you were in,' one Old Law Leeds bobby told me. In the immediate post-war years they were practically dragging them off the streets into the Municipal Buildings, then the headquarters of Leeds City Police, and police entry tests were comically simple. Policing had become a more attractive career as a result of the Oaksey Committee's settlement on pay scales, allowances and pensions. For the twenty-eight-year-old Ken Kitching it was a last chance to make something of himself.

He was born on 11 June 1922 in the Sheepscar/Chapeltown area of Leeds. His father was a slater's labourer; his mother had the Irish maiden name Manghan. He left school at fourteen and between 1936 and 1939 had a variety of unskilled jobs: clothing factory worker, garage attendant, shop assistant. He was a railway locomotive fireman during the war, a reserved occupation. He married Vera and they lived on a new housing development in the

Belle Isle area of Hunslet. It was built on a site where there had once been rhubarb fields and piggeries. He carried on working the railways until he joined Leeds City Police in August 1950.

Kitching hadn't performed any kind of military service, which set him apart from the great majority of his police contemporaries. Geoff Ellerker's route into the police was more typical. He was born south of the Aire at 61 Hunslet Road on 27 August 1933. His father was a grocer's assistant. He was educated at a secondary modern school, Brudenell Road in the Hyde Park area, leaving at fifteen. The best from his school went on to good apprenticeships: Ellerker joined the printing trade, one of Leeds's well-established industries. He was conscripted in 1952, serving in the RAF Police. The RAF Police had formations all over the world and during the period of Ellerker's national service (1952–4) had heavy security responsibilities in conflicts in Cyprus, Kenya (during the Mau Mau uprising) and the Canal Zone, Egypt. It seems likely that Ellerker served in one of these places and perhaps got his taste for policing. From the RAF, he returned initially to his trade, and was a compositor at Hunter's of Armley. Printing was a secure trade, buoyant in the post-war years, but two years later he joined Leeds City Police, soon after his marriage to Dorothy Masters, whom he met while on holiday in Blackpool. A proud policeman serving the city of his birth. The arms of the city and the motto *Pro Rege et Lege* were stamped on his police badge.

Like the overwhelming majority of Leeds bobbies in Old Law times, Kitching and Ellerker were Loiners and servants of their city. The first paragraph of the *Leeds City Police: Constable's Guide* told them: 'You are appointed under the Municipal Corporations Act, 1882, by the Watch Committee of the City of Leeds, as a Constable for the City and for the County in which the City is situated, but your powers do not extend beyond a distance of seven miles from the boundary of the City.' The Leeds police were close to the public in Old Law times. Even those who came to Leeds from outside were tied to the locality by the force rule which insisted that its police officers reside within the city boundaries. The bobby travelled to work with the rest of the workers on the bus or the tram, and with changing facilities non-existent in the poky stations he always went to work in his uniform. An ordinary citizen in uniform – that was the traditional understanding of the English bobby. It was the peculiar genius of English policing that the bobby's iconic status was enhanced, not diminished, by his close identification with the public.

Policing in the post-war years was intensely local. Leeds was one of 176 police forces in 1945; sixty years on there are forty-three and the number is likely to be reduced further. Even modest towns had their own police forces, jealously guarding their boundaries, cleaving to its traditions, reflecting the local chauvinism. Leeds City Police thought itself superior to the surrounding police forces – the West Riding Constabulary (as it was until 1968) and the Bradford City Police. Leeds men referred to 'the Riding' as 'donkey wallopers'; the Riding, in Leeds's opinion, 'did nowt but chase sheep shaggers all day'.

Though the crime rate was beginning to rise, 1950s Britain was not yet the 'high-crime society'. It was a relatively orderly society. Deeply embedded as they were in the community, Leeds City Police prided itself on knowing everything that was going on in the city which was criminal or untoward. Professional criminals in the pre-motorway days were not very mobile and the crime in Leeds was almost all down to criminals from the city who would invariably become familiar to local detectives. Leeds City Police's card index of 'villains' (or 'ganifs' as they were known in Leeds, a Yiddish expression), complete with nicknames, drinking habits, tattoos, was famous. Its criminal intelligence and its clear-up rate of the more serious crimes were second to none. Leeds City Police pretty much had the city under its control.

The social composition of Leeds City Police reflected the public it served. Though Leeds was never a solidly working-class industrial city, still 55 per cent of the city's working population was employed in manufacturing at the start of the 1950s. A majority of Leeds bobbies came from the ranks of the skilled and semi-skilled industrial working class, which also happened to be where the majority of British people were. Many recruits to the police force came with trades behind them.

But like the city it served, Leeds City Police wasn't quite a blue-collar monolith. A fair number came from the middle ranks, lower rather than upper. The majority had been through secondary moderns, but there was a fair sprinkling of grammar-school boys, if not the most academically able. University graduates were unknown. There was a middle-class prejudice that joining the police was a waste of education.

Yet for young men who might otherwise have ended up in mundane factory and office jobs, the police offered worthwhile, respected and varied work. It appealed to those who enjoyed working outdoors, who liked being part of a team. It was a perfect job for those who had taken to military service. Importantly, at a time when people married and 'settled down' at a younger age, policing in Old Law times offered secure employment, steady if not great pay, and a reasonable pension at a relatively early age. It offered working-class men like Ken Kitching and Geoff Ellerker the opportunity for social advancement and a solid place in a society which looked up to its authority figures. Only the monarchy stood higher than the police in public esteem. The English bobby was an exemplar of English manhood: dutiful, self-controlled, strong but never one to throw it around. He represented the British Way of Life. It was a myth, no doubt encouraged by the BBC's popular series *Dixon of Dock Green* (1955–76), but it had a powerful hold over Middle England in the post-war years. To that section of society the British police was undoubtedly the finest in the world.

Ellerker's and Kitching's careers followed very different trajectories. Geoff Ellerker was an ambitious young policemen working hard to advance himself; Kitching was a dour beat bobby seemingly content with his lot.

Kitching spent the first years of his service policing the community he lived among. He worked first in 'B' Division, which covered a large part of south Leeds. Harold Robinson, who got to know him at Meadow Lane station, recalled, 'He was not a particularly bright man, but that applied to many members of the force at that time. A real good, plodding police officer.' Yet he was seen by colleagues as aloof and remote, surly even. 'He was a loner. You'd have particular mates; I don't think Ken had a particular mate,' Dennis West told me. From Dewsbury Road, Kitching moved into traffic and then, in January 1956, was posted to Millgarth Street, headquarters of the then Central Division. That experience in traffic served him well in the city centre and he was remembered by one colleague, Frank Atkinson, as an 'enthusiastic pursuer of erring motorists. Go down well as a present-day traffic warden.' His vigour with traffic obstructions went down well with Superintendent Molloy, a stickler on such offences. Kitching was also deeply intolerant of public nuisances like drunks and beggars and tramps. At a time when it was unusual to spend so long in Central Division, Kitching was there from January 1956 to June 1967. According to his service record he then spent a few months at Ireland Wood (though colleagues can only ever remember him at Millgarth) before returning to the city centre.

Kitching was a hard-looking man though smartly turned out. He was around 5'11" and skinny with slicked-back, thinning sandy-red hair. Beaky nose, sticky-out ears and a slightly overshot jaw. 'Right sharp features,' an old colleague of his told me.

Kitching was fixed and comfortable in his small world: the city centre of Leeds; his semi-detached in Belle Isle which he had no desire to improve on; a couple of local pubs. Colleagues never heard Kitching talk about his home life. 'All he would talk about were the "old days" of his time as a PC or of other tales of old Millgarth,' one of the men on his shift told me. He wasn't approachable and was curt with those he felt were beneath him, whether probationer constables or members of the public. A former Millgarth colleague (who wished to remain anonymous) told me that he was off duty and walking up The Headrow when he saw Kitching ahead of him. A member of the public stopped Kitching to ask him something. Whatever Kitching said to him had left him looking dazed. The colleague asked him what had gone on. This member of the public, thinking it had been his helpful local bobby, had asked the time, to which Kitching had replied, 'Fuck off.'

Kitching was appointed sergeant in November 1965. Fifteen

years to achieve promotion wasn't so unusual then. Leeds was then increasing its establishment, bringing in men from outside forces, and more were getting promoted.

Geoff Ellerker came from little and bettered and advanced himself through hard work and application. A proper Samuel Smiles story. Ellerker was upwardly mobile and family-orientated – everything that Kitching wasn't (the Ellerkers would have two children, the Kitchings were childless). Though policing was never regarded as a middle-class profession, it had some of the trappings – job security, opportunities for promotion, greater credibility with the bank manager – and Ellerker, like most working-class men of the time, was eager to get on and up the ladder. Ellerker's rise took him from the smoky inner-city to a new three-bedroom Wimpey house in the suburbs. It was at a respectable remove from the dirty business of urban police work, a nice place to bring up the kids, good schools, pleasant neighbours. Ellerker was known locally as a committed policeman, a good neighbour, a churchgoer (he accompanied his Catholic wife to her local parish church) and above all a quiet family man.

After several years as a beat bobby at Millgarth he achieved his ambition to get into CID. Detective work was seen as exciting and higher status with little of the drudgery associated with the life of a patrol officer. CID also had an element of glamour: sharp suit made up by Dunn's on Briggate, trenchcoat, trilby hat. From May 1961 until his return to Millgarth as inspector in April 1968, all Ellerker's police service was in CID. He established a reputation as a highly capable detective. He was modern in outlook, knew the law and was good on paperwork. He steered clear, as far as it was possible, of the heavy pubbing culture of CID. In February 1964, after almost three years in CID in North-East Division, he was made sergeant. Whereas the usual practice was to be promoted back into uniform, Ellerker remained in CID. He was posted to North-West Division which had its headquarters at Ireland Wood station.

After being made sergeant he put his mind to further advancement. His determination and discipline struck colleagues.

He was promoted to inspector on 8 April 1968 at the relatively young age of thirty-four and returned to Millgarth Street. By contemporary standards, Ellerker was a high-flyer. It was just eleven years since he had completed his initial training, an unusually rapid rise through the ranks. He would certainly have gone further.

In personal appearance he was smart, though not one of the immaculate ones. He was around 5'11" with swept-back dark hair. For a slim man he had unusually chubby cheeks.

'He thought well of hissel',' one of his former colleagues at Ireland Wood told me. He was certainly confident and sure of his place in the world. He was a good bobby.

There were some big men in the intensely male society that was Leeds City Police. Intensely male because even as the Policewomen's Department began to grow and establish its value in the post-war years, policewomen remained marginal, their work mostly of a welfare nature. Intensely male because the traditional masculine attributes were prized. Chief constables wanted physically robust recruits. Bobbies were encouraged into competitive team sports; inter-force and inter-divisional rivalry helped to strengthen group identity.

Most of all the police wanted somebody who would be staunch in an 'up and downer'. Men like Eric 'Moose' Walker, Derek 'Big Red' Holmes and Eric 'Buffer' Brailsford were the archetypal Leeds bobbies. Buffer: an ex-miner, built like a tank, broken nose, cauliflower ears. Up Halton Moor and Gipton, he'd clattered some lugholes and the people there loved him for it. It was 'Mr Brailsford' to them. Buffer was given responsibility for 'liaising' with the travelling people. It was thought that he would communicate with them on their level. He did. 'The rudest, crudest man in Leeds City Police,' Harold Robinson told me. 'A frightening man. At one time we were have problems with didicois – travelling people. And many of these didicois were very violent men. If they wanted to stand up and fight he'd fight them all.'

The public were proud of their policemen precisely because they were bruisers. The memory of PC 568 William 'Rocking Horse'

Bartle, who policed the Richmond Hill/Bank area between 1907 and 1933, endured long into the twentieth century. Elderly residents of Quarry Hill Flats (built on the site of some of the slums he patrolled) remembered with affection the bobby who'd clipped their ears as kids; swinging his great cape round his head he'd scattered many a rabble. He preferred to avoid the starchy formalities of the law and settle the matter there and then with his lump-hammer fists. The Rocking Horse legend outlived even Quarry Hill Flats.

The sensitive caring bobbies were the unusual ones – they got called things like the 'Padre'. Most armed themselves with a protective coat of cynical humour. After dealing with some horrendous traffic accident or sudden death it was 'have a drink'. No counsellors in Old Law times.

Intensely male, intensely cynical. As the bobby got to know 'the Job', he picked up bits of common sense – that the woman who'd been knocked senseless by the drunken husband on the Thursday night would be cooking his favourite on the Friday. He began to divide up the public into the honest public and the 'toerags'. Our Old Law bobby tended to believe that society was going to the dogs and despaired when new ideas about the rehabilitation of offenders became Home Office orthodoxy in the 1960s. Experience didn't incline him to belief in the innate goodness of human nature. Toerags couldn't be reformed. People learned right from wrong not through moral exhortation but through the infliction of pain, starting during childhood with the clipped ear and the smacked bum. He preferred the time-honoured responses to human wickedness: he was invariably an advocate for the restoration of the birch ('I tell you, they didn't come back a second time') and was firmly opposed to the abolition of the noose (ditto). He believed that social order would crumble if criminals were no longer shocked and awed by the terrible majesty of the law.

Millgarth Street was a big man's nick. The ideal Millgarth bobby was as substantial as its front doors, as hard as its counter. At one time Central Division only took officers who were six feet and over and sent the smaller ones to the outer divisions, because it was in the heart of the city that a physical statement had to be made, particularly on Friday and Saturday nights when the livelier pubs on Vicar Lane (the Robin Hood and the Dolphin) turfed out. The annual crime figure returns regularly put Leeds second behind London in convictions for drunk and disorderly, which was less an indication of the power of Tetley's bitter than it was a statement of the Leeds City Police's social intolerance and its commitment to stilling the city early on. With his helmet adding extra inches to his height, the average Millgarth bobby towered over the average Leeds male.

In April 1968 the city's police divisions were reorganised. Central Division became Millgarth Street subdivision and was coupled with Ireland Wood subdivision to form 'A' Division. Millgarth subdivision would be reduced in area in June 1969, but in 1968 it extended beyond the city centre three-quarters of a mile northwards as far as the university. It was the smallest in area of the six Leeds subdivisions as well as the least populated. Its population was 16,000, the Quarry Hill Flats complex and properties north of the city centre accounting for this number; the residential population of the city centre itself was very low, consisting of the occupants of the hostels, pub landlords and live-in caretakers.

The east, west and southern boundaries of Millgarth subdivision coincided roughly with those of the central area of Leeds: Quarry Hill Flats to the east, Westgate to the west, the river and station to the south. Within this was a compact shopping area (much more so than Manchester's or Liverpool's or Birmingham's) bounded by The Headrow to the north, Boar Lane to the south, Vicar Lane and the markets to the east, Park Row to the west. West of Park Row were the banks, law firms and insurance offices; mixed industrial and commercial premises were along the east and south peripheries; north of The Headrow was the Merrion Centre and a lot of semi-derelict properties and warehouses, which is where David Oluwale slept out before he took to the shopping area.

South of Boar Lane, the streets slope gently down towards the River Aire. Paralleling the river was The Calls, one of the oldest streets in the city, described in 1835 as a 'gloomy road above the river', a description just as apt in 1968. At the eastern end of The Calls was the Church Army hostel which accommodated David Oluwale between 17 April and 4 July 1968. The Calls was a street of sorrowful legends. At one time there was a long, dark flight of steps which went straight down into the mucky river and the story was that a certain Jenny White, 'finding marriage vows as false as dicer's oath', ended her life there. The spot where she went in was known thereafter as 'Jenny White's hole'. Heading west, still parallel to the river, The Calls runs into Call Lane. In the late seventeenth century, one of Leeds's first dissenting chapels was established there, out of sight of the principal streets of the town, as if to symbolise, one historian of Leeds has observed, 'the exclusion of [its] supporters from the mainstream of civic life'. At the end of the 1960s, different kinds of outsiders from mainstream society were drawn to Call Lane: Leeds's gay pub, the Hope & Anchor (sometimes called the Grope & Wanker), was there. This dark, neglected waterfront formed the southern boundary of Millgarth subdivision.

This, then, was Inspector Ellerker's turf, which until 1968 was patrolled by bobbies on foot. At times there could be anywhere between twenty and thirty of them out and about in the city centre. Policing in Old Law times was all about a visible, physical presence on the streets. The 'bobby on the beat' was the bedrock of English policing, part of the street furniture. Each police division was divided up into beats and the bobby would plod dourly around his assigned patch for eight hours, keeping an eye out for anything untoward, an ear pricked for the unusual barking of dogs and the smashing of glass, getting to know every crack in the pavement and 'trying up' his property ('shaking hands with door handles') during the night. Policemen's time was strictly regulated. Bobbies kept their 'points', ringing in to the station at regular intervals (usually on the hour) from a police box or, after these were taken out of service, a public telephone. These were the days before personal radios. The bobby's little black beat book stipulated the precise route he should follow. For instance, at one time the officer assigned to number 5 beat in the city centre was directed: 'Return to Call Lane, right Pitfall

Street, return to Call Lane, right Call Lane, right Warehouse Hill, along riverside, return and cross Call Lane to Verity's shop, to Lower Briggate, right Lower Briggate, taking all yards to Duncan Street.' In this regimented way every obscure corner of Leeds was covered.

During the tenure of Chief Constable Alexander Paterson (1956–67), Leeds City Police had started using Velocette motorcycles (nicknamed the 'Noddy bike') equipped with personal radios. Even so, the beat officer making his 'points', relying on his whistle and the public telephone, remained the fundamental unit of policing.

However, when Ellerker took up his inspector's post in April 1968 a radically new style of policing had just been introduced – unit beat policing (UBP). UBP was a modernising Home Office initiative which aimed to deliver a more mobile and technologically driven style of policing in response to the growing mobility and sophistication of criminals and a spiralling crime rate. Although UBP tried to retain some characteristics of the traditional style of policing through the concept of an 'area constable' – a sort of community policeman – the real policing of the city was now carried out by round-the-clock motorised patrols. The car constable would normally patrol two adjacent areas and keep in touch with the area constable and the station by personal radio. After midnight the city was policed almost exclusively by car beat men.

Society would later lament the demise of the bobby on the beat and the loss of face-to-face connection between police and public, but in 1968 UBP was seen as a positive move in the 'war on crime'. Society was changing rapidly, the old monolithic working-class communities were breaking up and moving into housing estates which couldn't be policed the old way. UBP would prove popular with the younger generation of Leeds policemen who were far happier crawling the streets in a shiny new Vauxhall Viva panda than plodding round cold, solitary beats. Suddenly policing seemed more glamorous.

Inspector Ellerker took charge of a shift of men. A shift worked a combination of earlies, lates and nights over a four-week rota, and would normally have five days off in that period, referred to in Leeds City Police as 'Rotary Leave'. The early turn was, in the Leeds vernacular, 6 a.m. while 2 p.m., the late turn 2 p.m. while 10 p.m., and nights 10 p.m. while 6 a.m. This was the basic shift pattern, though a token number of officers would be on intermediate shifts, half-nights (6 p.m. to 2 a.m.) for instance.

A shift was a close-knit body of men who not only worked together, they took their leave together, and often socialised together. They were on the same wavelength, sharing a bantering, sarcastic humour impenetrable to 'civvies'. Between shifts there was great rivalry: which was the most efficient, which was getting through the most work.

In April 1968 Millgarth subdivision was divided into twelve area beats. The theory was that an area constable would be assigned to each beat with a car patrol superimposed on two adjoining beats. A shortage of manpower meant that an 'area man' was not always available. There was also a subdivisional van driver whose main task was transporting prisoners to Millgarth and the Bridewell.

Ellerker's shift was known as Group 3. He was supported by three sergeants, one in the station and two section sergeants who were out and about. The two section sergeants supervised six area beats each and were normally responsible, then, for three car patrols. On a nightshift, once the pubs shut, there were usually no officers on foot in the city centre.

When UBP came in, the idea was that a shift inspector would become a strategist, analysing crime trends, working out how best to allocate resources to meet crime problems. But this was too intellectualised an understanding of the role. Ellerker did what inspectors at Millgarth had always done. He was out and about, visible, leading by example, taking personal responsibility for failures or faults in his subdivision. In Old Law times even Superintendent Herbert Goult would get down to street level, exercising robust supervision, administering bollockings for anything out of place or overlooked. Ellerker was of that Millgarth mould. He spent at least half a tour of duty patrolling with his men; the rest of the time he was inside dealing with reports and administration. It was a steep learning curve for someone whose police life until then had been in CID, who had never been a patrol sergeant and who had never supervised men. He was dealing with completely different crime problems in a completely different working context, less autonomous, less relaxed than he'd had it in CID. Finding his feet again as a uniformed officer, he came to depend heavily on one of his two section sergeants, Ken Kitching.

Sergeant was a very powerful rank in those rigidly hierarchical Old Law times. To the green probationer constable it was the sergeants more than anyone who would determine whether or not he made the grade. Dennis West, who joined Leeds City Police in the early 1950s, told me that 'whatever you were told do to you did it. No questions were asked at all. It was particularly the sergeants who ran the force – forget the others. You didn't call them by their first names, make no mistake about that. They'd tell you what to do. They'd got your respect. And what they told you to do was good because they'd done it.'

Typically, the sergeant was a strict supervisor. Probationer constables would submit a crime report to the sergeant, who would vet it and send it back if it wasn't exactly how he wanted it. Even humdrum reports of minor traffic offences could get sent back three or four times, sergeants suggesting different words if he didn't like the way it had been put. The young policeman would be watched by a sergeant as he gave evidence in court, and his performance assessed. If two or three sergeants didn't think much of the probationer he was out of a job, no avenue of appeal.

In Old Law times, after parade, a sergeant would march his men out on to the beats. He would meet each of his constables at some conference point on the hour, checking how he was and whether he had anything to report. These practices were dying out in the late 1960s: marching, because military-style discipline was being relaxed, particularly its more anachronistic expressions; conference points, because the introduction of personal radios enabled the sergeant to contact his men at any time and place. But Kitching remained very much a sergeant in the old style. He saw himself as the kingpin of his domain, always visible on the streets, attending even the most trivial incidents.

There was a time when they wouldn't take probationer constables at Millgarth, the man's nick, but a shortage of manpower in the late 1960s meant it was no longer possible to be so discriminating. The car patrol constables were mainly younger men with few years' experience under their belt. A 1969 Leeds working party report on UBP found that the average age of its car beat constables was twenty-four years eleven months and that almost half were probationers. Under UBP, the theory was that sergeants would become tactical leaders, not so heavily involved in the minutiae. But a year after the new system was introduced, the working party found that sergeants, like inspectors, were operating much as they'd always done. The greatest amount of a sergeant's time was spent assisting individual constables with specific incidents or crimes and subsequent reports. This, it concluded, was due to the shortage of manpower and the relative inexperience and immaturity of car beat constables. Leeds didn't see this as such a bad thing – the sergeant, according to the report, 'had countless opportunities to display leadership by example'.

The probationer constable, no matter whether he came with some experience of the world, was soon made very aware of his lowly place in the hierarchy. 'Even senior PCs were gods,' one retired officer told me. 'You used to go in the canteen at Dewsbury Road and you couldn't sit in their chair. Senior PCs sat in particular seats and that was their seat. "Eh, you can't sit there, that's so-and-so's chair." "But he isn't here." "Don't care, you can't sit there."' Young PCs would soak up bits of practical wisdom in the canteen at 'grub time'. 'In the poky little police stations that you used to have, you'd sit on nights with your sandwiches and the older bobbies would be telling the tale,' another recalled. One of these senior bobbies asked him how he had got on at training school. He was telling him that he'd finished either first or second in the examinations when the old boy cut him short. 'You can forget all that, lad,' he said. 'There's only two things that matter: the Cloth and the Public.' The 'Cloth' was the police uniform, almost sacred.

Dave Sowden told me about his first posting to Upper Wortley station, then headquarters of West Division. In every station there would be an experienced constable with twenty years' service under his belt, who'd never sought promotion, who was happy with his lot and seemingly rooted to his spot. In those nervous first weeks, Sowden was helped through by such a man, PC Hepditch, a comic-book portly bobby who sang basso profundo in the police choir. Sowden called him 'Dad', he was the source of all wisdom. Another character was PC Fothergill. 'Do you drink, lad?' was his first comment. When Sowden said he didn't touch alcohol, Fothergill barked, 'I'm not talking about beer, lad. *Tea*. I mean tea.' When he went out with Fothergill it seemed at times less like a hunt for villains than an interminable quest for a cuppa. Blacksmiths, scrap merchants, garages – he would have a range of 'tea spots' and he'd chat and pick up bits of gossip. Coppering, he explained to Sowden, was all about being a nosy bugger. There was a lot of experience in that police station at Upper Wortley. Once, when Sowden was sitting in the canteen at grub time, Inspector Roddy commented that around that table they had a full crew for a Lancaster bomber. Roddy had been a bomber pilot, PC David Shackleton had been a flight engineer, and there was also a rear gunner, upper turret gunner, bomb aimer. This was a rare glimpse into former lives since canteen talk was usually about 'the Job', the here-and-now. The probationer constable could be made to feel like a boy among the men. It might be years before he was allowed to make up a four at the domino table.

He was an apprentice learning a trade and independent-mindedness was discouraged. It started at training school, usually thirteen weeks at Pannal Ash near Harrogate. Lots of marching. Beds turned over if bed-pack wasn't up to scratch, bulled boots, razor-sharp creases in the trousers. Regimentation continued in the classroom. The trainee's head was filled with a hundred statutory definitions of criminal offences, the basic law a bobby needed. The training sergeant regurgitated chunks of *Moriarty's Police Law*, the 'definitions', which ranged from robbery and infanticide to arcane pieces of legislation relating to birds' eggs and coinage, and these were copied out religiously into exercise books. No classroom discussion or feedback sessions. It was all drilled in. One ex-Leeds policeman told me about his first class at Pannal Ash training school. The training sergeant entered the classroom and without a word of warning smacked one of the bobbies hard across the head.

'What's that, son?'

'Don't know, Sergeant.'

'*That's* an assault.'

And it continued. Before going out on a tour of duty, bobbies would line up in the parade room and the shift inspector would check that they were smart and tidy, boots polished, everything in order, staff, cuffs, torch, right turn and marched out of the station by the sergeant until they arrived at their particular beats, dropping off one after another.

A young PC was made to feel like Leeds City Police had ownership of him. He required the permission of the chief constable if he wanted to get married and his partner was vetted. His accommodation was inspected. Special permission was required if he wanted to live outside the Leeds City Police area, but it was rarely given. Although the Royal Commission of 1962 insisted that the policeman 'is a fellow citizen and every encouragement must be given to enable him to live amongst his fellow men', most forces had their colonies of police houses. Very soon the bobby would find that he'd left his old mates behind. He was married to 'the Job'.

In the late 1960s, the recruits were entering the force at a younger age than in previous times. They didn't have national service or trades under their belt. Into the police straight from school, they hadn't seen much of life. They weren't as 'wick' as their elders.

Group 3 at Millgarth, Ellerker's shift, was a typical mix of innocence and experience. PC Keith Seager, who would be so heavily involved in the Oluwale case, was born in 1944, left his job in engineering to become a Leeds City Police officer in 1965, and was still a probationer constable when Ellerker arrived at Millgarth. He was of stocky build, looked more like a Teddy boy than a bobby and was always getting pulled up for long hair. PC John Ferguson, a former cadet, born in 1947, was a very youthful-looking probationer. His parents owned the Regent pub, a popular Irish boozer, a place where Sergeant Kitching, with his Irish blood, liked to drink and listen to the traditional music (Ferguson was an accomplished piano accordion player).

Less worldly-wise, these Group 3 probationers were keen to win the respect of the older bobbies and senior officers. There were two forceful Old Law bobbies in their late thirties they looked to in particular, PC Arthur Shackleton and PC Ron Woodhead. Woodhead, whose nickname was 'Chopper', was a well-regarded ex-army man with a boxer's nose. Since his posting to Millgarth in 1961 he had mostly performed subdivisional van duties, transporting prisoners between Millgarth and the Bridewell in a Morris J4 van, and had little ambition to progress beyond that. Arthur Shackleton joined in 1957 and all his service had been at Millgarth. He now patrolled the quietest part of the subdivision, away from the city centre up near the university. And then there was the longest serving constable on the shift, Ken Higgins. He joined in 1951 and like Kitching had spent most of his service at Millgarth. Because of his dumpy shape he got the nickname 'Glob', and though he sometimes seemed nearer to circus clown than policeman, Glob had a reputation as an uncanny thief-taker. One old Millgarth colleague recalled, 'He'd been working across Harrison Street and he caught three breaking into the back of the Grand Theatre; they started running away and he shouted, "Halt, or I'll fire." And they all stopped. So he marched them down to Millgarth at the end of his finger.' He was unable to progress further in the police because he was hopelessly incompetent when it came to paperwork, but he was content as a Millgarth PC. Glob was toothless and refused dentures, though his shift once clubbed together for a set from a second-hand shop.

At grub time, Shackleton, Woodhead, Kitching and Ellerker usually made up a card school (the card game of choice was hearts) or a four at bones (dominoes). They were sometimes joined by the station sergeant, Frank Atkinson, an amiable, easy-going man in his early forties who had twenty years' service under his belt.

The young PCs sat round the edges until invited in. PC Seager was the first of the younger constables to become a regular at the table.

To these younger bobbies, Kitching appeared to be the dominant personality on the shift. He was Millgarth to the marrow and knew the subdivision inside out. The other section sergeant, Dougie Carter, struck them as a weak character in comparison: he was certainly a less voluble, less enthusiastic officer than Kitching. In every respect Kitching seemed set in his ways. He looked and seemed like an old man. Indeed, he was as old as their dads. When the panda cars came in the rule was that officers were to wear soft flat caps when inside the vehicle and switch to a helmet when outside. Kitching's helmet remained fixed to his head. He wore it unusually low, so that it pushed his ears out at right angles. But in that helmet and black greatcoat he cut a menacing figure on the streets at night.

Kitching normally worked area beats 1–6, the busiest part of the subdivision closest to the station, where most of the shops and the pubs were. This was called 'bottom side' and it was where all the action was. Dougie Carter tended to work the quieter 'top side', 6–12. Normally a section sergeant kept to his turf, but even on those rare occasions when he was assigned to the 'top side' Kitching was prone to patrolling with Ellerker in the city centre. A shift inspector wouldn't normally patrol exclusively with one sergeant, but Ellerker and Kitching soon appeared inseparable. They almost always took their break together.

The men on the shift soon worked out that Ellerker was no manager of men. Sometimes he was the officious disciplinarian, delivering harsh reprimands for minor errors, the next minute he was round the table playing cards, laughing and joking and trying to be one of the lads. Ellerker couldn't work out what kind of leader to be and Kitching exploited the inspector's inexperience. Kitching once said to PC Seager, 'I've got him right here,' and made a gesture with his thumb.

In all his years in the heavy-drinking culture of CID, Ellerker had never been known as a boozer. If anything, he shunned the social side of 'the Job'. Working the night shift at Millgarth, he took to drinking with Kitching.

Pubs played a big part in Sergeant Kitching's dour life. Typically, when working the nights he'd get home about 6.30 a.m. and sleep until lunchtime opening. Then he'd bike it down to Leeds and visit his usual haunts: the Golden Cock, Brougham Arms, Star & Garter. After a few pints he would bike it back up to Belle Isle and sleep the beer off, then have something to eat, maybe a couple in his local, before biking it back down to Millgarth for parade at 9.45 p.m.

Ellerker and Kitching's night-shift drinking sessions were no secret. Once Ellerker had dismissed his men from parade at 10 p.m. the two of them would hit the pubs, having a few before closing time. There was always a reason to be around these pubs – public order problems, checking the licensing laws were being observed. They had certain pubs where they knew they would get a drink once the landlord had put the lights down and locked up: the Royal Oak, the Scarborough and the Jubilee were always good. They'd be seen leaving by the back doors. Although it was unlicensed, they could always get a drink at the Irish Club on Kirkgate; Kitching was tight with its one-eyed manager, Eddie Bolger.

Between 10 p.m. and midnight it was almost impossible for anyone to make contact with them on their personal radios. Sometimes they wouldn't be seen until grub time. Occasionally the van driver would be summoned to run them back to the station. Kitching always carried a packet of Terry's mints in a vain attempt to disguise the smell of drink.

The men on their shift learned to tread carefully around them when they returned from one of their sessions. Drink exacerbated Kitching's unpredictable, volatile nature. He could swing in an instant from being pleasant, happy and euphoric to surly, snarling and rude. He talked at his men rather than to them. His colleagues thought that he behaved like an aggressive big kid. Ellerker would try to portray a character of efficiency, picking faults even while the smell of drinking was coming off him.

David Oluwale's first known contact with Group 3 came on 17 April 1968 when he was arrested in the doorway of the Queen's Hotel by Sergeant Kitching and PC William Greenwood and charged with disorderly conduct. Greenwood was one of the younger officers on the shift, twenty at the time of this arrest, and already unhappy at Millgarth and with Kitching.

Between April and July 1968, when he was lodged at the Church Army hostel, Oluwale had no contact, according to the official record, with the police. That changed when he lost his accommodation on 4 July. The other residents had complained to the warden of the hostel of his poor hygiene and disgusting table manners. Raymond Bradbury, Church Army captain, would tell the investigation that Oluwale 'did not mix with the other men in the hostel, and had no friends that I knew of'. On a Sunday afternoon in May 1969, Bradbury was taken to the mortuary at St James's Hospital to see if he could identify the body of David Oluwale but couldn't because his face was so 'badly distorted'.

Within days of losing his hostel place, Oluwale was arrested for shoplifting from Marks & Spencer's. He was remanded in Armley and admitted to the hospital. The medical officer, Dr Bernard Green, found no evidence of active mental illness. In Green's view he was accountable for his actions. Oluwale received a suspended prison sentence for the offence when it came to court at the end of July.

He was back on the streets, sleeping in the same city-centre shop doorways; back on the streets at a time when Millgarth Street was coming under increasing pressure from influential traders to clear beggars and rough sleepers from the central area of the city. There was no room for the unwashed in 'Project Leeds'.

3

Robin Hood Forest

I

David Oluwale was a police problem – he offended the ideal of the salubrious urban environment. The word 'police' comes from the Greek word *polis* (city). Policing is all about making and maintaining clean, orderly cities. Edwin Chadwick, one of the principal early-nineteenth-century architects of our modern crime-detecting police force, was equally committed to bringing modern methods of drainage and sewerage to our cities. For Chadwick these were 'police' matters.

Oluwale was labelled 'vagrant'. 'Vagrant' is used as a synonym for a tramp, but it's better understood not as a single offence but as a 'social censure' of a variety of offences regarded as threats to orderly civic existence. The Vagrancy Act 1824 (and the modified 1935 Act), which was used against Oluwale on several occasions, covered a wide range of social offences including 'wandering abroad', fortune-telling, prostitution, 'exposing wounds or deformities to obtain alms' (returning soldiers wounded in the Napoleonic Wars had swollen the ranks of the homeless poor). Enacted during a period when the respectable classes were anxious about the rising and potentially disorderly urban poor, the 1824 Act was aimed at those who refused to bend to factory discipline. The main purpose of the 'new police', a response to the same anxieties, was to target those whose modes of life mocked the gospel of work, who threatened the order of cities and the smooth running of the industrial machine.

Oluwale was classic 'police property', one of those whose mode of life put him beyond the pale of respectable, majority society. Rough sleepers with a history of mental or drink problems, the young unemployed, prostitutes – all would constitute 'police property'. Society doesn't care how the police deal with this human waste – it is theirs to deal with as it sees fit; just as long as it is removed from public sight, no questions are asked. Oluwale was, to the police mind, someone who didn't work and fouled up the city. Someone whose very presence on the streets was obnoxious and intolerable.

Sergeant Ken Kitching was in a long English tradition. In 1818, at a vestry meeting of leading citizens at Leeds Parish Church, it was urged that 'the constables and special constables be directed to use every exertion to apprehend all vagrants'; when the Leeds Police Force began its operations on 2 April 1836 the suppression of vagrancy was one of its main priorities. But there is a longer history. Under common law, constables had always had a responsibility for controlling vagrants and for centuries they had been subject to harsh treatment. Itinerants in Catholic England had received hospitality in monasteries and almshouses, but after the Tudor dissolutions those uprooted from the land and cut free from ties of family and work came to be seen as a threat to social order. Terrible punishments were inflicted on vagrants, such as branding (a letter 'V' on the shoulders) and whipping. The Vagrancy Act of 1597 provided that dangerous rogues could be banished overseas. Hundred of youngsters were simply spirited from the streets and transported abroad – a pragmatic way of removing troublesome, surplus people from the urban scene. Vagabonds would find themselves in the Bridewell, a house of correction which aimed to reform through work. The whipping post and the practice of expulsion disappeared, but the 'undeserving poor' continued to be vigorously policed and punished in workhouses and prisons. The English have, as George Orwell put it, 'a strong sense of the sinfulness of poverty'.

Leeds dossers were tolerated if they kept themselves away from the smarter parts of the city. In the scruffier areas they could play out the role of 'character', adding to the local colour. It was rumoured that 'Woodbine Lizzie' had been the beautiful wife of a high-ranking naval officer, though it stretched the imagination as she wandered around Kirkgate Market in her heavy old coat. Equally mysterious was the woman they called the 'Sergeant Major'. She was 5'10", ramrod-straight, and everybody stepped out of her way as she marched determinedly down Briggate, military beret planted on her head. She lived off the waste vegetables and fruit piled up at the end of the day in the market's pinfold. Then there was Squeaker, so-called because of his old-fashioned hearing aid, a wooden box fixed to his chest and a speaker which squeaked constantly whenever it was on. Bill Kilgallon, then Fr Kilgallon, who started the first day shelter for the Leeds homeless, told me, 'If Squeaker was peeing on the floor and you went to remonstrate with him he would just turn off this contraption and say, "There, lad, tha' can shout all tha' wants."' Another, Barnsley Bob, was a great one for sleeping at the brick kilns south of the river near Elland Road. Policemen at Dewsbury Road would give Barnsley and his pals a morning call to ensure they weren't bricked up; at first light a hunched dusty procession would be seen making its way over Leeds Bridge back into town. When Barnsley Bob died in 1978 his *Yorkshire Evening Post* obituary, which affectionately recalled his broad grin, was longer than that accorded to many a city worthy.

Until St Anne's day centre was opened in December 1971 there was no place in Leeds where the homeless unemployed and the rough sleepers could go to get out of the cold and get a hot meal. And so they gravitated to the market area at Kirkgate where fellowship and warmth and a cup of tea could be got. There was little chance of being 'moved on'. Though Kirkgate Market contributed to the costs of having a police constable permanently on duty there, the 'market PC' was typically a superannuated bobby nearing retirement who would only stir if somebody was causing a serious public nuisance.

David Oluwale, who was living a very lonely life at this time, was known around the markets; his connection with this part of town went back to his early days in Leeds when he worked at the Public Abattoir and Wholesale Meat Market. He used the cafés, sometimes washing up for a meal; sometimes he'd be given waste food from traders at the end of the day, or he would pick over the goods left in the pinfold. He used the Market Tavern, a rough pub popular with the market traders and the slaughterhouse men known locally as the 'Madhouse'. John O'Dwyer, the landlord of the Madhouse, was one of the few to come forward when the Oluwale investigation was opened and he said that he typically saw Oluwale three or four times a week. He was always in the same scruffy donkey jacket. He would be in at opening time, and sat on his own in the same place – the right-hand corner next to the jukebox in what the landlord called the 'best room'. He would drink three or four pints of mild and leave at afternoon closing time. They never engaged in conversation beyond 'How are you keeping?' O'Dwyer said that 'he had something lacking . . . a bit mental and he never seemed to take an interest in the music or anything'. In this hard man's pub, notorious for fights, Oluwale, so it seems, wasn't troubled by anyone.

Millgarth police station, on the eastern flank and facing away from the markets, was not somewhere Oluwale entered voluntarily, but it was a magnet for many of the rough sleepers. 'Leeds Billy', a war hero with a metal plate in his head and his army pension down his socks, was always in and out with 'the usual story'. 'The usual story' – this is how it was recorded in the occurrence book – was that all the other residents at the Crypt and the Salvation Army hostel were thieves and layabouts. 'Are you going to get 'em tonight?' he'd say to some bobby about to begin his shift. 'They're all pitch and tossers [dossers]. They won't wash. They won't work. Get 'em tonight, kid.' Leeds Billy used to sleep under the stalls of the open market and would often pop into Millgarth to get warm and have a cup of tea. Sometimes he would get roughed up by drunks at closing time – the homeless were vulnerable to attack – so the police would clean him up and get him looked at if he was injured. Every Christmas Day, even if he was off duty, Mick Grubb, a famous Leeds City Police hard man, was known to take him a dinner with all the trimmings.

Sergeant Kitching delivered kickings. Vagrants, he believed, were a drain on society who needed firm police action. One of his men remembered him saying that it would be better if Blossom, an elderly rough sleeper, went for a swim in the Aire. He understood his task in very simple terms: it was to clear this human rubbish off his patch, out of the subdivision if he could, using any means necessary.

Kitching had never been much of a 'thief-taker' and his knowledge of the law was rudimentary, but he was regarded by his superiors as an active, highly efficient city-centre sergeant who was always ready to take the lead in operational matters as they arose. Traffic obstructions, disturbances at closing time, street nuisances – these were his forte, the mundane but necessary jobs which keep cities running.

One of his colleagues, PC Woodhead, the subdivisional van driver, would describe Kitching as a 'fanatic' when it came to 'trying up' property. Often, Woodhead drove Kitching round the city centre and, rather than leaving it all to the beat constables, he took it on himself to check the shops and the arcades for anything untoward. Kitching wanted to set an example for his men.

He saw himself as street cleaner, and was obsessed with removing rough sleepers from the subdivision. He would often patrol in the J4 van and go out looking for them, not just in the city centre but around the edges, to Warehouse Hill, the railway embankments, Marsh Lane and the bus stations. He looked for them in obscure places, waking them up with his boot. The most desperate cases, the meths drinkers and the bed-wetters whom no hostel would take, slept under the Dark Arches, trains rattling above them, river rushing underneath them, water dripping on them, feeding like the rats off scrap food from the bins at the back of the Queen's Hotel. Kitching even went down there. At the Garden of Rest he found vagrants sleeping on benches, tipped them off and gave them a kicking. Sergeant Dougie Carter would tell the Oluwale investigation that Kitching 'was most zealous in shifting vagrants and sleepers-out from his section. My view was that he was a hard man and ruthless and untiring in doing his job in this direction. I think he had a strong dislike for this type of man.' Kitching never doubted that he was doing right for Leeds.

In June 1968 Sergeant Kitching saved the life of a man whose car had crashed into the Leeds and Liverpool Canal. Kitching had jumped in to rescue him. This act of bravery was recognised by a Humane Society Award.

Oluwale was a joke among members of the subdivision, a talking point whenever he was seen out and about. Some of the bobbies used to rile him up for sport, watch him howl down The Headrow, shouting and screaming in his native tongue.

It was a way of passing the time after the city had shut down. Because these were the 'long hours'. That's what they called that stretch between grub time and the end of the night shift, when one hour seemed more like three. Few prisoners to be had, few 999 calls coming in. And they were coldest hours too: before panda cars the bobby would be out there in the elements, warmth from the grub-time pot of tea wearing off, watching the frost forming gradually on his cape.

There were always games to kill time. At Dewsbury Road it was medieval jousting by the Aire on Noddy bikes; or chasing rabbits on them, trying to knock their heads off with their staffs. There was a bobby at Millgarth, I was told, who used to clamber across all the rooftops to get to the bedroom windows of this pub on Briggate, the Ship. He used to peer through the curtains. Once he came down from the roofs, face beaming and triumphant. 'They were at it, they were fucking *at it*!'

Strange sights in these 'long hours'. Another Millgarth bobby told me that he had this tea spot near the Queen's Hotel. It must have been about 2 a.m., deserted, when out from the gloom came Jimmy Savile, orange-dyed hair, walking determinedly across City

Square until he came to the statue of the Black Prince, stopped, had a long look up at him, walked on; the very next night, same time and place, he appeared again, his hair green; night after that, tartan.

Another remembered a sight like a nightmare. He was patrolling Lower Briggate with his mate PC Kennedy when they heard this rising din of scrabbling and squeaking coming from the direction of Boar Lane. PC Kennedy recognised the sound and pulled him into the first raised doorway, and just as he did, this seething torrent of rats came round the corner. There were hundreds of thousands of them, moving fast; the whole road filled with a writhing dark mass, determined yellow eyes, scrambling over each other. They were fixed in that doorway like Lot's wife, he told me. Didn't dare breathe. Could have been completely overrun by them. His mate put it down to the ancient sewers collapsing near Trinity Church. 'It was like something from days of plague,' he told me. Seemed to take an age to pass as they made their demented rush down to the River Aire.

They had names for him at Millgarth. Sometimes he was 'Ussywale' or 'Ally'. Sometimes he was 'playmate' or 'playboy' or 'your friend', occasionally 'David'. Mostly he was 'Uggy'. Every bobby on Group 3 knew who Sergeant Kitching meant when he said, 'Let us know if you see Uggy.' Kitching made it known that if anybody found Uggy sleeping out they were not to move him on without informing him or Inspector Ellerker first.

The new technology introduced with UBP was very useful for this. Previously there had been few personal radios and every message went through a central information room at police headquarters. Under UBP the subdivision took over these duties and became the radio control. Having initially shared frequencies, each subdivision was provided with its own separate frequency. The subdivisional radio operator was in close touch with the car beat men who were each equipped with personal radios. All calls went through him. He decided who should attend to incidents and he recorded every call on a message form: name of caller, time and date, nature of offence, action taken. When UBP came in, the station became more of a self-enclosed world; the central information room often complained that these local radio operators were too independent and that they were being kept in the dark on operational matters within subdivisions.

Radio operators were typically constables of some seniority, who had close personal relationships with the constables they served, and who knew intimately the layout and problems of the subdivision. PC Ken Bennett, an experienced officer with almost twenty years' service under his belt, most of it at Millgarth, was one of the radio operators who took regular messages about Oluwale. He would tell the Oluwale investigation that it was invariably Ellerker, Kitching and PC Seager who concerned themselves with him. 'I can remember wondering at that time why it was that these three officers in particular seemed to get involved with Oluwale much more than any other members of the shift. It was common knowledge that none of these officers liked to have sleepers out and vagrants on the subdivision, but in particular they disliked having Oluwale sleeping out . . . I have often received calls in the wireless room over the air from either PC Seager or Sergeant Kitching asking for the attendance of Inspector Ellerker, most usually in The Headrow or Lands Lane area. It was common knowledge amongst members of the group that Oluwale most frequently slept out in the Lands Lane and Headrow shop doorways and whenever I received a call over the air from PC Seager asking for Sergeant Kitching or from Sergeant Kitching asking for Inspector Ellerker to attend in these areas when on night duty, with no further details given, it was almost certainly because Oluwale had been found sleeping out.'

The first known contact between Oluwale and the three policemen took place during the night shift, 6/7 August 1968. That night Oluwale was sleeping in the doorway of the Bridal House on The Headrow. It was past 3 a.m. PC Seager was crawling along The Headrow in a panda car when he noticed a vehicle parked outside the Bridal House. He pulled up and could hear Oluwale's shouts from the doorway. According to the statement Seager gave to the Oluwale investigation, he was shouting, 'You're always fucking picking on me. Why can't you leave me alone? I've got to sleep somewhere.' He saw Ellerker and Kitching playing a sort of tennis with Oluwale. One would push him towards the other, the other would push him back. Oluwale was clutching his dirty green duffel bag in front of him. Oluwale managed to wriggle free and ran off towards Briggate, shouting. Ellerker said, 'Leave him, we'll see him later.' Kitching told Seager, 'Give us a shout if you see him.'

An hour later Seager saw Kitching walking fast down The Headrow towards Park Row; Ellerker was jogging in front of him. Realising they were chasing Oluwale, Seager drove slowly alongside Kitching, who ordered him to 'Get down there and stop him'. Seager drove on and parked his car up in Cookridge Street, got out quickly and ran towards Oluwale. Oluwale swerved past him into the road but Ellerker caught up with him and, according to the statement Seager made to the investigation, leapt on him and brought him to the ground.

They bundled him into the back of Seager's car, drove up Woodhouse Lane, passing the university, up the Otley Road, through Headingley, to the ancient village of Bramhope, seven miles away from Leeds, and to a quintessential English pub, the Fox & Hounds. Seager could see that Oluwale's cheek had swollen; Oluwale was saying, 'What are you going to do now? Why are you doing this to me?' They pulled up in the car park and Ellerker said to Oluwale, 'We're going to have to leave you here for a few minutes because we've got to go to the police station.' Ellerker pointed to the door, which was in darkness, and said, 'If you go and knock on that door they'll give you a cup of tea and we'll be back in a few minutes to pick you up.' Oluwale thanked them and walked towards the pub door. Ellerker got back in the car and said to Seager, 'Right, get your foot down.' They had a good laugh about it on the way back to Millgarth, imagining the publican's surprise. The car journey to and from the Fox & Hounds took forty minutes.

Kitching would boast and laugh about this incident later at Millgarth. PC Bennett, the radio operator, told the investigation:

'He never said who was with him when this was done, I never asked him because to be honest I didn't agree with this sort of conduct and I didn't want to know any more about it.'

That week the same three took Oluwale for another drive.

In the early hours of Sunday 11 August, around 3.30 a.m., Kitching woke Oluwale with a kick. He was pulled up from the ground while Ellerker stood watching. He clung on to his duffel bag.

Seager, who was patrolling nearby in a panda car, had received a message over the radio ordering him to go to the Bridal House. When he arrived, Ellerker and Kitching led Oluwale by his arms into the car. Oluwale was protesting that he didn't want to go back there again. They were telling him that they were only going for a ride.

Seager asked Ellerker where he should go. Kitching suggested Middleton Woods and Ellerker said, 'That'll do.' Ellerker got in the front seat, Kitching was in the back with Oluwale. They drove across the bridge over the Aire into south Leeds, passing the foundry where Oluwale had worked after his release from Menston in 1961. They drove for about twenty minutes.

Kitching was enjoying the game, acting the Dutch uncle. He asked Oluwale about his mam back in Africa, what she would have thought of him always getting himself nicked, never working. Oluwale kept repeating, 'I don't know, I don't know.' He began to cry.

When they got to Middleton Woods – about five miles from the city centre – the driver took the left-hand fork and kept driving. Deep into the dark heart.

Sergeant said, 'This'll do,' and they stopped. Inspector got out of the car. Oluwale refused to get out, pleading, 'You said you wouldn't do this.' Inspector and sergeant had to prise him from the car.

Ellerker told Oluwale, 'It's going to be you that suffers if you don't stay away.' According to Seager, Oluwale started shouting and swearing at them. 'You cunts, you never leave me alone – I've got to sleep somewhere.' Kitching told him to shut up and pushed him in the chest with such force that he fell back four paces into a tree.

They got back in the panda car and drove off leaving Oluwale stranded. As they made their way back to the city centre Kitching said that Oluwale wouldn't like it there, it was dark and he would lose his way. He said that one day he'd learn that he wasn't wanted in Leeds.

Back at Millgarth, PC Bennett asked Kitching, 'What did you do that for, was it to make him think he was back home?' Kitching replied, 'Well, he should feel at home in the jungle.'

To their colleagues it was Kitching more than Ellerker who seemed to derive pleasure from tormenting Oluwale. Kitching once told Seager that Oluwale loved to be got hold of by his coat and shaken – that it was 'his favourite pastime'. Kitching would grab hold of him and tilt his head back, make a fist and say, 'Shall I do it then? Where do you want it?' Oluwale would stand there speechless. Kitching loathed all dossers, but he was only ever that vicious with Oluwale.

Back in the mess room at Millgarth, Ellerker and Kitching used to joke openly about their encounters with Oluwale. The incidents which are known about, and which led to criminal charges, were probably not the full extent of Oluwale's miseries. There was a story that he was put into a dustbin and rolled down one of Leeds's Victorian shopping arcades. Another that Sergeant Kitching urinated on Oluwale as he slept, Ellerker holding the torch so that Sergeant could see where he was aiming. Another story from PC Arthur Shackleton was that Ellerker and Kitching found Oluwale at the doorway of John Peters and set fire to the newspapers he was lying on. Since the assaults on Oluwale invariably took place at the quietest time of the night in secluded places it's not surprising that there was no corroboration for these allegations; however much they seem to fit into the pattern of abuse, torment and ridicule, these stories were never established as 'fact'.

No one, not even Dougie Carter, the other section sergeant, reported the incidents Kitching and Ellerker were openly bragging about. Though many felt uncomfortable and unhappy working under them, nobody who knew about the maltreatment of Oluwale did anything about it.

Oluwale's only respite came when Group 3 was on the early and late turns. Oluwale was not, as far as is known, subjected to harassment by any other groups of officers at Millgarth.

Until his next contact with Ellerker and Kitching in the early hours of 4 September 1968, Oluwale left few traces. He signed on regularly for his £5 10s weekly social security. On one occasion he gave his address as 'The Shop, Albion Place'. Nobody at the Eastgate Employment Exchange questioned it.

Bertram Leng was one of two permanent nightwatchmen at Lewis's on The Headrow. He often saw Oluwale sleeping in the doorway of the Bridal House. He referred to him as 'Lame Darkie' because he walked with a limp. He'd tried to speak to him on a number of occasions to find out how he was doing, but Lame Darkie would become excitable, speaking in a strange language. Leng thought he was a 'mentally deranged chap'.

He would tell the Oluwale investigation that there was one week when Lame Darkie slept out in the Bridal House every night. The police would arrive and move him on, and off he'd go muttering to himself, only to return as soon as the police were out of sight. He remembered one particular night, which detectives would later establish as 3/4 September 1968. Lame Darkie was standing outside the shop with two officers, a sergeant and an inspector. A police car was parked up. Lame Darkie was quiet until the inspector said something to him and then he 'blew his top'. A few minutes later Leng saw a police van pull up beside the car. He heard the van door close and then no one was left at the scene. About a week after this incident he asked a bobby how they'd got on with the darkie; the bobby told him that the darkie had bitten the inspector's thumb so they'd had to take him in.

The van had been sent by the radio operator, PC Ken Bennett, in response to a request for assistance from PC Seager at around 12.30 a.m. Seager had been patrolling The Headrow when he came across Ellerker and Kitching struggling with Oluwale at the Bridal House. Bennett sent PCs Newstead and Woolliams. Woolliams

was not long in the force, twenty years old, and often heard Ellerker and Kitching asking where 'the dirty little bugger is tonight'.

Still shouting and screaming, Oluwale was shoved into the van. According to Woolliams, Oluwale cowered inside looking 'like a scared animal'. Kitching and Ellerker started punching him. Oluwale was shouting 'Leave me alone'. Kitching took out his torch and hit Oluwale a number of times over his head; he hit him so hard the glass fell out. Newstead, the driver, could hear punches and slaps all the way to the Bridewell. He heard Kitching say, 'I can't get his mouth open.' Oluwale had got Ellerker's hand in his mouth. At the Bridewell, Ellerker had to stop Kitching from inflicting further damage on Oluwale. 'The cunt got me as well,' Kitching was heard to complain. 'We'll charge him with me as well.' 'There was some reference made to Oluwale's teeth,' Seager would tell the investigation.

Ellerker and Kitching ended up in the casualty department of Leeds General Infirmary. Ellerker had grazes on his face and superficial grazes on his left thumb; Kitching, who had been wearing gloves, had a very minor abrasion of the left thumb and an abrasion to the left forearm. Both received tetanus jabs. Kitching was thankful for those gloves. He always tried to avoid personal contact with dossers – anxious not to get loused up. He used his boots where possible.

Many months after the incident one of the officers at the Bridewell, PC Phil Ratcliffe, would recall that 'in the eyes of the officers who worked here in the charge office, Oluwale was looked on as a bit of a hero for doing this, and Inspector Ellerker was not well liked for the way he treated him'. PC Bennett told the Oluwale investigation, 'I remember laughing at Inspector Ellerker, who was clearly upset, and thinking to myself it was just retribution for what Inspector Ellerker and Sergeant Kitching had done to him previously.'

Oluwale was charged with two counts of assaults against policemen and disorderly conduct and remanded in custody. The Armley medical officer, Bernard Green, saw the prisoner on 11

September. Oluwale told Green that he'd found it difficult to get rooms after prison and couldn't understand why he wasn't allowed to sleep out. He seemed to Green to be heading for a breakdown. Green saw him again a few days later and by this time he'd settled down. Green knew of his history of mental illness but, in his opinion, it was not 'active' at this time. He regarded him as 'a man of poor but not subnormal intelligence'. He noted: 'Insists police frequently take him outside Leeds and leave him in the "Forest".'

Just a few days before the violent altercation on the way to the Bridewell, Oluwale had called in to the Citizens' Advice Bureau to complain of an assault. The woman who helped him on 28 August scribbled down the 'vague details'. It seems likely that he was trying to tell her about the incidents at Bramhope and Middleton Woods. She advised him to go to the magistrates' court and lodge a complaint.

As an avenue for redress this was only marginally more promising than going through the police's own complaints procedures, which, since their introduction in 1964, very rarely vindicated complainants. The relationship between the police and the magistrates was intimate in Old Law times, so much so that the magistrates were almost an extension or arm of the police force.

The great majority of those who appeared before the magistrates pleaded guilty to the offences with which they were charged. For those charged with low-status offences such as drunk and disorderly, 'wandering abroad', disorderly conduct, it was usually a night in the Bridewell's stinking 'long form', which was situated in the basement of the town hall, and then straight up the spiral staircase into the magistrates' court for prosaic justice in the morning.

Prisoners (as soon as an individual was arrested he was referred to by police as a 'prisoner') were turned round quickly in Leeds. A thief arrested at 9 a.m. would be taken to the station where a clerk would complete his 'front sheet', so that by 10 a.m. he was at the Bridewell. His previous convictions would be pulled out from the 'blue card' system. By midday, after a swift court appearance, he could be on his way to Armley with six months. Leeds City Police prided itself on the efficiency with which it disposed of prisoners.

It was production-line justice. This seamlessness wouldn't be disrupted until the 1980s when criminal prosecutions were taken out of the hands of the police and handed over to the Crown Prosecution Service.

Old Law bobbies still speak of one stipendiary magistrate (the permanent magistrate) with great affection. Ralph Cleworth was 'Stipe' between 1950 and 1965. He referred to Leeds City Police as '*my* policemen'. If anyone assaulted one of '*my*' policemen' it was well known in the city that he would be going to prison for several months. If the police bent it a little, Cleworth recognised that it was probably in a good cause. His antipathy to the criminal and his championship of the police only intensified after he and his wife were robbed on a train journey up to Leeds. 'I feel like refusing everyone bail,' he told one police officer. And for some time afterwards this quietly spoken man handed down draconian sentences for minor offences. Cleworth's successor, John Randolph, was never as popular with the police. He was, according to those who had dealings with him, a cooler, less approachable man. Since he had himself been a policeman before entering the law he had a less idealised view of the force than Cleworth. But though more realistic, Randolph was still prosecution-minded.

It was Randolph whom Oluwale appeared before in September 1968 on charges of assaulting police officers. Usually when Oluwale appeared in court it was for vagrancy offences such as 'wandering abroad', to which he pleaded guilty and took his punishment. On this occasion, however, Oluwale pleaded 'not guilty' to all charges. It was clear from the comments he made to the Armley medical officer, and presumably the Citizens' Advice Bureau's officer, that he was feeling very aggrieved at his treatment at the hands of Ellerker and Kitching, that he couldn't bear any more drives out of the city and that fighting back had been his only option. Ellerker and Kitching would still have been confident that when it came before court their version of the events of that night would prevail.

The little that can be gleaned about this court appearance reveals much about Oluwale's powerlessness.

His own solicitors didn't understand him. They found him to be 'excitable' and 'almost unintelligible'. Barrington Black (now a judge) still remembers Oluwale as a sad, shambling character, probably mentally ill or on drugs. Defending such a man against charges of assault on the police was hopeless. To suggest that the police were themselves the violent aggressors was a non-starter, and Black did not attempt it.

Sergeant Kitching, like all policemen of Old Law times, knew his way around the courts and was confident in giving his evidence. He told the court that they had tried to direct Oluwale to St George's Crypt – the correct procedure for a sleeper-out – but that he 'went berserk, shouting, screaming, like an animal, lashing out with fists and feet'. He told the court that in trying to restrain Oluwale, Ellerker had received a bite to the hand and that he, Kitching, had also received a bite on the hand which cut right through his leather gloves. Kitching said that he had used reasonable force to restrain him.

Few of Oluwale's words have been recorded for posterity. However, there is a partial record of what he told the court that day: 'I haven't got an address in Leeds. The last address I had was a hostel. I remember 3 September. I tried to get some sleep in a shop doorway. At 12 o'clock he came and told me to get up. I said, "Why are you taking me tonight?"* He still wanted me inside the car. There was a scuffle between me and the police. I went inside the car and sat down. They locked the car. He hit me when I got inside the car. I didn't bite any finger. I scratched his face inside the car when he was doing something to me.' The written record doesn't quite convey Oluwale's struggle to make himself understood. Oluwale tried to tell the court about the drive to Middleton Woods some weeks before. Only he didn't know it was called Middleton Woods so called it 'Robin Hood Forest'. He knew his English myths from school. Randolph wanted to know why Oluwale was telling them about a forest when they were talking about an incident on The Headrow. He told Oluwale that as far as he knew there were no trees on The Headrow.

* It seems more likely that Oluwale said, 'Where are you taking me tonight?' But this is what was recorded.

PC Seager remembered Kitching having a good laugh as he described Oluwale's confusion in court. The trees on The Headrow and Robin Hood Forest.

In sentencing Oluwale, Randolph asked that an inquiry be made into the possible repatriation of the prisoner. The idea of returning to Nigeria had been on Oluwale's mind for some time. It seems likely that his lawyer, on sentencing, had raised the possibility rather than Randolph, the scheme not being well known.

Oluwale was the kind of person the British state would have been very happy to have been rid of. Repatriation was an idea that was bandied around much more freely after Enoch Powell's speech, and as such had racist connotations; in late 1968, Powell had even mooted the idea of a 'Ministry for Repatriation'. But a National Assistance Board (NAB) scheme to support the voluntary repatriation of those who had become incapacitated had been introduced as long ago as 1949, the year of Oluwale's arrival. Since then a steady stream had been sent back by the British government, the bulk of them psychiatric patients. To give an idea of the number, in 1962 seventy-eight mental hospital patients from Commonwealth countries, mostly from the West Indies, were repatriated. Before the general election of 1964, when anti-immigrant feeling was high, the Home Office had even considered instructing NAB officers to be proactive in identifying suitable cases for repatriation, not just the criminal and mentally ill but the long-term unemployed. There was unease in some government departments that this might look like a 'veiled form of deportation of Commonwealth citizens whose usefulness to Britain had come to an end', and in the event the change of government stopped any extension of the scheme. But the NAB repatriation scheme was still in place in 1968 and, having expressed an interest, Oluwale should have been a prime candidate. Of course, nothing was done. Whenever Oluwale raised the question with officials he was told that it wasn't their responsibility but if he went to that office, called that person, filled in that form . . .

Oluwale couldn't even secure his repatriation.

While Oluwale served his prison sentence, Sergeant Kitching

vowed revenge. 'Counting the days,' Kitching used to say. 'It won't be long before David's out. I'll get him. I'll have him again.'

Once the Oluwale investigation opened, the younger officers on Group 3 made known the depth of their dissatisfaction working under Ellerker and Kitching. But at the time the disgruntled ones had a moan among themselves and accepted their lot for the sake of their careers. Authority wasn't questioned or challenged then.

But the respect which a sergeant and an inspector should have commanded had all but drained away. If there was a significant turning point it was Christmas Eve 1968. Group 3 was on nights and Ellerker began the tour of duty with a homily against drinking on duty – he didn't want them 'falling by the wayside'. Ellerker and Kitching then went out and proceeded to get drunk, and for several hours the radio operators tried in vain to contact them. Kitching was found sprawled out on one of the stalls in Kirkgate Market in the early hours. Some of the bobbies had seen him lying there earlier but, fearing a violent reaction, had decided against stirring him. There was also a feeling that Kitching deserved to land in trouble. 'I left the station after a meal at 2 a.m. and saw the outline of a policeman slumped against a stall in the open market, but I didn't go near him,' PC Bill King told the Oluwale investigation. Kitching was only stirred when a member of the public went into Millgarth to report that one of their men looked to be unconscious. At this time, Ellerker was slumped in the canteen, red-eyed.

Resentment grew among the men of Group 3. Some went to Sergeant Dougie Carter requesting transfers to another shift. A few weeks after the marketplace incident, and with the nocturnal drinking sessions continuing, Carter reported his concerns to Chief Inspector Mather, who passed on the complaints to Chief Superintendent Goodhind, who told Inspector Ellerker to cut out the card games.

II

Dirt, the anthropologist Mary Douglas observed, is 'matter out-of-place'. Shoes are not dirty in themselves, but shoes are dirty when someone sticks their feet up on the dining table. Food isn't dirty in itself, but when it's splattered down your shirt it is. Dirt offends against order, Douglas said, and its removal is a positive effort to organise the environment. Orderly society depends on clear boundaries which have to be respected. Transgressing these lines is a kind of pollution, endangering others, and it's up to the order-makers of society to ensure that those who threaten to pollute stay on the other side of the line.

Oluwale, sleeping in shop doorways, was 'matter out-of-place'. It was his very being which caused the offence, not his personal behaviour, though at the trial of Ellerker and Kitching a great deal of attention was paid to Oluwale's terrible toilet habits. On this subject, though, it's worth quoting from a real cleaner, rather than from metaphorical ones. Olive Bradbury, who had worked for eight years as a cleaner at John Peters' furniture shop, gave this statement to the Oluwale investigation, but she wouldn't be called to testify at court.

I first saw Oluwale sleeping in the doorway about five or six years ago when I arrived at the store.

On this occasion Oluwale was sleeping on the floor behind the display unit in the Lands Lane entrance. He was wrapped in newspapers and he was using a bag as a pillow. It was like a shopping bag made of carpet material. We roused him because the doorway has to be cleaned and he went away quietly, he never spoke to us.

Each time I found Oluwale sleeping I would rouse him and he would get up and go away. He would give a little salute with his hand as if to say thank you, but he never made any conversation, he always walked up Lands Lane towards The Headrow. The last time I saw Oluwale was about two years ago, I can't remember which month it was but I remember the mornings were dark and it was cold weather. On this occasion I found him sleeping in his usual position in the doorway. I think he roused himself on this occasion when he saw me. At this time I think he was dressed in an old overcoat and he had a bag with him. (He always had a bag with him.) He did not speak to me and walked away towards The Headrow. I have not seen him since.

Oluwale never left any mess in the doorway and I never made any complaint to the shop manager, Mr Widdop, or to the police . . .

I have never seen Oluwale in the company of any other person.

Prior to his discharge from prison on 10 January 1969, Oluwale had a meeting with the Preston prison welfare officer to discuss his 'Discharge Plan'. Oluwale, almost unintelligible to Miss Duckworth, said that he was going to return to Leeds and hoped to find digs; he told her that he hadn't worked for a long time, though he didn't seem unduly bothered by this. She noted: 'Is of low intelligence and I would think could be very aggressive, and is going to have great difficulty in staying out of trouble on release.' His file stated that he faced an uncertain future, that he had been hospitalised, that he had been unemployed for years with doubtful prospects of work and that he would have a problem finding accommodation on his release. He returned to Leeds and the streets.

The John Peters' furniture shop, formerly the Scala Cinema, was the successful business of Manny Cussins, the most powerful figure on the board of Leeds United. The Lands Lane entrance to the shop was deep and wide (about twenty-five feet across). The double doors were set some way back from the pavement and were reached by two passages on either side of a central glass display unit. The passages went round the back of this display unit to form a U shape. There was a good six-foot gap between the main doorways and the rear of this glass display unit, and it was in this space that

David Oluwale slept, surrounded by his few belongings. Not only was he concealed from public sight, it was a relatively warm place. The shop's lights remained on at night, which meant that small infra-red heaters in the ceiling were also on. Nowadays, no shop would present itself as such an attractive spot for rough sleepers. There was room for perhaps a dozen people round the back of that display unit, but the morning cleaners who used to stir Oluwale only ever remembered him being by himself.

The problem with John Peters was that Group 3 knew it to be one of Oluwale's favourite spots. It was here, two days after his release from prison, that he was next arrested. The arresting officer that Sunday afternoon was PC Ferguson, who had just started the late turn. He saw Oluwale acting in 'a suspicious manner' and, according to Ferguson, when asked what he was doing, Oluwale shouted, 'Fuck off, I'm going to sleep here.' He then went berserk and started 'kicking and throwing his arms about'. He was charged with disorderly conduct. The next morning at the magistrates' court he was given the choice of fourteen days in prison or a £5 fine. He took the prison.

For some of the older rough sleepers in Leeds any roof, bed and regular meal was better than the streets. The notorious George Arthur Lindstrum, a frail elderly homeless man, would commit offences simply to get locked up, and never paid his fines. He knew the inside of Armley better than any man alive. In winter months he'd practically beg the magistrates to send him down. George Arthur made the *Guinness Book of Records* for the most court appearances (over five hundred). Oluwale wasn't like him. He didn't welcome these bouts of imprisonment, paying his fines when he could, and I suspect that Oluwale wouldn't have been a popular cellmate. This particular fourteen-day sentence was cut short when he found the money to pay part of his fine.

I suspect also that Oluwale resented the intrusions of probation officers and prison welfare officers, who advised but appeared from the evidence to have actually delivered very little. Armley's prison welfare officer met him at the beginning and end of his sentence. At their first meeting, Oluwale told him that he hadn't worked for

six months, that he was a labourer and that he was married with two children; he said that he hoped to return to them on his release. He gave his address as 15 Oxford Street, Sheffield, the place he'd lived for a short time in 1951 (actually the address no longer existed – the house had been pulled down in a slum-clearance programme). Prior to his release, Oluwale told the officer that his wife and children didn't want him, that he had never worked since coming to the United Kingdom and that he was of 'No Fixed Abode'. His plan was to return to Leeds and to try and find a job in a foundry. He had no clothing and he said that he would like to receive aftercare. He was released on 23 January 1969.

In the early hours of Sunday 26 January he was arrested again. This would be Oluwale's first known contact with Sergeant Kitching since the biting incident back in September of the previous year. Again, it was a violent encounter.

After grub time Kitching received a message from Millgarth's van driver, PC 'Chopper' Woodhead. Chopper had been cruising around Leeds in the J4 van when he came across Oluwale sleeping out at John Peters. He dutifully put a message through to the radio operator, who contacted Sergeant Kitching. It was 3.45 a.m. Kitching's duty book records: 'Told to move out went berserk, shouting screaming lashing out with fists and feet, bit me on hand but did not penetrate glove was fighting mad. Struggled all rolled on ground, arrested with PC 410 to M/St and charged then to Charge Office.' Chopper's version was that when they told Oluwale to move on he was violent, screaming and extremely excitable; that he tried to bite Kitching's thumb and that they had to subdue him. They only used the necessary force to overpower him, he claimed.

Officers on duty at Millgarth station that night remembered Oluwale being brought in by Kitching, Chopper and Inspector Ellerker. A WPC, Hazel Dolby, gave the most vivid account. She was standing behind the long counter when she heard a commotion from the area between the outer and inner doors. One of the inner doors was flung open and the prisoner was sent sprawling in front of the counter. Kitching and Ellerker came into the charge area.

Ellerker kicked the prisoner between the legs 'with such force that Oluwale was lifted bodily off the floor'. Oluwale was screaming. Kitching and Ellerker lifted him off the ground and draped him over the counter. Oluwale was 'holding his private parts, tears were streaming down his face and he was crying bitterly'. WPC Dolby didn't want to see any more and left the office for the radio room.

Another witness to that night's incident was PC Ruddick. An experienced constable in his mid-forties on office duties, Ruddick had only ever worked at Millgarth since joining the force in 1953. Ruddick heard screaming coming from outside the station. He saw Chopper half carrying Oluwale to the charge desk. Ellerker and Kitching were behind. All three officers appeared out of breath. Chopper released his grip on Oluwale, who fell on to the floor, blubbering. Chopper had to drag him to his feet to get his details. Oluwale was treated well in the station, according to Ruddick.

Sergeant Frank Atkinson, the senior officer on station duties, was present. One of his main responsibilities was the supervision of prisoners in his custody. Atkinson heard Ellerker saying, 'You won't bite me again' as he and Kitching set about the prisoner, punching and kicking him about the body and private parts until he was subdued. Oluwale was screaming throughout. Atkinson did nothing to stop the attack.

PC Arthur Shackleton, who had also been there, claimed that he left the station as soon as Oluwale was at the counter but that he heard Ellerker say, 'You won't bite my thumb again.'

PC Keith Seager told the investigation that Kitching's attitude towards Oluwale 'got worse after the incident when Oluwale had bitten him'.

Oluwale was charged with disorderly conduct. Convicted, he was, again, given the choice of going to prison for fourteen days or paying a fine. He served some of the sentence before, again, paying part of the fine and was discharged on 5 February. According to official records, he left prison with private cash of 4s 9d and no discharge grant. He gave his address as Lands Lane. Next of kin 'none', clothing 'nil'. The notes and comments of the prison welfare officer, Reg Morton, painted a miserable picture: unemployed, never worked, on benefit, no settled way of life, no place to lodge. 'Deteriorating all the time. Poor material, lacking in concern for himself' – this was Morton's considered view. 'Intends to stay in Leeds and find accommodation. Can write and read English. Strong persecutory feelings of anti-authoritarian. Difficult and unreasoning at this time, gave no opportunity to talk out his problems.'

Owen McHale, an unemployed labourer, was one of the handful of people who came forward with information about Oluwale as a result of Polly Perkins's appeal in the local press. McHale knew him as Olly. He often saw Olly around Eastgate Employment Exchange. McHale once gave him 6d for the price of a cup of tea. His shoes were all worn down. A few weeks later, he saw him leaning against a barrier at the bottom of Eastgate, they talked and he seemed happy and spoke about signing on. The last time McHale saw him was at the market, sitting on a table near the Rhodes café. His clothes were all torn, he had a bit of a beard on his chin and he looked 'a right state'. He spoke about going for voluntary treatment at a mental hospital, to get out of the cold weather, he explained. He said he had a wife somewhere, and said she was called Olga. He said that he'd been in the Salvation Army hostel at Darlington and the workhouse at Sheffield.

Lucky Akanidere, living in Dewsbury then, saw his old friend for the last time early in 1969, near the railway station. 'I remember I took the wife to see *The Sound of Music* at the Majestic and it was the last week it was shown. When we were catching the train back home, I saw Olu and gave him five shillings. He had with him a brown leather briefcase which contained his belongings. He seemed fairly normal and I gave him my address and asked him to visit me. He did not seem depressed.' Lucky told the investigation that Oluwale 'used to hate the police and often talked about what they had done to him, you know, beating him up and sending him to the asylum'.

On 10 February, Oluwale was treated in hospital for abrasions to his right thigh. Later that same day he was on Park Row and, according to PC 'Glob' Higgins, was shouting at a young woman standing at the bus stop and waving his fists at pedestrians and making 'animal-like noises'. When Glob arrested him, he claimed that Oluwale began to lash out at him with his duffel bag. Glob radioed through to Millgarth and Ellerker turned up with the J4 van (he thought, though he couldn't be certain, that Kitching was also present). According to Glob, Oluwale was calm by then, but Ellerker grabbed him by the hair and pulled him into the van. Oluwale ended up on the floor, face down. Ellerker was kneeling in the back, still holding Oluwale's hair. He lifted Oluwale's head and banged it repeatedly on the floor of the van. Glob was sat on one of the bench seats in the back of the van, watching. Oluwale pleaded not guilty at the magistrates' court the next morning, but was found guilty and fined £5.

Higgins's report of this incident would interest the Oluwale investigation. The words 'I asked him for his name and address and I was ignored' had been inserted into his report. The handwriting was different from Higgins's and it was never discovered who made the addition. Leeds detectives on the case told the Yard men that this line had been included to bring Oluwale within the provisions of the Leeds Corporation (Consolidation) Act 1905. Under section 27 of that Act, all persons whose conduct was disorderly could be summoned, and if they refused to give their name and address they could be taken in to the police station so that they could be ascertained.

Oluwale was consistently being charged with disorderly conduct. It was this local law, rather than the cumbersome and antiquated vagrancy laws, which Leeds City Police were now using against him. The Municipal Corporations Act 1882 had given the municipal boroughs the power to make bylaws for the 'good rule and government of the Borough, and for the prevention and suppression of nuisances'. The Leeds Corporation (Consolidation) Act gave considerable powers to the Corporation and to police to exert control over a wide range of social nuisances which threatened the 'health and local government of the city', for example: blowing horns in the street to announce an entertainment; abusive language; burning any offensive material within a hundred yards of any dwelling house; 'calling' newspapers on a Sunday. Leeds City Police found disorderly conduct a particularly expedient offence since it could cover almost any kind of public behaviour it found objectionable. As every probationer knew from the local procedure course, disorderly conduct was "owt that's not orderly'.

The intensification of efforts to remove Oluwale from the streets, by violence and by Leeds law, is bitterly ironic. This came at a time when arrests for street offences in Leeds – rough sleeping, drunkenness and disorderly behaviour – were actually falling; when the force, in response to the concerns of influential city-centre traders, was starting to question whether Unit Beat Policing, by removing men from the beats and putting them in cars, had not reduced its ability to tackle antisocial behaviour and street offences.* And at a time when urban policing was becoming more anonymous, more impersonal, Oluwale had become the object of a highly personalised campaign.

Oluwale was next arrested at City Station, not for disorderly conduct on this occasion but for trespassing and 'refusing to quit the premises'. The arresting officer that day, 18 February, was transport policeman Ernest Padgett. He saw a lot of Oluwale in the early part of 1969, sleeping during the day in the station waiting rooms until he was removed at night. Sometimes he would find Oluwale sleeping in one of the arches under the station. Padgett knew that Oluwale had a history of mental illness. He described him as walking with a strong limp, always in a dark overcoat with a cloth cap and usually carrying a sling duffel bag. In court the next day he was given a choice of a £10 fine or imprisonment and took the fine.

The next officer to arrest David Oluwale was the youngest on Group 3, Gary Briggs. Briggs had been a cadet in Leeds City Police before becoming a constable on his nineteenth birthday in September 1968. He was not long out of training school and struggling to get on the right side of the 'moody' Sergeant Kitching.

---

* In June 1969, Millgarth subdivision reverted to foot patrols and started to regain control of the streets. In 1970, there were almost twice as many prosecutions for vagrancy offences as there had been in the previous year.

PC Briggs was on car patrol in the early hours of Sunday 23 February when he found Oluwale on Bond Street. Briggs pulled up, got out and Oluwale started to shout and swear. Briggs nicked him. Sergeant Kitching saw Briggs at grub time and went mad when he found out that Oluwale had been brought in without anyone telling him. PC Gott overheard Kitching say, in a vicious manner, 'Briggsy, don't you lock up Oluwale again without sending for me and Inspector Ellerker first.'

Disorderly conduct again. The charge sheet was completed. It was never established who scored out the typed 'BRIT' on Oluwale's charge sheet and scrawled 'WOG' in biro in its place. The Oluwale investigation never got to the bottom of it. The station sergeant, Frank Atkinson, said that he, as the arresting officer, had typed in the 'BRIT' but said that he had nothing to do with the 'WOG'. The office clerk who assisted Atkinson, PC Ruddick, also denied it, as did Chopper who transported Oluwale to the Bridewell at 4.30 a.m.

This time Oluwale took his fourteen days. At Armley he was seen by W. Hallas, the prison welfare officer, who noted that Oluwale wanted assistance to find digs. Hallas thought that most of Oluwale's problems were down to lack of accommodation and that if lodgings could be found it might help him keep out of prison, though he would require work. 'His colour of course may be against him in his own endeavours,' Hallas added.

Oluwale left prison on 8 March with a discharge grant of £1 5s 11d and 18s of his own money. He had given his address as 'Bond Street, Leeds'.

On 11 March he visited his probation officer, Rose Briggs, coincidentally the mother of the police officer who had last arrested Oluwale. Oluwale asked whether she could find him accommodation because he was banned from the hostels. He became angry when she said she couldn't supply him with any money. He said he didn't want to stay in Leeds and asked her whether she could help him to return to Nigeria. She made a phone call and told him that there was a scheme run by the Ministry of Social Security and that he would need to make a personal application. Oluwale became agitated, said it was a waste of time and walked out of the office.

At 7.15 p.m. that same day he was arrested by PC John Ferguson at the doorway of John Peters. According to Ferguson, Oluwale became 'hysterical' and abusive, shouting, 'You fuck off, in my country you can fucking sleep outside.'

The prisoner's nationality was again shown as 'WOG' on the charge sheet. This time it had simply been typed in. The typist was never identified.

On 12 March, he was sent to Armley for thirty days, other offences being taken into consideration. It would be his last stint there. On 27 March, Oluwale had his pre-release interview with W. Hallas, the prison welfare officer, and Wilfred Hoyle, a probation officer from outside who was there to try and persuade Oluwale to accept voluntary aftercare on his release. Hallas recorded that Oluwale had nowhere to go on his release and was rapidly becoming a social problem, in and out of prison, unable to make any sustained effort at a job. 'It is increasingly obvious that he is completely unable to function on the outside.' The welfare officials couldn't get through to Oluwale and formed the opinion that he didn't know what the conversation was about. To Hallas he seemed 'schizoid'. Hoyle told the Oluwale investigation, 'I was sure the man was mentally ill, but it is difficult to be sure about anything when there is a language barrier.'

On 10 April, Oluwale was discharged from Armley. He had £1 19s cash. In a plastic bag his possessions: a blue shirt, one plastic cup, two reels of cotton, one hymn book, one form U1 40, one leather purse, one form EC4, two photos, one form P45, one out-of-date bank book, rosary beads and a ballpoint pen. All of these items were in a plastic bag. Other details were noted. Address: living rough. No job on release. Domestic problems: nil. He was wearing:

brown check cap
green check single-breasted overcoat
grey-striped single-breasted jacket
blue long-sleeve pullover
yellow tartan collar attached shirt 'Longer Last' make

green check waistcoat
green fancy necktie
brown suede rubber-soled shoes
black fancy socks
green check trousers
elastic braces and plastic belt

Most of his clothing was in a poor condition.

From Armley he went first to see his probation officer, Wilfred Hoyle. Hoyle noted: 'He was most excitable, and it was almost impossible to understand him. He said that he had £1 19s which was his own money and that he would have no difficulty in finding an address if he gets some more.' He then presented himself at the area office of the Ministry of Social Security on St Paul's Street to apply for benefits. He was given £4. From there he was sent to the employment exchange to sign his U1 80 B form. He would sign on again on 11, 14, 15, 16 April. Oluwale's human contacts were fleeting, official. His final social security payment was £1 8s, received on 17 April.

III

Thursday 17 April 1969. In Leeds that night the shop girls and skinheads were dancing to a new tune. Desmond Dekker sang of the rejected, stripped, hunted 'Israelite' – it was the first reggae song to top the UK charts. The papers were saying that reggae music might stop racial prejudice.

According to Sergeant Dougie Carter's duty book, it started out as a fine dry night, though there would be light showers. Group 3 was on and paraded at 9.45 p.m.

Unusually, Sergeant Kitching was working 'top side' that night, with Sergeant Carter taking the busier 'bottom side'. There were eight constables out, six of them in panda cars; Chopper took the J4 van and PC Gary Briggs was on foot patrol until grub time (1.15 a.m.) after which he transferred to a panda car. Two constables, Bill King and Arthur Shackleton, went off duty at 2 a.m. Ellerker was the patrol inspector. Sergeant Frank Atkinson was the station officer.

The Oluwale investigation later pieced together the movements of officers on that tour of duty by examining their duty books. Geoff Ellerker was the only person on that shift not to turn his over. He claimed to have lost it.

The duty book was used by every officer to keep a detailed record of all parts of his daily duty. It was a sort of diary. In it an officer would record his working days, days off and leave; he would note his beat; he would give brief details of the statements made by individuals interviewed in the course of his duties. Inside the duty book were supplementary books in different coloured paper recording details of stolen vehicles, persons wanted and the most significant crimes. Each officer had to keep a full book and produce it for inspection on demand by supervisory officers.

In his duty book the officer would also pencil in the time of visits from supervisory officers. 'Stick me one in' or 'Put me one in' an inspector or sergeant might say to a police constable, which was an instruction to record a visit. The Oluwale investigation hoped to reconstruct the movements of Ellerker and Kitching from the duty books of their shift members.

How reliable certain duty books were was another matter. The Oluwale investigation discovered that a number of officers on Group 3 were given to making false duty-book entries, recording so-called 'slippy visits' (visits which had not actually taken place) so as to disguise real movements. Kitching in particular was notorious for encouraging his men to record 'slippy visits'. In addition, Seager would give evidence during the trial that on several occasions Ellerker had asked him to put false entries in his duty book and that he colluded, and that on other occasions he omitted significant incidents involving Oluwale. These admissions would ultimately put a serious question mark over Seager's credibility as a witness.

The first entry in Kitching's duty book for this particular tour of duty was a visit to PC 895 at 10.20 p.m. at Central Hotel on Little Queen Street. PC 895, who was patrolling beats 7 and 8 in a panda car, was William Greenwood, a twenty-two-year-old officer who had been present when Kitching first arrested Oluwale in April 1968. The sergeant didn't stop to chat, just said, 'Put me one in.' At 10.40 p.m., Kitching records visiting the Jubilee pub with Inspector Ellerker. 'Statements and enquiries re prize for amusement machines,' his duty book noted.

At 11.15 p.m., PC Seager took a prisoner at Park Square East, and Kitching went to assist along with Chopper Woodhead. Until grub time at 1.15 a.m., Seager and Kitching, according to their duty books, were occupied with this prisoner: questioning him, charging him, completing the necessary paperwork. Half of the shift joined Seager and Kitching for their grub: Chopper, Ellerker, Sergeant Atkinson, PCs Greenwood and Briggs. The cards came out. Forty-five minutes of hearts.

After grub time, Seager continued with his reports and had Ellerker sign them off. He saw Kitching leaving the back entrance of Millgarth for the garage where sergeants' and inspectors' cars were kept. At 2.40 a.m., Seager resumed his patrol, driving around the Merrion Centre and then into The Headrow, left down Albion Street, left into Albion Place and then left into Lands Lane where he intended to check Thornton's and Queen's arcades. He claimed that he saw one of the sergeants' cars parked up outside John Peters. He pulled up and saw Kitching coming out of the shop entrance. The sergeant told Seager that Oluwale was in there fast asleep. Kitching got on to his radio and told the radio operator, 'If the inspector's not engaged, will you ask him to join me in Lands Lane – he'll know what for.' Seager claimed to hear the radio operator saying that Ellerker was there and that he would let him know.

When later questioned about the night's events, Sergeant Frank Atkinson recalled that a message came into the station that 'he' had been found in Albion Place. No names were mentioned but Atkinson assumed that it was Oluwale. He saw Ellerker leave the station to attend to it.

PC John Bowes was the radio operator on this tour of duty, an experienced officer in his late forties. He claimed to have no recollection and no record of any such call from Kitching, though he acknowledged that it was possible – it was the sort of call which came through.

Kitching's duty book indicated that he resumed his patrol at 2.30 a.m. and then visited PC Greenwood at Marlborough Towers at 2.50 a.m. Marlborough Towers was right at the very western edge of the subdivision, a mile away from Lands Lane. PC Greenwood recorded a visit from Kitching at 2.30 a.m., not 2.50 a.m.

Seager was still at the scene when PC Briggs pulled up in his panda car and Inspector Ellerker got out. According to Seager, Ellerker said, 'I'll see you later, Gary,' and Briggs drove away. Kitching said, 'I've got him,' and Ellerker grinned.

Briggs gave the Oluwale investigation a number of statements about this drive, revealing a little more detail each time. In his penultimate statement – when he told what he claimed was 'the whole truth' – he said that at 2.40 a.m., while patrolling beats 1 and 2, he received a call from the radio room to return to Millgarth. Ellerker was waiting for him and told him to take him to Lands Lane. On the way there Ellerker said, 'There's a coon in John Peters,' and asked, 'Do you know Oluwale?' Briggs told him of the times he had arrested him. Ellerker asked, 'What do you think of him?' Briggs commented that he could be violent. Ellerker said again, 'I've been told there is a coon in John Peters,' adding, 'That's the way to get on in the Job.'

Ellerker asked for Briggs's staff. 'I'm not going to take any chances with him.' Briggs knew that Ellerker had been bitten by Oluwale and thought that he wanted to 'get his own back on him'. When they arrived at John Peters he handed over his staff. He put the visit into his duty book and drove away quickly 'because I thought Oluwale was going to get some hammer' and 'didn't want 'owt to do with it'. In his duty book he made the entry '2.55 Visit – Inspector E – Thornton Arcade'.

In a statement he gave on 17 November 1970, Seager said that he was stopped from going into the entrance of John Peters by Ellerker, who told him to remain where he was. From the street, Seager could hear Oluwale's voice. He could hear blows and Oluwale shouting 'Fuck off' and repeating 'Let me alone'. Sound of blows, smacks. As Seager said in his statement (though it should be emphasised again that his reliability as a witness would be called into question in court):

> I saw David Oluwale come out by the showcase and the pillars. He ran out of the left-hand exit to the arcade – I recognised him as Oluwale. He had his right arm hand wrapped round the back of his head. He didn't have a cap on – which he normally wears – he was wearing an overcoat I think – but it could have been a mackintosh. Most times I've seen him he has been wearing an overcoat – if he wasn't wearing the overcoat he normally had it with him. He ran up Lands Lane – he was screaming out loud – he ran up towards The Headrow.

Seager claimed that Ellerker and Kitching came out from the left-hand entrance to John Peters 'smiling and looking quite happy with life'. Ellerker asked him where Oluwale had gone. His statement continued:

> I got the impression they were going after Oluwale again and for that reason I didn't tell them I thought he'd gone down Queen's Arcade, but merely pointed up towards The Headrow. Sergeant Kitching opened his car door and said, 'Are we going then, Sir?' It appeared to me that Sergeant Kitching was in a hurry to get after Oluwale again before he got too far. Inspector Ellerker said to Sergeant Kitching, 'Yes just a second.' He started to walk to the passenger door of Sergeant Kitching's car – when he turned to me and said, 'Stick me one in – 2.55 Brills.' . . . Brills is in Bond Street and some way away [about two minutes' walk away] from John Peters' shop in Lands Lane.

Where Ellerker and Kitching went to in the hour after this incident isn't known, but at 4.10 a.m. Chopper recorded a visit in his duty book from Ellerker at Woodhead's seed shop at the bottom of Kirkgate. At 4.20 a.m., Kitching recorded a visit to PC Newstead, at the back of police headquarters on Grace Street. Newstead remembered Ellerker being in the car with Kitching.

Kitching's duty book records that between 4.30 and 5.30 a.m. he was searching 'the Well Closes and area' in the 'top side' of the subdivision for a missing child, Christopher Middleton. This would later be shown to be a false entry. The Well Closes were in the area patrolled by PC Shackleton. At the beginning of the shift three of the Middleton children had been reported missing. Two were soon found. As Shackleton went off duty at 2 a.m., he informed Kitching that one was still missing. This seems to have provided Kitching with a convenient alibi. The missing boy (who returned home around breakfast time) doesn't appear to have been an urgent police priority: the father was out scouring the streets with his dog until 4.30 a.m. and recalled seeing no police officer apart from Shackleton earlier that night.

At the time he claimed to be scouring the Well Closes for missing children, PC Terry MacLean recorded seeing Kitching very far away from that area. At some time between 4.30 and 5 a.m., MacLean saw Kitching in a vehicle outside the Griffin Hotel on Boar Lane, which was over a mile away from the Well Closes. Kitching asked MacLean what he was doing and then drove off towards City Square. He couldn't recall who had been with Kitching, or in what vehicle. In his first statement he said he thought Kitching had been in the J4 van with Chopper and Ellerker. In a second statement, MacLean said that it could have been a car, but he was very definite that Kitching was present, if uncertain about the others. Between this sighting and the end of the shift at 6 a.m. it is not known for certain where Ellerker and Kitching were.

The first workers – newspapermen, postmen, bus drivers and conductors – began to appear in the city from 5 a.m. Following the opening of the investigation into Oluwale's death, George Merrion, a postman, came forward with what looked like a pertinent piece of information. He had finished his night shift and caught the 5.12 bus home from the Corn Exchange. It took him down Call Lane. He saw a police vehicle – at first he thought a car, later he said that it might have been a van – parked down the path leading down to Warehouse Hill. He claimed that he had a conversation with a young bus conductor. The bus conductor told him that he had earlier seen a man being chased by two policemen down to the river.

Following investigations, that bus conductor was traced. David Condon recalled walking down Lower Briggate towards Swinegate bus depot to begin his shift when he saw two policemen talking to a man near the junction of Call Lane and Leeds Bridge. The man, who Condon would describe as scruffy, ran away from them down Call Lane, the policemen in pursuit. He lost sight of them and assumed that they must have run down the alleyway which led towards the river. This chase took place some time between 5 and 5.10 a.m.

At Millgarth, about ten minutes before dismissing from duty, PC Briggs picked up his staff from Ellerker. He overheard Ellerker say to Kitching, 'Oluwale won't assault me again.' Briggs claimed that the varnish covering was newly cracked and dented in places ('It looked as though it had hit something hard'), although later in court he was unable to direct the jury to any significant markings. He explained to the Oluwale investigation that his earlier reticence about the events was because, 'I thought that I would be done for not reporting it before.'

Group 3 was on the late turn the day Oluwale was pulled from the Aire. Sergeant Kitching read out a teleprinter message during parade. He had a strange sort of grin on his face, PC Seager recalled. 'I wonder how he got in there?' he said, or something to that effect. Others on parade that day also remembered Kitching in a light-hearted mood. PC King told the investigation that Kitching remarked, 'Did he fall or was he pushed?' Glob thought he said, 'It looks as though we will have to find another playmate.'

Sergeant Frank Atkinson explained later he thought it strange that Oluwale had not been brought into the station in the early hours of 18 April 1969. 'I would have expected him to be brought to Millgarth rather than be taken to the charge office because when Inspector Ellerker and Sergeant Kitching dealt with him, Oluwale got rough treatment, which it would be easier for them to do at

Millgarth as opposed to the central charge office because Mr Ellerker was in charge at Millgarth.' After Oluwale's death was announced, Atkinson remembered saying to Sergeant Dougie Carter that it was strange that Oluwale hadn't been seen since they had last been on nights. Carter agreed. Soon after Oluwale was pulled out, Carter said to Kitching, jokey, so as not to rile him, 'You didn't push him in, did you?' Sergeants Carter and Atkinson did nothing with their suspicions: they were for the quiet life.

Kitching was at the Bridewell when one of the officers there commented that they hadn't seen so much of him since his 'friend' had been dragged from the Aire. Another, PC Phil Ratcliffe, joked that it wouldn't surprise him if Kitching hadn't pushed Oluwale in. According to Ratcliffe, Kitching appeared shaken by that and said, 'I'll have to find somebody else to pick on.' Ratcliffe put this conversation to the back of his mind.

WPC Marilyn Brooks was in the Traffic Department when Kitching's name cropped up in conversation. A colleague who had served at Millgarth, though she couldn't give the name when questioned, said something like 'I have something I could pin on him'. He told her that Kitching had thrown or pushed a man into the river. She didn't take it seriously at the time.

'The general opinion was it would be on Sergeant Kitching's conscience,' Terry MacLean told the investigation when asked how the news of Oluwale's death had been received by Group 3. MacLean, who left the force in April 1970, had presumed that it was suicide.

Nobody came forward to ask questions about Oluwale. His death was talked about in a humorous manner. Several months later Ellerker was transferred to Ireland Wood subdivision, but on one particular tour of duty was covering both subdivisions in 'A' Division and took his grub at Millgarth. He was in the canteen with Seager, Shackleton and Kitching, laughing, reminiscing about Oluwale, playing hearts. Oluwale had become a fond memory. 'There'll never be another like him,' was the refrain. Of the homeless, Kitching was heard to say, 'These people would be better off if they ended up in the river like David.'

PC Briggs had his suspicions. But since he had no hard and fast evidence to link Kitching and Ellerker to Oluwale's death he said nothing. Why lose your job over a man like Oluwale? He nursed his suspicions until a night in September 1970 when he told Brian Topp, who told an eighteen-year-old cadet called Gazzer Galvin.

4

The Night-Soil Men

I

When the town hall was opened by Queen Victoria in 1858, Leeds arrived as a great town. The building was an impressive statement of business energy and local patriotism, proof that manufacturers could raise their sights beyond mere moneymaking. It was a demonstration of that zeal for improvement and liberty which Edward Baines, legendary editor of the *Leeds Mercury*, insisted could be found in 'huge, unsightly mills, unwashed artifices, smokey towns, and streams running as black as ink'. Who could not be impressed by the town hall's massive dimensions, its Corinthian columns and pilasters, those imperious stone lions which flanked the twenty steps? The maxims of that civic age were inscribed on the frieze of its lavish Victoria Hall: 'Industry overcomes all things'; 'Goodwill towards men'; 'Honesty'; 'Except the Lord keep the city, the watchman watcheth but in vain'.

'Magna Charta' and 'Trial by Jury' were up there too. The town hall was built so that it could accommodate the courts of justice, and when Leeds became an assize town in 1864 – somewhere where the most serious criminal cases could be heard – it was another mark of the town's arrival. In 1971 the town hall still accommodated the courts, although the autumn assize that year would be the last.*

The first day of the assize was always a grand civic occasion. The High Sheriff and Lord Mayor would be in attendance. The judges – High Court judges – would be driven in from Carr Manor in a procession of Rolls-Royces and greeted at the town hall steps with a fanfare from the Sheriff's trumpeters. A white-gloved Leeds City Police officer of appropriate rank would then lead the scarlet-robed judges through the front doors, into a vestibule adorned with the words 'Europe-Asia-Africa-America'. Imperial pride pressing down. 'Stand on one side, stand on one side,' the policeman would call out, and there would be lots of bowing and scraping as the judges peeled off to their particular courtrooms.

Monday 8 November 1971, several weeks into the autumn assize, and there was little sense of occasion, though the Union flag flew over the town hall as it did on every day of the session. On this wet and blustery, biting cold morning, the judges made their way into the building by the back entrance. Among them was a short, stocky septuagenarian, Mr Justice Hinchcliffe, who made his way to Courtroom 1. Over the next thirteen days he would preside over Regina v. Geoffrey Ellerker and Kenneth Kitching, jointly charged with the manslaughter of David Oluwale.

Manslaughter not murder, that was the decision of the Director of Public Prosecutions (DPP) after considering the final report of the investigating officer, Detective Chief Superintendent John Perkins, and after much deliberation with counsel.

Perkins's report had described an escalating campaign of violence culminating in the alleged assault on Oluwale at John Peters around 3 a.m. on 18 April 1969. After Oluwale fled from the scene holding his head – the last known sighting of him – Perkins believed that Ellerker and Kitching went hunting for him. He said that Kitching and Ellerker were seen at the Griffin Hotel somewhere between

* The Courts Act 1971 abolished the system of periodic assize and quarter sessions and established a single permanent Crown court for England and Wales.

4.30 and 5 a.m., a matter of minutes away from Leeds Bridge, where, around 5.10 a.m., David Condon saw two policemen chasing a man along Call Lane and down to the waterfront. Around a thousand Leeds officers gave 'negative statements' to the effect that they were nowhere near the river at that time. Perkins said that Ellerker and Kitching were the only policemen on duty that night who couldn't account for their movements at that time: Kitching had given false duty-book entries for that crucial hour between 4.30 and 5.30 a.m. and Ellerker claimed to have lost his duty book. In his opinion there was evidence to suggest that Ellerker and Kitching had continued their chase of Oluwale down to Warehouse Hill and that as a result Oluwale had jumped or been forced to jump into the Aire. According to the statement of a civil engineer, John Tinkler, the height from the surface of the river to ground level at the quay at Warehouse Hill at the time and on that date was 6'6". It would be almost impossible for a man – especially a small man like Oluwale – to get out unaided at this point. Finally, Perkins drew attention to the comment of Ellerker to Kitching, overheard by PC Briggs just before 6 a.m., that 'Oluwale won't assault me again'. This was said, Perkins believed, in 'full knowledge' that Oluwale was dead.

Though there was no direct evidence that Ellerker and Kitching had chased or thrown Oluwale into the river, there was, in his view, strong circumstantial evidence: the prior conduct of Ellerker and Kitching towards Oluwale; the alleged assault at John Peters; the sighting of two policemen near the river and the chase.

After assessing the evidence, Kenneth Dowling in the DPP's office reported that it was very doubtful a charge of murder could be made to stick. The case, in his view, rested on the 'somewhat dubious' evidence of an assault at John Peters and the 'doubtful' evidence of two unidentified officers chasing a man whose colour could not be determined some hours later. PC Seager's general unreliability and untrustworthiness as a key witness worried him. There was also a suspicion that the officer had taken 'a more active part than he will admit in the previous harassment of Oluwale'.

Counsel's opinion was sought. The DPP instructed John Cobb

QC and Donald Herrod. Though agreeing with Dowling that the quality of much of the evidence was poor, they believed that there was a prima facie case for murder against both men and prima facie evidence to support other lesser charges. And though they recognised that it would be wrong to put a man on trial for murder if the quality of evidence was so poor as to make acquittal virtually inevitable, they also believed that the public interest demanded that police misconduct and misbehaviour not be covered up.

Manslaughter was the pragmatic middle course. A jury was unlikely to convict individuals of murder – even more so policemen – if there was any doubt in their minds. But they might be prepared to convict on a lesser charge. Herrod was instructed by the DPP to draft charges of manslaughter and other offences in relation to Oluwale. On 13 April 1971, Ellerker and Kitching were served with summonses. There were other serious charges as well as manslaughter on the indictment. Ellerker and Kitching were charged with assaults occasioning actual bodily harm (ABH) on 7 August 1968, 4 September 1968 and 26 January 1969. These charges related to the attack on Oluwale prior to his removal to Bramhope; the attack in the van on the way to the Bridewell (when Oluwale himself was charged with assaulting Ellerker and Kitching); the attack on Oluwale at Millgarth station which left him in tears on the floor in front of the counter. This last incident (26 January 1969) also led to charges of assault occasioning grievous bodily harm. In addition, Ellerker was charged with causing Oluwale ABH on 10 February 1969 (the head-banging in the J4 van witnessed by PC Higgins). Finally both were charged with causing Oluwale ABH on the night of 17/18 April 1969 at John Peters' shop, just hours before it was believed he was chased or thrown into the Aire.

The trial began at 10.30 a.m. on 8 November 1971. Leading counsel for the prosecution John Cobb gave his opening speech to the jury of ten men and two women. In his cool, understated style, Cobb outlined the Crown's case against the defendants, speaking for over three hours.

Cobb knew that David Oluwale was a problem. He was a tainted victim, someone the average *Daily Mail* reader would disdain. Someone who these Leeds jury members might themselves have seen about town, mumbling to himself in a strange tongue, snot down his coat. However crude and rough their methods, respectable citizens would be expected to line up behind their policemen against a man like Oluwale. Cobb was alert to the possibility that defence counsel might seek to smear the victim. Cobb's strategy was to disarm the defence by being very frank about the kind of man Oluwale was. He appealed to the jury's innate sense of fair play and justice: that Oluwale, though flawed, was a citizen and a human being and deserved better treatment than he got.

Cobb said of Oluwale: 'almost the first English air he breathed was that which found its way within prison walls'; that he was of fairly poor intelligence though probably not subnormal; that he was a loner who, as far as it was known, was not married, and that he had few, if any, friends; that he had a long history of mental illness. 'He seems to have lived between 1949 and April 1969, a wretched, miserable existence.' The court was told that Oluwale, 'variously known abbreviatively as Ally, Olly, Uggy and Lame Darkie', had been in prison on many occasions for assaults on the police, disorderly conduct and for 'wandering abroad', and that he had often shown violence to those who crossed his path. Cobb said that he was a man with few social graces and that no hostel would have him. 'He was a dosser who slept rough, using newspapers as bedding, with his duffel bag as his pillow; he never worked, but relied on social security payments: these he used mainly for drink, but occasionally for a more solid form of nourishment.' This was David Oluwale. Not the sort of man a respectable person would want in his house. Not the sort of man you would normally sympathise with.

Cobb then detailed the alleged assaults which culminated in Oluwale's death. He said that in the last year of his life Oluwale came into frequent contact with Inspector Ellerker and Sergeant Kitching. These two senior officers, who might have had more weighty matters to deal with, made it their business to make life as unpleasant as possible for Oluwale. 'They hounded him, harassed him and assaulted him: they teased him cruelly, and they made a torment of his life ... The case for the Crown is that these two assaulted him grievously over the nine-month period from August 1968 to April 1969; and that, by their conduct towards him in the early hours of Friday 18 April 1969, they unlawfully brought about his death by causing him to fall or jump into the River Aire, whence he never emerged, save sixteen days later as a corpse.'

Cobb closed by saying that gossip and rumour had 'run riot' in Leeds during the last twelve months. He urged the jury to leave outside the court anything which they may have heard. 'Bring in with you only your knowledge of the layout of the City of Leeds: your common sense and your open minds untarnished by any platitudes such as "there's no smoke without fire".'

On the defence side there was confidence that on the manslaughter charge at least the prosecution had a weak case. Ronnie Teeman, the solicitor representing Sergeant Kitching, had been surprised that it hadn't been thrown out by the stipendiary magistrate during the committal proceedings in May 1971. Teeman's submission had been: there was no evidence that Oluwale was at the scene; no evidence as to how he got into the river; no evidence as to where he went into the river; indeed no evidence that anyone went into the river on that date, at that time, and that place. 'If it cannot be proved that Oluwale went into the river at five o'clock the prosecution fails,' he had said. To Teeman's disappointment the committing magistrate, John Randolph, took a different view. Randolph later admitted to Teeman that though he agreed with his arguments he thought that a matter of such public interest had to be ventilated at the assizes. As an ex-policeman, Randolph might have been vulnerable to accusations of covering up police misconduct. Though it had not gone their way at the committal hearing, the defence team was confident that their argument was unanswerable.

The interest which the case generated in Leeds was nevertheless a worry for the defence. Though it attracted the national press (the *Daily Mail* calling it 'The Case of the Lame Darkie'), more than anything it was an intensely local affair involving one of its major institutions. Every Loiner was fascinated by 'The Kitching Sink Drama'. 'POLICE HOUNDED "LONER" OLUWALE TO DEATH – QC,' was the striking headline in the *Yorkshire Post* after the first day's proceedings. It was something out of the ordinary.

The defence team was acutely aware of lingering local prejudice against the city's police force after the previous year's conspiracy case. Since Geoff Ellerker was one of the convicted officers, there was a concern that he might already be tainted in the minds of a Leeds jury, and the defence had tried to have the trial moved away from the city. Mr Justice Hinchcliffe had been good-humoured about it when Kitching's counsel Gilbert Gray QC and Ronnie Teeman made their submission. 'Where do you want the trial to go, boys? Totnes? Winchester? Don't you think I'm experienced enough to direct the jury on these matters?'

It stayed in Leeds, played out in the city's moral centre in front of a jury of Leeds people, followed intently by the Leeds public. And so, David Oluwale, an obscure figure in life, became a household name. Even the Elland Road Kop sang his name. To the tune of 'Michael, Row the Boat Ashore', thousands of fingers pointing at Leeds City Police officers lining the terraces:

The River Aire is chilly and deep – Ol-u-wa-le,
Never trust the Leeds police – Ol-u-wa-a-le.

Another, to the tune of 'My Old Man (said follow the van)':

Policeman said 'Get in the van, don't dilly dally on the way!'
They had him in the van and in half a minute
They were down by the river and they chucked him in it.
Cos he dillied and dallied, dallied and dillied
Lost his way and dint know where to roam
And you can't trust a copper if your name's Oluwale
When you can't find your way home.

Despite the local interest, Leeds was too busy a city to fill courtroom galleries on wet weekdays in November. Only when the jury delivered its verdict was there a packed public gallery. Most days it was half empty. The trial was played out in understated style in front of an unremarkable judge.

This wasn't a case in which forensic evidence played a significant part. Clothing and equipment had been taken from Ellerker, Kitching and PC Gary Briggs a few weeks into the investigation. A senior forensic scientist had found nothing of 'evidential value' (such as bloodstaining) on the clothing of Kitching or Briggs. The staff which Briggs had handed over to Ellerker on the way to John Peters yielded nothing either. When Briggs went into the witness box on the fifth day of the trial and showed the staff, he couldn't point out the marks which related to that incident. There were small areas of blood-smearing and tearing on items of Ellerker's uniform, but the distance in time between Oluwale's death and the opening of the investigation vitiated its value as evidence. It was a case which rested largely on the evidence given by police officers on Ellerker and Kitching's shift. It would boil down to the credibility of these witnesses, the bystanders.

Ellerker would be defended by Basil Wigoder QC and Arthur Myerson. Wigoder came from a distinguished Jewish family and was one of the leaders of the criminal Bar at the Old Bailey. He was the only one of the protagonists who came from 'off Circuit'. Ellerker's solicitor, Peter Fingret, and Myerson had wanted leading counsel of national importance, Ellerker having been disappointed with his representation in the earlier corruption trial. Wigoder, rather like Cobb, was not a demonstrative advocate. 'He was one of the quiet and decisive types, calm and authoritative,' Myerson told me. As far as it was possible given the nature of the allegations, the defence team wanted a prosaic trial. And this is what they got. There were few moments of high drama.

Gilbert Gray QC defended Sergeant Kitching; his junior barrister was Harry Ognall. Gray was very different to Cobb, the remote Wykehamist, and Wigoder, a former President of the Oxford Union. He was the son of a Scarborough butcher; Cobb was the son of a surgeon, Wigoder a doctor. Gray hadn't been to an ancient university; he'd been to Leeds and the student union he presided over had produced no prime ministers. Gray was an exceptional jury advocate and a vivid phrase-maker, but the Oluwale trial didn't make too high a demand on his skills.

PC Keith Seager was the most important prosecution witness. He entered the witness box on the second day of the trial. He was a problematic witness: he had done the driving when Oluwale was taken out of Leeds to Bramhope and Middleton Woods and dumped; he had stood by on several occasions when Oluwale was being beaten. Yet he had said nothing.

Seager was uncomfortable in the witness box, perhaps inhibited by his sense of loyalty to his colleagues. He described a litany of abuses against Oluwale. He said that Oluwale had become Ellerker and Kitching's 'plaything'. He described the kickings Oluwale received in the shop doorways, including the alleged incident on 18 April 1969 when he claimed to see Ellerker and Kitching coming out of the entrance of John Peters smiling and looking 'contented with themselves'. Yet under cross-examination, Seager said that Sergeant Kitching was one of those solid down-to-earth men who could always be relied on to stand by his men. He concurred with Gilbert Gray's characterisation of Kitching as 'a sergeant of the old school, an old-fashioned bobby in his approach'. He said that when Oluwale was being driven out of the city, Kitching had talked to him with concern, asking him about his family, trying to point out that his way of life was no good. When asked the question, Seager said he didn't think Kitching could have been responsible for his death. He admitted that whenever the subject of Oluwale's death arose it was discussed by everyone in a light-hearted way. Gray asked Seager, 'He [Kitching] did not start like a guilty thing on a dreadful summons when the name of Oluwale was mentioned, did he?' Seager replied, 'No.' Seager agreed that he was in a difficult position because he had had so much contact with Oluwale. He'd moved him on so many times. Seager acknowledged that Oluwale was a filthy character, both in his personal habits and his language, not the sort of man one wanted to grapple with too long or too close. He was fluent in the use of four-letter words.

Ronnie Teeman told me that the defence strategy was to hammer away at some very obvious points. If the police officers testifying were telling the truth, why didn't they do so much earlier? How much of that testimony had been advanced to excuse their own behaviour and to move themselves from the firing line? As Basil Wigoder would point out in his closing speech, 'How does it come about that throughout the whole of this alleged history of ill treatment of Oluwale there was never a single murmur or complaint such as "Look here, Sergeant or Inspector, isn't that going a bit too far?"'

In his cross-examination of Seager, Wigoder put it to him that he was trying to wriggle out of blame by heaping it on the most vulnerable target he could find. He suggested that Seager was getting back at the former inspector for all those lectures he'd received about the length of his hair, dirty shirts and unpressed trousers. Seager denied Wigoder's suggestion that he was in it 'up to the hilt' in the ill treatment of Oluwale, that he had kicked him and had received a severe warning for this from Ellerker.

Seager couldn't defend himself against the accusation that he had falsified duty-book entries for Kitching. The drives to Middleton Woods and Bramhope had not been recorded. Seager said that he did not think these were proper things to record. Wigoder said that his duty book contained 'ten deliberate lies and deliberate dishonest omissions'. It had been a tough five hours in the witness box for Seager, and his performance confirmed the prosecution's concerns about his reliability.

PC Ron Woodhead – Chopper – went into the witness box next and said that never in his many years' service had he witnessed anybody being violent towards Oluwale. Chopper was a highly respected police officer but during the investigation Polly Perkins found him to be uncooperative. Perkins always suspected that Chopper, as the subdivisional van driver on the night of 17/18 April 1969, knew far more than he ever let on, and formed the opinion that his loyalty to colleagues was greater than his regard for the truth.

On the fourth day of the trial, the prosecution called PC Cyril 'Les' Batty. The incident he went on to describe was not the subject of any criminal charge, but the prosecution believed that his testimony illustrated the defendants' complete disregard for Oluwale as a human being. PC Batty thought it was May 1968, not long after Ellerker arrived at Millgarth. He was off duty in the city centre after a night out with his girlfriend. It was sometime around 2.30 a.m. and the streets were deserted. As he walked back to his car he saw Kitching and Ellerker turning right into Lands Lane from Albion Place. They appeared not to have seen him. Batty got into his car and drove up Lands Lane towards The Headrow. He heard shouting coming from the doorway of John Peters, slowed down to have a look and saw that the two officers were standing over Oluwale. Batty had his window slightly down and he could see that Oluwale was trying to get up off the ground. He saw that Ellerker was shining his torch on Oluwale, while Kitching was urinating on him. He could see steam coming off Oluwale's clothes. Cross-examined by Gray, PC Batty was asked why he had said nothing about the incident at the time. 'Not a single horn blow or flash of the lights to try to stop it. Nothing at all?' Batty replied, 'No, sir.' He said that he thought his word would have counted for nothing against two officers of higher rank: 'I was looking after my career.' 'You seem to be worse than the Pharisee who passed by on the other side,' Gray said. And he added, 'You know, don't you, that Oluwale was a man given to biting and scratching? You don't stand over a man like that urinating.' That was what was known as a 'good jury point'.

Later that day, William Greenwood was in the witness box. Harry Ognall, for Kitching, asked Greenwood about an occasion when he took part in an arrest of Oluwale. He asked him what Oluwale's demeanour had been, and asked Greenwood to refer to the court report. Mr Justice Hinchcliffe intervened: 'I would have thought that had been established a thousand times. It is accepted on all hands that he was a dirty, filthy, violent vagrant.'

Throughout the trial Hinchcliffe could neither conceal his distaste for the victim nor his disappointment that police officers were up before him. He was the most powerful judge on the North-Eastern Circuit, a High Court judge since 1957; not a towering intellect but someone regarded as having common sense and a way with juries. Knowing his limitations he always played it safe, one eye on the appeal court. Nobody can recall a judgment of Hinchcliffe's being overturned. He was more modest about his abilities than many High Court judges of that era and wasn't a monstrous tyrant like some – no Melford Stevenson – but he had some of the vices attached to that office: he was pompous, an incorrigible snob and punctilious. He once damned a junior member of the Bar by saying that he was 'a dreadful man – he gets his linen from Austin Reed's'. Some detected in Hinchcliffe more sinister prejudices: why throughout the trial did he insist on pronouncing Basil Wigoder's name, very emphatically, as 'wig odour'? Having been Recorder of Leeds prior to his elevation to the High Court bench, Hinchcliffe knew the city's police force well and had a high regard for it. He believed that the judiciary should be completely behind the police.

On the fourth and fifth days of the trial came further evidence of the indignities and violence suffered by David Oluwale. PC Ken Higgins – Glob – went into the witness box. He'd put a set of dentures in for the occasion. He told the court of a head-banging ritual which he had heard Kitching and Ellerker boast about in the Millgarth canteen. They talked of making Oluwale perform a 'penance'. According to Higgins, Ellerker would force Oluwale to kneel before him and bow. Oluwale would then have to bang his own head. Sometimes Kitching would administer the penance. So many bumps. Several officers were present, Higgins said, when this ritual was described. Then he told the court of the assault in the police van on 10 February 1969 when he saw Ellerker bump Oluwale's face repeatedly on the floor of the J4 van. Higgins may have looked a 'doilum' but he was very comfortable and natural in the witness box. Perhaps because he looked so gormless there was a presumption of honesty. Later, the defence would try to paint him as an inept clown. Ken Kitching would inform the court that Higgins's nickname was Glob and that this was used in 'good-natured contempt'. For the jury though, the six commendations Higgins had received throughout his career – for bravery, diligence and tenacity – told their own story.

Sergeant Frank Atkinson, who was on station duties for the relevant period, made a far less assured witness. It went smoothly enough at first. The court heard that in the early hours of 26 January 1969 Oluwale was brought into the station by Kitching and Ellerker. Oluwale was behaving violently, he said, and the officers were forced to restrain him. They punched him to the floor and when he was down both kicked him 'in the region of the private parts'. According to Atkinson, Ellerker said that Oluwale wouldn't bite him again. He went on to describe a second assault, which he believed took place weeks later on 23 February (this was not the subject of charges), when Oluwale was again punched to the floor by Kitching and Ellerker. During cross-examination, Wigoder accused Atkinson of 'lying in your teeth'. Ellerker, Wigoder said, was off duty on sick leave when the incident was supposed to have taken place. At this point, Atkinson complained of feeling faint. As an usher gave him a drink of water, it was observed that the sergeant's eyes rolled before he slumped down heavily in his chair. He was unable to carry on giving his evidence.

Atkinson was recalled the next day. When Wigoder again accused him of inventing the whole incident, Atkinson rather limply said, 'I have been awake all night, thinking, thinking, thinking.' Superintendent Len Barker, who had the rotas, was recalled. To Atkinson's relief, Barker produced duty slips which showed that Ellerker went off sick at 6 a.m. on 23 February, which was at the completion of the shift. But the jury were left with that image of a big man, an experienced sergeant with twenty years' service, crumpling in the witness box under cross-examination.

'I got the impression that [Oluwale] was a man of very limited intelligence who'd had a very hard time in life,' Donald Herrod, now a retired judge but then John Cobb's junior, told me when we met to discuss the case. 'He was obviously mentally ill in some way to be living the kind of life he was living. And I just felt he had deserved better than what he'd got.' Herrod wonders why no one in the magistrates' courts thought of sending him for a mental examination. 'All right, he was making a nuisance of himself, using shop doorways as lavatories and dossing down in others. And he must have been a nuisance to the police because they were getting it in the neck from the shopkeepers when they arrived the next morning. But they didn't deal with him the way they should have dealt with it. He wanted to be dealt with with sympathy and understanding rather than violence.'

By the standards of the profession, Donald Herrod's upbringing was modest. He studied for the Bar in the evenings while working at Civic Hall in Leeds. But there would be no hint of an ordinary Yorkshire background in his speech; in court his demeanour was imposing, suave and patrician.

Herrod had also been led by Cobb in the first trial involving Ellerker. That case – the length that police officers had gone to protect a senior colleague, the lies that were told – had disturbed his previously unquestioning faith in the integrity of the police. After that he was less trusting; when defendants alleged that confessions had been beaten from them he was prepared to give such stories credence.

'To treat him the way they did was unforgivable,' Herrod says of Ellerker and Kitching, 'and I suppose I had the feeling that they're not going to get away with this.' But throughout the trial, Herrod sensed little regret for the life that had been lost. The two defendants had 'a very arrogant attitude right to the end: that he was a vagrant who was making a nuisance of himself in public premises and they were entitled to move him on and do so harshly if that was demanded'. The police witnesses also gave a sorry impression. 'One had a feeling all the time that you may not be getting the full story. I think Seager was a reluctant witness who had to be pushed into what he was saying. Maybe we never did get the whole story from him.' Sergeant Frank Atkinson he remembered as 'a thoroughly unimpressive witness. I remember hearing a bump and turning round and he wasn't there . . .'

There was one exception to this sorry parade, according to Herrod. That was Hazel Ratcliffe (née Hazel Dolby).

Hazel Ratcliffe had resigned from Leeds City Police in December 1969 on the same day as her husband, Phil Ratcliffe. In a statement to the Oluwale investigation, Phil Ratcliffe, who was working in the central charge office during the relevant period, cited the ill treatment of Oluwale as one of the reasons he got out of the force. Not that he said or did anything about it at the time. After seeing the television report on the inquiry and the appeal for witnesses, he had discussed with his wife whether he should assist. She was expecting her first child and persuaded him not to, that no doubt the police would be in touch in due course. They were finally questioned in late January and February 1971, Hazel Ratcliffe giving her statement from Lincoln Maternity Hospital.

Phil Ratcliffe was also called to give evidence at Leeds Assizes. 'I have never seen a man crying so much and never utter a sound,' he said, describing one occasion when Oluwale was taken into the Bridewell, Kitching pushing him up to the counter by putting his knee into the prisoner's back. He said that Oluwale was placid, far from violent. In fact, he seemed withdrawn and subdued, a broken man. It was Phil Ratcliffe, after the death of Oluwale, who had asked Kitching whether he had pushed him in. It was said in a 'jocular' way, Ratcliffe explained in court.

While her husband had seen the aftermath of the assaults on Oluwale, Hazel Ratcliffe had witnessed an attack on Oluwale first-hand at Millgarth in the early hours of 26 January 1969, which had led to charges of ABH and GBH against Ellerker and Kitching. She saw him punched to the ground and kicked, a hard kick which 'lifted him a little and moved him'. She told the court, 'He was holding his private parts with both his hands and he was crying.' She admitted that she had left the office for the radio room because she couldn't bear to watch. During cross-examination, Wigoder suggested that Oluwale was very violent when brought into the station, that he went 'absolutely berserk, flailing his arms about and legs and screaming and shouting' and that the officers were barely able to restrain him. Hazel Ratcliffe was firm that this wasn't how it had been, that when she saw Oluwale he had been in no position at all to offer violence. She said that she had wanted to say something at the time but had been afraid to stand up against her superiors. Despite her failure to act at the time, Herrod remembers her as a powerful witness. He recalls looking across at the jury. 'I knew that they believed her evidence. Hazel Ratcliffe turned the tide.'

Compelling as Hazel Ratcliffe had been, she was a witness to an assault, not a manslaughter. As the trial went into its second week, attention focused on that question. What would the jury infer from the events taking place around 5 a.m. on 18 April 1969?

On 15 November, postman George Merrion and bus conductor David Condon gave their evidence. Merrion told the court about his conversation with a bus conductor, who he was sure was Condon, and of seeing a police vehicle parked in an alleyway off Call Lane facing down towards the river. Condon described a chase in the early hours of 18 April 1969: a scruffy man pursued by two policemen down Call Lane. It was dark at the time and he admitted that he couldn't identify those two uniformed men as Kitching and Ellerker; he couldn't say what ranks either of the policemen were; one was wearing a raincoat with the collar up. He couldn't identify the pursued man as Oluwale; he couldn't say whether it was a white man or a black man, all he could remember was that he was a smaller man than the policemen, 5'6" to 5'8", medium build with broad shoulders, and that he was wearing a jacket with a large collar which covered part of his face.

The next day the court heard from PC Ian Haste, the frogman who had recovered Oluwale's body from the Aire. Cross-examined by Gray, Haste said that he had doubts as to whether Oluwale could have gone into the river at Warehouse Hill, since the body would have had to have travelled over two weirs to arrive at Knostrop. The investigation had proved otherwise but Haste's testimony went unchallenged.

PC Albert Sedman entered the witness box and read from the sudden death report he had prepared after Oluwale's body was recovered. Sedman said that he saw a large lump on the Nigerian's forehead, cut lips, bleeding from one eye and a bruise on the right arm.

On 17 November Dr David Gee, Senior Lecturer in Forensic Medicine at Leeds University, testified that in his opinion Oluwale's death had been caused by drowning. He thought it was probable that the injury to the head had been inflicted just before or a few hours before death. He said that in his view it was likely that the body had been immersed for a period between one to two weeks, though he didn't rule out entirely the possibility that it had been in the river slightly longer. Gee, cross-examined by Wigoder, said that though Oluwale had received a head injury before death there was no indication that it was a 'substantial' one; in his opinion a blow from a truncheon would have done more damage than he found. Of the marks on Oluwale's face noted by Sedman, Gee said that the layman could have taken these for injuries, but that in his opinion they were due to putrefaction.

The court then heard from Dr Carty, consultant psychiatrist at High Royds. He told the court about Oluwale's history of mental illness and of his behaviour on the ward, of the lions with fishes' heads whom he thought were going to kill and eat him. 'From time to time he kicked, he struck, he bit, he scratched and he spat in people's faces,' Carty said. Cross-examined by Gray, Carty told the court that two members of his staff had suffered biting by the Nigerian, and that when he was admitted to the hospital initially he would defecate on the ward floor and in the corners. Oluwale had lost jobs through fighting, Carty said, and had once boasted to him about attacking a police officer. Cross-examined by Wigoder, Carty opined that he would not have been unduly surprised if Oluwale had committed suicide. He agreed that Oluwale was 'particularly fond' of biting fingers. Carty said that Oluwale had complained of being persecuted by the police when he was admitted in November 1965, but that he was confused, irrational, giggling and childish at the time. Carty claimed that when he calmed down he withdrew the accusations.

The prosecution called John Thomas Wall, a station sergeant at Ireland Wood. Radio operators' daily duty sheets and wireless message slips for both subdivisions in 'A' division were kept at his station, and the investigation had hoped to trace relevant ones for April 1969. Other than the entries in officers' duty books, the wireless slips often constituted the sole record of an incident. It was hoped that these slips would support the allegations made by PCs Seager and Briggs, by placing Ellerker and Kitching at John Peters around 3 a.m. on the night of 17/18 April; it was also hoped that they would provide some indication of officers' movements during the remaining hours of that tour of duty. Sergeant Wall told the court that there had been an intensive trawl of daily duty sheets and wireless message slips for 1969, but that some were missing. However, Wall said that the only common date when both duty sheets and message slips were not to be found was 17/18 April. Wall admitted that he had no idea how they came to be missing: they could have been called for other inquiries and not returned; anyone at Ireland Wood station had access to them.

Once all the prosecution witnesses had been heard, both defence counsel moved to have the manslaughter and grievous bodily harm charges thrown out. In their view the Crown had not presented sufficient evidence to support a case. Wigoder submitted that while there was some suggestion by inference that the two policemen chasing a man along Warehouse Hill on 18 April 1969 were Ellerker and Kitching, there was no evidence at all that Oluwale was the man being pursued. The prosecution had to prove that not only was Oluwale the man being chased, but that he had met his death on 18 April. This, in his view, had not been established. 'To make a case of manslaughter at all, to suggest that Mr Ellerker or Mr Kitching unlawfully caused Oluwale's death, one is really left with such a vast area of speculation and guesswork that it would not be right to allow a charge of this grave nature to go to the jury.'

Gray then made his submission on the manslaughter charge. Referring to the evidence of the frogman, he said that it was not certain that Oluwale had even gone into the river at Warehouse Hill; even if he had done, nobody knew what circumstances had led him there. 'It might have been manslaughter, it could have been an endless range of accidents, it could have been the negligence of someone, even possibly the gross negligence of the police officers in not fishing him out if they knew he had gone in. It might have been suicide. A man swimming away for some reason who could not keep swimming and sank. The range of reasonable possibilities and explanations is without limit.' Gray said that it was not open to anybody to seek to infer how David Oluwale met his death. There was a total absence of eyewitness evidence or indeed any circumstantial evidence of a nature and quality to exclude other explanations.

After hearing the submissions, Hinchcliffe said that in due course he would direct the jury to find the defendants not guilty of GBH (the ABH charge relating to the same incident at Millgarth remained). There had been no evidence, Hinchcliffe said, to indicate that Oluwale had sustained serious injury as a result of an assault. Turning to the manslaughter, he said, 'I am driven to the conclusion that there is no evidence that Oluwale was at the scene. There is no positive evidence that the two accused men were at the scene.' All that could be said was that 'two unidentified men were talking to an unidentified male person'. Hinchcliffe concluded, 'There is no evidence at all as to how Oluwale came to be in the river, or that he went into the river at Warehouse Hill, or that he met his death on 18 April 1969. To say that the two men with the unidentified third man could have been the two accused men is not a foundation for a charge of manslaughter. It is my duty as the judge, as I understand it, that no one shall run the risk of being convicted on suspicion, rumour and gossip. In the circumstances I shall direct the jury to return a verdict of not guilty.'

On the defence side there was little surprise. Essentially, Hinchcliffe had accepted the argument made by Ronnie Teeman at the committal hearing earlier that year. 'We always thought that the manslaughter charge would fail because there was nothing to connect Oluwale's death with the petty persecutions to which the police had subjected him in the months before his death,' Arthur Myerson told me. 'I didn't think the jump was justified. And I agreed with Hinchcliffe that there was a great deal of rumour and speculation which had to be discounted in a judicial decision.' Gilbert Gray recalled of the trial: 'The atmosphere was such that when that frogman said what he did, that was game, set and match to us. It really was.'

'I always thought he was a very fair judge,' Herrod says of Mr Justice Hinchcliffe. But the prosecution were deeply disappointed, having felt that there was sufficient evidence for a jury to consider. 'We were disappointed we hadn't proved as much as we set out to do,' Herrod told me.

II

Of the 120 individuals subpoenaed, only a third of them actually went into the witness box. Most of the ones who weren't called were police officers who had little to contribute other than testifying that they were not involved in any chase by the river on 18 April 1969. But a seemingly interesting, and arguably relevant, witness who was not called was Bill Wheatley. He was a member of the ambulance crew who had been present when Oluwale's body was recovered from the Aire. Long retired, Wheatley was glad to have a chance to tell his story. 'A funny business from the outset,' he told me.

Bill Wheatley had been a lorry driver before joining the Leeds Corporation Ambulance Department in 1966. He took a drop in pay to do what he thought was a more rewarding job. Through his work he got to know Oluwale. One of the tasks of the ambulance crews was to visit the Crypt and the hostels and places frequented by rough sleepers, then take the verminous ones to the deinfestation centre at Stanley Road. Though Stanley Road had no record of ever having treated Oluwale, Wheatley remembers taking him on a number of occasions. He would pick him up at his doorway on The Headrow or Lands Lane, take him to Stanley Road for a 'damn good bath and all that' and then to the hospital for a check-up.

A 'tubbing', that's what they called it. 'You'd put them in an ambulance,' Wheatley told me. 'Of course you got loused up and all. So the ambulance had to be stoved out. Blankets had to be put into autoclaves. 'Owt in there doesn't live. Uniforms never fit after that.' Before it was filled with hot water, sulphur was sprinkled into the bath; the verminous person would use a carbolic soap. 'It stiffened your skin up,' Wheatley tells me. 'They used to look forward to it. Hot bath, hot meal, any medication they needed they got it. To them it was a relief. In general they respected ambulance crews. They knew we were there to help them. Somehow there were that bond there.' He remembers Oluwale as a lonely soul, though one who smiled readily and didn't appear to be broken or mentally ill. 'Big shoulders. He were quite a boy. Kept much to himself. Totally harmless fellow. We didn't have a bit of trouble from him.'

He was the ambulance attendant on Sunday 4 May 1969 when they received the police call. His mate Bill Stockill was the driver. According to the statement Wheatley gave to the investigation in November 1970, they arrived at Knostrop at 3.30 p.m. to find a huddle of policemen standing on the riverbank. They parked the ambulance close by and took a look at the body. 'Didn't recognise him,' Wheatley tells me. 'His face were blown up with water. He were blown up enormous. It's not so much water as gas.' What he remembers noticing most about the condition of the body was this dent on the forehead. Wheatley remembers that it was very quiet at the scene, little was said, which was unusual for policemen. 'I said to my mate, "He belongs to somebody." You talk like that.'

In view of its condition they called for a mortuary van to take the body away to St James's Hospital. 'Another thing that stood out – and you don't often see it – a young doctor came out, he looked at him and said, "life's extinct". He just put "life's extinct" such-and-such a time and then he just put underneath "R.I.P.". You don't often see that. And I thought that were a nice touch, like, you know. Little things.'

At the mortuary they stripped his body and searched him, finding in his clothes a yellow unemployment card which had been missed by the policemen who had gone through his pockets. 'I says, "Bill, you know who it is?" He says, "Oh no." Got him all put away and everything. Cleaned up. A few weeks later I got a call, *return to base*. And there were two CID officers in governor's office. He says, "Did you find 'owt untoward?" I says, "Why? Untoward about what?" I said, "The only thing that were untoward about David Oluwale was the dent in his head. Right there." No more was said.'

Normally, in what was known as a 'continuity case', the ambulance man would have been called to give evidence before the coroner, covering every potentially relevant step from the recovery of the body. Wheatley was never called at the hearing. As he puts it, 'The continuity were broken.' He didn't get a chance to give his evidence at the trial either. Presumably the prosecution decided that he had little to add given his lack of medical expertise and the conflicting expert medical evidence which downplayed the significance of the head injury.

Perhaps if Wheatley had been called he would have told the court of the placid, softly spoken man he had known, albeit fleetingly, as he went about his job.

III

Every so often there comes a trial which catches the nation's attention and defines the times. But the case of David Oluwale, though it was covered by the nationals, didn't shake Black and White Minstrel Britain to its core. It didn't rouse much anti-racist sentiment. Activists didn't pack the public gallery. The Leeds case was eclipsed by a well-publicised trial taking place at the Old Bailey at the same time, the 'Mangrove Nine' trial. This was where the serious anti-racist statement was made. The Mangrove restaurant in All Saints Road, near Ladbroke Grove, was a fashionable spot for politicised black Londoners, regarded with suspicion by the Metropolitan Police and subject to frequent raids. When one of these raids ended in violence, a number of Mangrove regulars were charged with serious criminal offences. Against the received legal wisdom, a number of the accused eschewed representation in court and conducted their own defence. Black community groups up and down the country, emboldened and radicalised by Powellism, rallied to the cause. When the all-white jury found the defendants not guilty of all but a few minor offences, it was celebrated as a major blow against racist oppression. The trial being heard two hundred miles north didn't appear, at least at the time, to have anything like the same social and political significance. In this fraught year — a year which saw internment introduced in Ulster, the 'Oz' obscenity trial, monster demonstrations against the Industrial Relations Bill, and the 'Angry Brigade' attacks, raids and trial — David Oluwale didn't feel 'historic'.

During the trial there was a complete silence around the subject of racism. The prosecution either didn't think or didn't choose to highlight racial prejudice as a motivating factor in the vendetta against Oluwale. The 'NAT: WOG' charge sheets were not presented as evidence at the trial, though they had concerned the investigating officer enough to make him want to establish the authors. Even with this piece of information, the investigation had not probed into the attitudes of Millgarth officers towards black people, perhaps to avoid greater scandal; it preferred to see the attacks on Oluwale as a product of Sergeant Kitching's unusually vindictive feelings towards vagrants, and Ellerker's desire to get his revenge after being bitten. A tale of two 'bad apples'.

Colour entered into it in just one way, Gilbert Gray QC told me when I met him to discuss the Oluwale case. There was a question mark over the one black jury member. The defence considered whether to have him taken off (defence and prosecution had at that time the right to have a jury member stand down without having to offer any reason). The thought was: would this man's colour predispose him to sympathise with Oluwale? Was he more likely to be anti-police? They decided to keep him on: if there was any prejudice around, any distaste for the victim and the way he lived his life, this solitary black man, sitting among these white middle-aged and middle-class property owners, would want to distance himself from Oluwale.

It was not bad psychology. In 1971 Britain was still very much in thrall to Enoch Powell. If the debate on immigration wasn't as intense as it was in the wake of the 'Rivers of Blood' speech, that was only because politics had moved in a Powellite direction. The Conservative Party's success in the 1970 general election was in no small part down to its pledge to stop permanent large-scale immigration. The 1971 Immigration Act, which finally slammed the door on black New Commonwealth immigrants ('non-patrials' to use the language of the legislation), was a sign that, though there was no place for Enoch in the Cabinet, he was very much there in spirit. That legislation was the final instalment in what had been a decade-long steady reversal of the liberal immigration policy Britain had pursued since 1948.

To Gilbert Gray, whose illustrious career at the Bar goes back over half a century (he still practises), the case of David Oluwale seemed nothing more than a squalid little local affair. 'It didn't really stand out for me. It wasn't a cause célèbre. Because there wasn't much to celebrate – a tramp lying in a pool of vomit and other things. I don't think it was a race issue as such. What was at issue: I've never forgotten what Alf Robens said – Chairman of the National Coal Board, if you remember. He said, "It's not colour that matters, it's conduct." And I think I used that in my closing speech. And I also used what I think Archbishop Joost de Blanc said when he was sent to South Africa as archbishop. They said, "How are you feeling?" He said, "I'm feeling splendid, but I have one disadvantage, some people might think." "What's that?" "I'm colour-blind." So, you work two of those things in, dropping your voice appropriately, the jury then are left . . . *no question of colour prejudice at all.*'

It all boiled down to character: the character of the two officers and the character of Oluwale. Gray had seen him in the shop doorways on The Headrow. 'Nasty piece of work. He was so filthy, rank, stinking, and smeared with anything unmentionable. And if a copper went near him to help him he'd let him get so near and then he'd bite his leg or gob on him or whatever. I could well understand that the policeman on his lonely beat having filthy teeth sunk into his calf and having some shit hurled at him was not amused.'

'I'm sympathetic towards policemen in general,' Gray told me. 'My father during the war was the commandant of all the special constables in Scarborough. So I have some feeling for them because they have a bloody awful job and they're supposed to know the law better than the judges in the court of appeal. I *so* wanted to help.'

If the defence couldn't portray Kitching to be the friendly local bobby, it could try to show him to be a tough but effective policeman doing a dirty but necessary job for the Leeds public. The court had earlier heard Superintendent Len Barker testify that vagrants were an 'infernal nuisance' in Leeds, and that Oluwale had used doorways as a bedroom and a toilet. He said that it wasn't enough to tell them to move on, they had to be told in language they understood. Barker said that while the citizens of Leeds were sleeping comfortably in their beds it was men like Kitching who were having to push men out of the city centre and make sure they never came back. To show that Kitching was not without friends in Leeds City Police, Barker also told the court of Kitching's Humane Society Award. (Kitching would remind the jury of this act of bravery when he went into the witness box.)

From the outset of the investigation, Kitching had never denied that he'd been violent towards Oluwale. One of his former colleagues told me that Kitching had once advised him that if a prisoner alleged an assault during the course of an arrest, rather than try to deny it and risk being found out, it was far better to simply admit it and then justify it. Despite his limitations, Kitching's straightforwardness had served him well when giving evidence in court over the years, and he invariably came over as confident and convincing.

What remained after Mr Justice Hinchcliffe's intervention were the ABH charges. Defence counsel's strategy was to show Oluwale to have been someone completely beyond the pale of civilised society, thus mitigating the violence shown towards him. 'It is always a rather unenviable job to speak ill of the dead and that is why it is not nice when anybody has to start criticising David Oluwale, he now being dead,' Gilbert Gray QC said as he opened Sergeant Kitching's defence. He said that he would be calling a nurse from High Royds who would tell of Oluwale's indiscriminate violence. 'You would not bend over,' said Gray, 'because as quick as a flash and as lithesome as may be, David Oluwale would leap up like a miniature Mr Universe and have hold of you, scratching and biting with a mouthful of the biggest, dirtiest teeth Mr Dent had ever seen in his life.'

Earlier in the proceedings, during the examination of Detective Superintendent Jim Fryer, the transcript of Detective Chief Superintendent Perkins's first interview with Kitching had been read out. During the course of this interview, Kitching had described his dealings with Oluwale. 'I have put him out of doorways and kicked his behind. Under Leeds Library in Commercial Street. Brill's, Bond Street, in Baker's in Trinity Street, in John Peters in The Headrow, Bridal House in The Headrow, the Empire Arcade in Briggate and Trinity Church in Boar Lane.' 'Tickled him with my boot', 'never hit him really hard', 'kicked him gently', 'just a slap', 'booted his backside out of it', 'good slapping' – these were the phrases he used in that interview. He didn't try to hide his disdain for Oluwale. 'A wild animal, not a human being,' he had told the investigating officer.

Eric Dent, a Menston staff nurse, was called to the witness box. Dent, now an important defence witness, had only gone to the police with information after the trial had started. He was concerned that too much sympathy was being shown towards the victim and believed that the true horrible nature of the man should be revealed. Dent's was powerful testimony. He described in vivid terms a dirty, snarling, biting man possessed of superhuman strength.* When Mr Justice Hinchcliffe said that he didn't know the phrase 'Mr Universe', Gray explained, 'It is a title like that of Miss World except it means the most muscled male body in the universe.' When Gray asked Dent how, in his long experience of nursing violent patients, he would rate Oluwale, the reply was 'very violent, very unpredictable, very dangerous'.

Kitching told the court that Oluwale was a filthy individual whose trousers were often sodden with his own urine. After touching him Kitching would have to take off his tunic and wash. On one occasion he caught vermin off Oluwale. He told the court he'd been punched, kicked, bitten, scratched, spat upon by Oluwale. Usually he tried to avoid direct physical contact. He put his gloves on whenever he dealt with him. He said that he could have arrested

* For Eric Dent's statement, refer back to pp. 60–2.

Oluwale every time he found him sleeping out, but that he didn't want to tie up the courts. That's why they drove him out of the city. 'Here you were, getting him off your patch,' Gray suggested. Kitching agreed. Cross-examined by Cobb, Kitching said that it hadn't been brutal or cruel to leave Oluwale at Middleton Woods. It was actually a 'fine August night'. He himself lived up that way and it was a nice spot to sit out. Less woods than park. The idea, he told the court, had been to keep Oluwale out of the city. He called it an 'experiment that failed'.

Kitching admitted that he'd punched Oluwale on more than one occasion, but that he had employed no more force than was necessary. 'Was that force from the sheer delight of it or necessary in the course of your duty?' Gray asked him. Kitching replied, 'It was necessary in the course of duty. Had his behaviour been different he would have been treated properly.' If he had used too much violence, he added, wouldn't the station sergeant, Frank Atkinson, have stopped it?

Asked about the alleged incident at John Peters on the night of 17/18 April 1969, Kitching said he could not remember the date, but he was sure that he had not harmed Oluwale. 'We did not do violence to David Oluwale. I never saw Inspector Ellerker use a truncheon on him. I did not do anything unlawful to make him squeal and scream.'

Cross-examined by Cobb, Kitching poured scorn on the officers who had testified against him. He said that PC Higgins was reliable only in the sense that 'If a sergeant said to him go in the middle of City Square and do traffic duty until I have you relieved, he would stay for a week'. He professed not to remember the incident at Millgarth on 26 January 1969. He had no memory of Oluwale 'crying copiously'. Cobb asked, 'Is that because you have seen him crying copiously on many occasions?'

Asked whether he agreed that the last time he saw Oluwale alive was the night of 17/18 April 1969, Kitching replied that he couldn't remember, but agreed it must have been sometime during the week commencing 14 April.

Kitching agreed that he had become overinvolved with vagrants.

Cobb asked him whether any thought had been given to arranging for mental health workers or social workers to take an interest in Oluwale. 'They had shelved the problem,' Kitching answered. 'I agree it is essentially a social problem but they didn't want to know.' 'Did you ever do anything that was kind to Oluwale?' Cobb asked. 'What could I possibly do?' came the reply from Kitching.

During the trial it was noted by the *Yorkshire Post* that Ellerker sat bolt upright throughout, often taking notes, looking the professional. Following Mr Justice Hinchcliffe's intervention, the bleaker scenario which Ellerker had feared – seven years – had lifted.

Though the more accomplished and articulate of the two defendants, Ellerker was a more difficult individual to defend than Kitching. Whereas Kitching was still a police officer, albeit one under suspension, Ellerker was a discredited ex-copper with a criminal conviction. He failed to do certain things he should have done, was how he delicately put it when Wigoder raised the issue at the outset. Another difficulty was that Ellerker had been an inspector, someone who was expected to display intelligence and judgement and be above the dirty business of tangling with tramps.

Despite a superior grasp of language, he was less confident in the witness box than Kitching. 'Putting oneself across in a criminal trial is not an easy task – and it wasn't something that Ellerker was good at,' Arthur Myerson said of his former client. 'He was a forceful personality but he didn't really portray himself in that way. There are some occupations which lend themselves to appearance in the witness box: estate agents and second-hand car salesmen who are used to selling themselves as well as the product. And some policemen are like that; but Ellerker wasn't. He was a very private man.'

Having refused to cooperate with the investigation, this was the first opportunity to test Ellerker's story. Examined in chief by Wigoder, Ellerker explained that the reason he had not cooperated was that he was in prison, convicted on the basis of 'rumour and speculation', and that as far as he was concerned the Oluwale inquiry was just so much more 'rumour and speculation'.

'I was something of an unusual inspector in as much as I had different views to other people who held the same rank as I,' Ellerker told the court. 'It is my experience that people reach the rank of inspector and are content to sit back and become an administrative machine. I take the view that as an inspector running a shift you should become involved in anything that happens and be alongside the men, no matter how serious or trivial.' He said that Group 3 was not a very good shift and that he had been forced to 'crack the whip a little' to get his men moving. That may have made him unpopular, he said.

He denied being involved in the urinating incident alleged by PC Batty. He denied being involved in a 'head-bumping' ritual, and said that PC Higgins was probably thinking of Robert Milne (aka Barnsley Bob). There used to be talk in the Millgarth canteen, Ellerker said, of Milne doing his 'penance' by bumping his head. He denied Higgins's allegation that Oluwale's head was slammed on the floor of the van on the way to the Bridewell; Higgins was a 'confused' officer. He denied kicking Oluwale between the legs at Millgarth. Asked about PC Seager, Ellerker said that he had to tell him off on many occasions for failing to do his work and had taken him to task over his scruffy appearance. Once, he had had to reprimand Seager for kicking Oluwale up the backside when moving him on from John Peters. He denied chasing Oluwale down The Headrow on the early morning of 7 August 1968 and bringing him down with a flying tackle. He said that he had never taken Oluwale outside the city against his will: 'It would have been improper to do so.' Asked by Wigoder about the alleged assault on 4 September 1968, Ellerker said that Oluwale had gone berserk and had bitten his hand. 'He came towards us like a hurricane. His legs were going, his arms were going. He scratched my face in a half-punching clawing movement. He was screaming like a lunatic.' After this incident, Ellerker instructed the shift that if anybody found Oluwale in shop doorways they should contact him. Given his propensity for violence, Ellerker explained that it would have been irresponsible of a senior officer to have left his men to deal with Oluwale on their own.

He admitted to Wigoder that he had been violent towards Oluwale when arresting him, but that he had never used any more force than was necessary. Oluwale was a very difficult individual to deal with, he told the court. 'He was always excitable. You couldn't hold a rational conversation with him. He used to shout and carry on at the top of his voice. I considered him to be a very violent character.' He denied that he had been pursuing a vendetta against Oluwale.

The next day Ellerker was cross-examined by Cobb. He explained that he had gone around with Kitching so much because he was the 'bottom side' sergeant. He denied that he and Kitching took a delight in 'hounding' Oluwale out of doorways and teasing him. When Cobb asked, 'If Sergeant Kitching found him did you find that he radioed for you to come?' Ellerker answered, 'No, sir.' Getting involved heavily with tramps could be seen as beneath the dignity of an inspector, Cobb suggested. 'Nothing should be beneath his dignity that is not beneath the dignity of a PC,' Ellerker replied. He repeated that the policemen giving evidence against him were either confused or embittered members of his shift seeking to heap dirt on him. He named Sergeant Atkinson and PC Seager as the main conspirators.

Cobb questioned Ellerker about his allegation that Seager had kicked Oluwale up his backside. Cobb asked him whether this was not 'a very serious matter indeed', calling for disciplinary action. Ellerker replied, 'I would not say it is a very serious matter. It is obviously a matter for concern, something that should be tackled. It depends on the way the kick is administered.' 'Isn't it a very serious matter for a police officer to assault a citizen?' Cobb asked. Ellerker replied, 'Vagrants are, to say the very least, a difficult job in this city, and on this occasion I put it down to PC Seager being a little too exuberant.' Cobb said that he seemed to be suggesting that 'there was one form of treatment that could be dispensed to vagrants and another to other citizens'. Ellerker said, 'Yes.'

Ellerker insisted that he remembered nothing of the night of 17/18 April 1969. Asked about the alleged incident at John Peters, Ellerker said that he believed that witnesses had been confused with a similar incident which happened in the January or February. It was not long after he had been bitten by Oluwale, and he recalled that he had thought it prudent to take a truncheon along with him. 'I have said quite openly that I would make sure that Oluwale did not assault me in future and if necessary I would use a truncheon on him because he was of such a violent nature.'

Throughout the trial there was nobody called to give a good word for David Oluwale. No friend to speak for him. Nobody to challenge the image of the dirty and dark and threatening presence. But many police officers had had dealings with him without witnessing animal-like behaviour or meeting with a violent response. PC Michael Hargreaves, a Millgarth officer on Group 1, had told the Oluwale investigation, 'He didn't offer any objection to being told to move on and went on his way without giving any trouble.' 'Never had any trouble with him,' PC Denis Moran had told the investigation. 'He always went on his way,' said PC Stephen Clarkson. 'He always moved on, he was never violent, he just picked his bag up and went away chuntering,' recalled PC Peter Smith. 'He went without much trouble but used to jabber like a witch doctor,' according to PC Barry Clay. 'I never had any trouble with him, although he did used to grumble incoherently,' PC Brian Higgins said. Leeds Assizes didn't hear from any of these.

On 22 November, counsel gave its closing speeches. For the Crown, Cobb spoke for over two hours. He asked the jury to consider whether Kitching was indeed just an old-fashioned bobby. 'Is that a proper description of him or not? On his own admission he trifled with Oluwale's liberty. On his own admission he regarded Mr Oluwale as an animal, not a human being, and on his own admission gave him a slapping on at least one occasion.' Cobb added, 'If anyone deserves to be labelled as an old-fashioned bobby, it is PC Higgins.' He said, 'No effort has been spared to denigrate Mr Oluwale. Oluwale had been described as mentally defective, dirty, awkward, physically strong and frightening. Is he really as bad as the defence would have us believe? Perhaps much of it is justified, but perhaps some of it isn't. He has not been heard at all. He cannot be. He might well have a point of view which he might like to have ventilated. He liked sleeping out. He did not like to conform to the standards we all know. He was a nuisance.' Oluwale, Cobb said, was 'part of the flotsam of life for over twenty years', not the sort of man who had been vociferous in making protest and complaints. He stressed that the case could not be of 'greater importance when one looks at basic principles'; that the quality of justice in this country 'must remain if possible more pure than fine gold'.

In his closing speech, Wigoder said that the case had raised an 'enormous volume of smoke' and that it was the jury's task to blow it away and see what was left. He said of David Oluwale: 'Mr Cobb refers to him a citizen. What right have we to call him a citizen? His only claim to being a citizen was that every now and then he was lodged in the local prison.'

Gilbert Gray is known for his gift for the striking phrase. When I asked him about one particular phrase that he used in his closing speech, Gray told me that he borrowed an idea from a song that was sung at Bar Mess, a regular social gathering of the legal elite. 'Her Majesty's Solicitor-General Sir Harry Hylton-Foster, superior human being if there ever was one, elegant aquiline features, slender hands – he used to come to Mess in the Leeds Club and we used to have songs and I used to play a trombone,' Gray told me. 'And he used to sing "The Night-Soil Man". And we'd all get behind him in a conga and he would sing as he went round the tables:

> The Night-Soil man he does what he can
> And he rings his bell of warning
> He shovels up the shite in the middle of the night
> And he takes it away in the morning
>
> Going down the sewer
> Shovelling up manure
> I love to hear his balls go clang, clang, clang
> He always does his bit
> shovelling up the shit
> He's the foreman of the gang, cor blimey!'

In his closing speech, Gray said, 'Nobody, it seems, was ever kind to David Oluwale. Then you may think he was not very kind himself – fighting, scratching, kicking, spitting. This was not an abandoned baby, who demands cosseting, care and correction, but a miniature Mr Universe as lithe as a panther, who could leap up from the ground and grab you.' Kitching had his job to do in the very centre of Leeds where the dossers were found, Gray said, 'to move them on and kick them out of it'; it was not criminal to use force unless too much force was used intentionally. The 'police officer', Gray said, 'is faced with the unlovely task of going down dark alleys at night. They have to stand foul-mouthed abuse in the street and call their foul-mouthed abuser "Sir". They, in a real sense, are the night-soil men of society.'

On 22 November, Hinchcliffe began his summing-up. He declared the police to be 'a fine and splendid profession. Without them there could be chaos and anarchy. They do their best to keep the peace and they do their best to enable people to sleep in their beds safely.' He said the remaining charges of assault were 'not the most serious' in the criminal calendar, but it was 'bad enough if and when it is committed by a police officer'.

Hinchcliffe asked the jury to consider whether the prosecution had proved that Ellerker and Kitching had used more force than was reasonable in the circumstances of effecting the lawful arrest of Oluwale. He told the jury that sleeping out would not be an arrestable offence but that an assault on the police in the execution of their duty would be.

Of the victim, Hinchcliffe had little to say other than that he was a 'menace to society' and 'a frightening apparition to come across at night'. He asked the jury to 'not let their nausea and outrage at the shocking conduct of Oluwale cloud their judgement'.

The next day the jury retired to consider its verdict. They deliberated for four and a half hours. When the jury returned at 3.20 p.m. it found Ellerker and Kitching guilty by a unanimous decision of the assaults on 7 August 1968, 4 September 1968 and 26 January 1969; Ellerker was also found guilty of the 10 February

1969 assault. But both men were found not guilty of ABH on Oluwale at John Peters on 18 April 1969.

Mitigation pleas were made before Hinchcliffe passed sentence. Jailing Ellerker for a total of three years, and Kitching for twenty-seven months, Hinchcliffe said:

> This must be a grim moment for both of you, as indeed it is for me, but this has been a most unpleasant case. If these had been assaults by one civilian on another they would have been bad enough, but when committed by senior police officers with the duty of behaving firmly and properly towards those with whom you have to deal, the matter becomes one of real gravity. By your wicked misbehaviour to this coloured vagrant, you bring disgrace and shame not only on your wives and family, but on the whole of the police force of this country. The verdict of the jury today will add fuel to the fire of those who spend most of their time sneering at police officers and making brash criticism against the police force. You will understand that these are matters which cannot be overlooked.

Ellerker picked up his coat, turned quickly round and disappeared down the dock steps. Kitching, slightly stooped, picked up his raincoat and trilby hat and followed him.

IV

Kitching took his sentence well, shaking hands enthusiastically with his solicitor Ronnie Teeman, who went down to see him in the cells. It was as if he'd had a lucky escape.

Dorothy Ellerker packed her children off to relatives in the north-east. They'd been teased at school, their father called 'Murderer'. Hate mail was sent to the home. The neighbours rallied round though, and the church was a great support. She told the press that she would stick by her husband, that nobody is sent a cross they can't shoulder. She said that he 'couldn't have slept like he did if he had anything on his conscience'. She said that he had a gift for figures and was thinking he might train to be an accountant.

Armley was too dangerous so her husband went to HMP Birmingham (Kitching went to Lincoln), locked up all day for his own safety, then on to Stafford. She visited him with the children just after Christmas. They commented on how thin he'd gone. He was looking to the future, talking about doing A levels so that he could start a new career.

In Leeds, some comfort was taken from the fact that police officers had rooted out their own bad apples. Nobody could cry 'cover-up'. The trial was even proclaimed as a vindication of the British sense of fair play. 'Is there any country in the world that would have bothered about David Oluwale?' the *Yorkshire Evening Post* asked. The 'faceless nobody' from 'humble fisherfolk in Lagos' had been given justice 'that no VIP could expect'. 'A triumph for British Justice,' wrote one reader.

Vindicatory feelings surfaced. One J. K. Krufthoffer complained that the *Yorkshire Evening Post* appeared to be 'arousing sympathy for a useless vagrant'. 'Leeds has its share of do-gooders as views on the Oluwale case have shown,' a Mr Fellows wrote to the same paper, 'but surely it would never have arisen if he had been deported when found to be a vagrant and this stigma would never have clouded the city.' At this testing time the police found many sympathisers. In his parish magazine *Orbit*, the Vicar of Meanwood declared that the trial had been a travesty of the truth and that the highest traditions of policing had been maintained. The *Yorkshire Evening Post*, which published many letters of support for the police, urged its readers to remember that 'Oluwale demonstrated that the policeman, the average man, is expected to clear up all sorts of messes while the public sleeps'.

In Chapeltown, 'Remember Oluwale' was daubed on a wall near the Hayfield pub, but in truth Chapeltown never really knew him. In what sense was he really part of a 'black community', any community for that matter, this man who died on the streets protected by nobody? This man who twice went to the grave unmourned?

He became a symbol. For black people, in Leeds and beyond, his death carried a message and a warning about who really belonged to the British nation. The indignities heaped on Oluwale, the less-than-human, the non-citizen, spoke to their experiences. When the Select Committee on Race Relations and Immigration took evidence at Leeds Town Hall in February 1972 both the Indian Workers' Association and the Muslim Council began their submissions by referring to David Oluwale's case. His story touched all those who had struggled to make a new life for themselves in the city.

The Oluwale case demoralised the Leeds City Police. 'Among police forces in the North of England it had become a bad joke,' one officer told the *Daily Mail*, describing his experiences on a training course. 'When it was announced that I was from Leeds the class held their nose and grinned.' 'Leeds Murder Squad – whom do you want murdering today?' was one of the jokes. Dave Sowden told me, 'It left a nasty taste. When you stopped people or when you pulled people for offences, instead of the usual phrase "Go and catch some robbers", "Go and throw a few more in the river".' 'A terrible incident which left a blight on all Leeds City Police officers,' Glyn Wide, who served in the force, recalled. But another told me, 'Friends outside the police were not much concerned with Oluwale; they seemed to think a great deal of time, effort and money was being wasted. And many of these were professional people who one would expect to have a bit more concern about the way society was being policed.'

Leeds's six MPs called on Home Secretary Reginald Maudling to appoint a public inquiry into the state of the city's police force, a deputation which included political heavyweights Denis Healey; Keith Joseph, the Conservative minister for social services; and Merlyn Rees, who had had ministerial responsibility for race relations in the last Labour government. The response of the Leeds City Police's top brass was defensive and grudging. The Chief Constable dismissed them as 'a gaggle of politicians'; his defiant stance was supported by a majority on the Watch Committee. Influential local opinion, including both newspapers, came out against a public inquiry, the *Yorkshire Post* arguing that it would provide an opportunity for 'malicious accusers' to attack the police. The Lord Mayor said that further public scrutiny was unnecessary in the light of the trial.

There were questions in the House of Commons on 2 December. Reginald Maudling admitted 'there is a feeling that in general there is something that should be investigated'. But Maudling saw his role as one of sustenance and assistance to a beleaguered police force; a force which increasingly saw itself as the underpaid, unappreciated last line of defence against the forces of disorder in society – trade union militants, football hooligans, black power activists, student protesters, Irish Republicans, home-grown anarchists. Not wishing to see the police further demoralised, Maudling decided against a public inquiry, opting instead for a special inspection to be carried out by HM Inspectorate of Constabulary. It would be the police investigating the police, not that this reassured the Leeds City Police; there was an expectation that a highly critical inspection would spell the end of the force, that Oluwale would provide the pretext for its immediate dissolution and amalgamation.

In January 1972, J. Starritt, Assistant Commissioner of the Metropolitan Police, carried out the inspection at the behest of the Chief Inspectorate of Constabulary. He found Leeds City Police to be an efficient force, made recommendations for extra staff, new buildings and better equipment, advised that it pay attention to cultivating better public relations. The critical parts of the inspection were not disclosed to the public. Leeds City Police survived the immediate crisis, but it was clear by then that the idea of maintaining a separate force was no longer credible.

1 April 1974 would be talked about in Yorkshire as though it was the beginning of hell and not just a landmark day in the organisation of local government. An intimate sense of civic pride and local feeling was lost. Leeds was reduced to a mere metropolitan district in the administrative county of West Yorkshire. The 138-year history of Leeds City Police also came to an end that day. It was amalgamated with Bradford and West Yorkshire to form the West Yorkshire Metropolitan Police. Dennis West, who joined Leeds City

Police in 1951, described it to me as 'the saddest day'. 'We used to take a pride in the Leeds City Police. I've often said, when I go you put in my obituary "former Leeds City Police officer".' Millgarth police station was finally closed in 1976 and was demolished in the 1980s; there's now a car park in its shell, and a few rows of the white-tiled cell walls can still be seen down one side. A new Millgarth stands opposite the site of the old one, a utilitarian slab just as forbidding.

The two disgraced former policemen returned to their communities on release from prison. Kitching went back to a changed Hunslet: industries gone, houses bulldozed, dozens of shops closed, no more rugby at Parkside. The new Leeds South-East Urban Motorway, which carved through the community, went right past his street. He found security work at Hepworth clothiers, that once great Leeds institution. His old neighbours on the quiet cul-de-sac told me that he 'kept himsel' to himsel'', 'wandered about looking bleeding lost', 'never looked at anybody'. Joyce Callaghan told me that 'no one would entertain him', though occasionally a police car would pull up outside his house and stay there an hour or so. He continued to booze in the same pubs. He died alone in September 1996. A great-niece signed the death certificate; his occupation was recorded as fireman.

Geoff Ellerker's old police colleagues lost touch with him. I was told that he became a teacher; another thought that he worked in a nursing home or a hospice. He lives with his wife at the house they moved into forty years earlier when he was an ambitious young policeman with a promising career ahead of him. He accompanies his wife to church every Sunday; they also attend scripture class. They are a quiet couple, very close. I approached Geoff Ellerker in November 2004 in person (as he was hosing down his driveway) and again in September 2005 by letter in the hope of getting his story, but he didn't wish to speak. This is a shame because it would be good to hear his comments on the matter, for the record. That said, he was found not guilty of manslaughter, served his time for the assaults, and so one can understand his desire for privacy.

*   *   *

Nationally, the story of David Oluwale soon faded from public attention. Middle England was largely unmoved; society was left unchanged. Outside Leeds it was possible to have been a reasonably aware person yet remain ignorant of the name.

Leeds wanted to forget him. 'A name that will haunt Leeds police for years to come,' the *Yorkshire Post* said of Oluwale. There was shame that such a thing could happen on the streets of Leeds, right under the noses of its citizens. Blacks ending up face down dead in rivers was the kind of thing that happened in the Deep South, not Leeds. There was shame that the crimes should have been committed by officers of *their* police force; shame that experienced officers had stood by and let it happen; shame that the crimes would have remained hidden but for an eighteen-year-old lad.

Leeds was surging forward, hard as Billy Bremner, fast as Sniffer Clarke. Motorways driving into the heart of the city. The old and derelict flattened. The air cleaned of soot. A programme of civic renewal was started by the city council called 'Operation Eyesore', part of the 'Project Leeds' promise to create a more aesthetically pleasing centre. Work began on the town hall. They called this part of the programme 'Operation Revelation'. There'd been a few dissenting voices urging that the building should stay exactly as it was; that even the stone lion with the smoke-damaged left eye and nostrils should remain untouched, a permanent reminder of Leeds's industrial heritage and its heavy environmental price. But Civic Hall had no desire to memorialise sooty pasts. Leeds Cleaning Company got the contract and soon after the Oluwale trial the scaffolding went up. A dilute acid solution was brushed on to the stonework to loosen the soot and dirt, then low-pressure pumps sent jets of water on to the masonry. It took 100,000 gallons to wash off the muck of ages.

EPILOGUE

Remembering Oluwale

Roy Pledger, ex-Leeds City Police: I don't think the population of Leeds were that bothered. Generally people didn't think Oluwale was a big loss.

He was a doorway man. I think that was his downfall. He was prone to shop doorways, and the people who owned the shops didn't like it. That was why there were so many complaints about him. All the city centre knew him. He was a total pest.

Bill Kilgallon, Chief Executive of Social Care Institute for Excellence (in 1971 he was a Roman Catholic priest in Leeds and founded St Anne's Day Centre for the homeless): He was well known at the cathedral because a lot of homeless people used to call in or shelter there during the day. My impression was that he was essentially someone on his own. It was relatively unusual to have a black homeless person. He'd not had great treatment from society as a whole. It was evident that he hadn't been given much support.

It was a case that did hit people in Leeds, and I think quite shocked them – the fact that it happened in the city.

[I asked Kilgallon about the link between the case of David Oluwale and the opening of St Anne's Day Centre weeks after the trial.] There wasn't a direct link. But there's no doubt that in generating support in the city to open the centre, getting volunteers in, getting resources to do it . . . there's no doubt that his death had a significant impact on that.

[I asked Kilgallon, 'Could something like this happen again?'] Yes it could. You've still got homeless people. There are still examples of people being mistreated in all sorts of organisations. I think it's much less likely to happen now. And certainly much less likely to happen by the police. Their culture has changed radically. Better leadership. Better public scrutiny. The whole view of society about the police is different. Back then people didn't question greatly what the police did.

All the places that they chased him and kicked him would now be on CCTV in Leeds. Virtually every yard of Leeds is covered. There'd be tapes of it.

Maurice Brayson, ex-Leeds City Police: Whereas today perhaps you'd see social services stepping in at an early stage, thirty years back you'd get the debris of society and nobody wanted to know. Such as Oluwale.

Exactly the same with murders. You get a prostitute murdered, or a homosexual murdered, you can forget any help from the public because they're not interested – they think they brought it on themselves.

Ronnie Teeman, solicitor for Sergeant Ken Kitching: The police station for a busy centre of a metropolis was subject to a great deal of pressure to keep the city clean and tidy. It must have been a source of continual complaint by traders that the conduct of Oluwale – sleeping out in their doorways, defecating in the streets – was affecting them. We did not have any place where these people could be sent – that was the problem.

Oluwale would squeal and run around the city and many shoppers would be frightened of him.

Arthur Myerson, defence counsel in the Oluwale trial: My memory was that Oluwale was perfectly harmless. He wasn't a criminal. He didn't go around thumping people. He wasn't a druggy. He didn't harass people passing by. He wandered around a lot talking to himself. He slept in doorways.

I always thought the trigger for the whole thing was the fact that he had a nasty habit of pissing and shitting in the doorway before he moved on in the morning. And that's how the social side begins to boil. Shopkeepers complain to the chief constable, chief constable complains to the superintendent, the superintendent says, 'Aha, who's the inspector in charge of the nightshift?' and says, 'Who will rid me of this turbulent nogoodnick?'

[It was] the story of an ambitious policeman who could not see any way of solving the problem other than forcing the man away from the city centre. I think Ellerker came to the conclusion that there was no sensible way of dealing with him. Because you couldn't frighten him away. You couldn't send him somewhere else.

[Oluwale] was a sad figure in many ways. I have a feeling he was even *persona non grata* at the Crypt. I mean, they literally took anyone.

He was very good at living out on the street. I think one of the things people did fear was that as his mental condition deteriorated – which I think it was doing – he would commit an act of unprovoked violence which could fall upon anybody. He was obstreperous.

People came together who between them created a situation with which neither side could cope. I strongly suspect Oluwale couldn't cope with what was being done to him, and he wasn't prepared to go. I would have thought that he knew that what they wanted him to do was simply to go away. But he wouldn't or couldn't – because this was his home.

But what happened that night I don't think we shall ever know.

Peter Fingret, Geoff Ellerker's solicitor: My lasting memory is of how the two trials involving Geoff Ellerker took over my life and that of my staff for those two years. Police and lawyers are notorious gossips at the best of times and these events sparked rumour after rumour, some true but many far-fetched. The search for the truth seemed to be an endless uphill struggle.

I have a vivid memory of carrying Ellerker into the town hall for his first committal proceedings on a stretcher, as he was unable to stand following a back injury.

I have a memory of a burly desk sergeant from Millgarth fainting in the witness box under ferocious cross-examination.

Today, when I stay at a smart hotel in The Calls, my mind always goes back to those days, when only the foolhardy would step into that area near the River Aire.

Bernard Atha, Leeds Labour councillor, and Deputy Chairman of the Leeds Watch Committee in 1971: I had this rather idealistic view of the standards the police should attain and maintain.

I was horrified when the story broke. The abuse of that poor soul had been going on for a long time. It was known to policemen at Millgarth and it was almost a joke. But no one did anything.

I just saw it as a racially motivated process of abuse. The fact that so many in the force knew what was happening to this poor sod and no one did anything to intervene, except an eighteen-year-old lad, then there was something wrong in the service. There were some decent folk on the Conservative side – they weren't in any way nasty folk – they didn't quite have those same views. I wanted it right out and it was quite clear that wasn't going to happen. The Conservative's attitude when the Oluwale story broke was *yes, these two are guilty, they must be punished, but let's leave it at that.*

There were a lot of people saying 'the bugger's better out of it'. Because he was neither use nor ornament. He was a problem and a cost, an expense, a nuisance.

Maureen Baker OBE, designer of the Leeds Scheme: He was a lovely young man. He was like so many of the Nigerian students: young, bright, articulate. He was unlike many of them in that he was small. Very bright, very articulate, very good dancer. Didn't stand in the corner waiting, just came to the bar, had a drink, had a chat, spoke to other people there. He said he was a student.

David said he got into trouble at Armley and got badly beaten up. He fought back. He was very bitter over the drugs he'd been given. And my husband, who was a pharmacist, the first time he met him when he was eventually released, the first thing my husband said was, 'He looks as though he's had a lobotomy.' From the drugs. He was quite different.

He became far more visible. He didn't have a home to go to.

He would wander around Chapeltown, or round the bottom of Meanwood here. There was a factory run by a Gambian, and he would leave the back door open so when he was round that area he would have somewhere warm to sleep. I used to see him on the corner here at Hyde Park. St George's Crypt wouldn't have him. He couldn't sleep under the arches because the white vagrants would throw bottles at him. Hostels didn't want him. The other vagrants didn't want him.

That's why he slept in the Bridal House. He used to go there deliberately. It was almost as if he was challenging them. *I'm not going to run away and hide from you.* There was a streak of determination in him. He knew what would happen if he went in the Bridal House.

What we didn't get was justice; what we did get, I think, was a watershed in terms of relations between Leeds City Police, as it was then, and the African-Caribbean community. That was when the police realised they had to do something. That the community had changed and they had to change with it.

Max Farrar, former Chapeltown resident, sociologist and activist:
The media and the civic authorities were aware that there was a race problem in Leeds. And the establishment was extremely defensive and pretty much in denial about the whole thing. So when a police officer says race had nothing to do with it, I would frankly suggest that those police officers are either consciously or unconsciously in denial. You won't find anyone over the age of forty-five who doesn't remember it and they all speak of being absolutely chilled by it. *Scared. Alarm bells ringing.* An awful lot of people thought, *Oh hell, life in Britain.* Black activists in Chapeltown and one or two white supporters ensured that David's death was investigated and they attended the trial of Kitching and Ellerker. In the early 1970s the words 'Remember Oluwale' were painted on the wall on Chapeltown Road in huge white letters. I noted them every time I walked past. I'm sure David's death and the trial had some impact not just on black people and white radicals, but on the city as a whole. The police were forced to think again, at least at senior levels. But it wasn't till after the 1981 violent urban protests in Harehills and Chapeltown that things noticeably changed.

Leroy Phillips, formerly a psychiatric nurse at High Royds, now a senior probation officer: Probably if you look at it some things haven't changed for the better. If one goes back to the amount of black people who die in police custody: *has anything really changed?* Nothing seems to happen. At least thirty-odd years ago something did happen. But now nobody gets convicted of anything.

Basil Haddrell, ex-Scotland Yard detective, on the Oluwale investigation team: Some say the police failed to deal with Oluwale in a professional manner, and indeed evidence was adduced to support this claim. However, by the number of occasions he appeared at the magistrates' court, I can't understand why the social services didn't adopt a course of robust and proactive action to rehabilitate him. In the cold light of day it's my belief that they seriously failed in their duty towards him. I always considered Oluwale to be principally a victim of the society of that time, in that he fell between a number of support systems designed to assist persons who proved unable to help themselves.

Oluwale frequently became violent and acted in a socially unacceptable manner, but other than incidents of misguided verbal abuse there was no real evidence to suggest his demise was racially motivated.

Sad. Nobody would wish that on anybody. He was hounded.

There were about six or eight, I can't remember, probably six Leeds City telephone directories inside the coffin which – I can only surmise – had been left there by the undertaker to get rid of them. Which is a bit unfortunate because they weren't expecting them to be found eighteen months later. They were probably an inch and a half thick – it's a big city, Leeds. Clearly they shouldn't have been there – but this is life, you know.

David Stanton, ex-Leeds City Police: If you look at David Oluwale, he's a down-and-out and he's coloured. There was nothing going for him. And there wasn't a support system there. Everybody washed their hands of him. Social services certainly weren't helping him. David Oluwale had some responsibilities to himself, but whether he was capable of going down this accepted way of life . . . I don't think he was capable at that stage of looking after himself. He was homeless, he was destitute, he had nowhere to go.

He couldn't, or he didn't want to, help himself, probably because of his mental health problems or the fact of how other institutions had dealt with him.

He didn't need violence. He just needed to be firmly told to move and he would move.

I was told he used go round the caffs [round Kirkgate Market] and he probably did a bit of washing-up and they gave him food. But he didn't seem to have any means of support. I don't know whether he was drawing unemployment or any form of benefit or welfare. It was a low, lonely existence. He didn't seem, other than the times I saw him sitting on the bench outside the Holy Trinity Church, to be really talking to anybody. Just shuffling around. He was no problem. He used to acknowledge me.

Sometimes I feel if I had done a little bit more for him . . . But you don't know. He ended up how he ended up.

Gayb Adams, old friend: Nice person. Very naive. He would do anything for a laugh. Kick a fence down for a joke. Bit of craziness in him. If I'm wrong, God forgive me.

Tony Harney, *Yorkshire Evening Post* reporter: He was really liked. Very popular young bloke. There were not many people like David hanging about. And David used to sleep late in the morning, often till about nine, and barristers and people like that walking past used to leave money in the doorway. He was in no way an aggressive man; he liked to talk about religion and various things. He'd talk about where he came from. I think he was a bit bemused about how he'd arrived here. He asked about the Roman Catholic cathedral and whether he would be able to go in there and I told him many times that there'd be no door closed to him in a place like that. I know that David used to go in there to pray. David always struck me as being an educated Christian-type guy; all right, slightly confused I'm sure. He'd arrived in a country he couldn't equate with; he couldn't fit in. The startling thing about his death is, despite the fact that he was a nobody if you like, and sleeping in the doorway, today those sorts of people would be . . . well, I don't think there'd be a tremendous amount of sympathy when they'd passed on . . . but with David it was different.

I wouldn't have said for a second he was mentally ill. I think he was a guy who found himself in a country that was completely alien. Having said that, he wasn't an angry beggar. He was an extremely proud man. He was proud of where he came from. He was probably ashamed of what he was. If he had been offered positive help I'm sure he would have taken advantage of it.

Mrs H. L. Franks of Moortown, letter written to John Cobb QC, dated 21 November 1971: Oluwale would often sleep in the doorway of the shop next to my husband's premises in Thornton's Arcade, as it happened to be the largest doorway in the arcade. He impressed my husband as being essentially a very pathetic little man and quite inoffensive, that my husband always bade him goodnight. Had he been of the criminal and tough aggressive type he would not have felt comfortable in mind about leaving him next door to his premises all night in a quiet arcade.

Ann Ogbonson, wife of Christmas Ogbonson, old friend, in a November 1971 interview: Before he went into hospital he was just an ordinary man and worked for some months with my husband at West Yorkshire Foundries, Leeds. He came to my house several times and spoke to my husband in his own language quite often. He liked children and looked after mine. Then he disappeared and we did not find out for some time that he had gone into hospital.

David was a good man and a very lonely one and in the last few years of his life he weighed no more than about nine stones and was only a small man.

Even in these years he did work occasionally and at one time I saw him sweeping up leaves at Woodhouse Moor.

The last time I saw him was a few days before he died and he was sitting in the centre of Leeds eating a loaf of bread.

Joe Okogba, old friend: It was a shock for everyone. We couldn't believe it. He was easy-going and cheerful. We called him Yankee.

Bill Wheatley, one of the ambulance crew who recovered David Oluwale's body: I don't know whether his soul's resting in peace. I can't see it cos there's been no real justice done.

He had a right fetching smile if he smiled. It used to go from ear to ear. Oh aye. You know, when he smiled . . . he had a cheeky bloody grin wi' him.

Very quiet voice. 'You are my friend,' he used to say. 'You are my friend. You are good people.' And I always remember he used to nod his head, you know. 'You are good people.'

POSTSCRIPT

Not long before this book was first published in June 2007, I heard the news that Geoffrey Ellerker had died. I'd found out little of note about his life after prison – an internet search threw up an item from a 2001 edition of the *Northern Echo* which noted that the Ellerkers were amongst the participants at a Harrogate murder mystery weekend, a 'quiet, elderly couple' from north Leeds. But as a result of the book's publication I was contacted by a number of people wishing to share their stories and I discovered a little more about Ellerker. Other lingering questions were answered, and a few gaps in my knowledge filled.

On his release, Ellerker reverted to his original trade, finding a position at a small printing firm. There were some in the trade union who didn't want Ellerker re-admitted. But one senior member – a justice of the peace – brandished the rule book and argued that since he'd left the union with a clean bill there was no reason to bar him. Ellerker rose to a supervisory role but didn't endear himself to his fellow workers. 'He didn't appear ashamed and repentant. The feeling was that he'd got away lightly,' Tom Howley, a union representative, told me. When he was made redundant in the early 1980s, he was very much abandoned by the trade: 'If somebody was out of work the union would help, but it wasn't the case with Ellerker.'

At the court of public opinion, if not Leeds Assizes, Ellerker and Kitching were damned. I learned of another song sung at Elland Road, this one to the tune of 'I'm a Knock-Kneed Chicken':

'They're the boys from Millgarth and they don't care
They threw Oluwale in the River Aire
They don't give a bugger and they don't give a damn
They are the Millgarth . . . Boot Boys!'

Kenneth Kitching also presented a hard front to the world after his release. Ian Duhig, a poet from Leeds, who worked for a time at the same place as the former sergeant has vivid memories:

When I moved to Leeds in 1974, the city's reputation for coldness and brutality was of mythic dimensions even among poets. Martin Bell, who came and stayed until his death execrated the place in a sequence he called 'The City of Dreadful Something', which included the line parodying Marlowe, 'Why, Leeds is Hell, nor am I out of it!' Never in it, even on a visit, Patrick Kavanagh could nevertheless define despair as 'like winter alone in Leeds'.

My first job locally was as a casual labourer in Hepworth's cloth warehouse in Claypit Lane, just up from the Merrion Centre ('with its special subways for mugging' – Bell). In fact, my workmates were very friendly to me, only setting off the more their coldness to a security guard who worked there called Kitching, which I didn't understand. Then they told me his story. Apart from his crimes, which they felt shamed their city, they resented this soft job he'd walked straight into after a soft and short time in open prison. I looked at him more closely in the light of this. He was a shadow of the bully his ruined physique still suggested he was once good at, and his eyes were beginning to hollow out because of the drink. But we were all haunted by Oluwale, whose name would be hissed after him in much the same way that it was chanted at police by the Elland Road Kop, as abuse of abusive authority.

I worked a lot with homelessness agencies in Leeds after this time and the example of what happened to Oluwale lay before them all as demonstrating the depths to which the city's inhospitability could sink if it wasn't challenged. Kitching remained a different kind of example for me, an example demonstrating the truism that we become like what he hate: he treated Oluwale hatefully as a pariah, then Kitching was a hated pariah. And that is how he will be remembered in this city.

One of the few reassuring features of the Oluwale case was the tenacity with which Detective Chief Superintendent John Perkins and his team pursued the truth. Perkins's granddaughter contacted me after reading the book, and through this I was introduced to his younger son, John Victor Perkins, an officer in the Suffolk Constabulary, and Jennifer Warren, his eldest daughter. I'd shown their father to be an unusual character, and though they had no great quarrel with my portrait they wanted to tell me about the man of courage and compassion – the 'true copper' and devoted family man.

The case wasn't something the family talked about much at the time – one of the few memories of their father's stay in Leeds was that he'd been taken to see 'The Good Old Days' at the City Varieties Theatre where he'd met Eddie Waring – and the photographs and papers from that period had gathered dust in boxes.

It was a testing time in their father's career. In the summer of 1971, soon after completing the Oluwale investigation, Perkins was sent reluctantly to Hastings on another difficult assignment. Whilst there he was taken ill and had to seek psychiatric help, which in the police force at that time carried a stigma.

His son and daughter never discovered what had happened at Hastings, their father never talked about work in front of the family. But they got a sense from their mother that the Oluwale investigation had been more than usually stressful. According to their mother, Perkins felt himself under intense pressure to suppress the truth.

Never one of the lads, Perkins knew well that he risked turning himself into a hate figure at the Yard. The expectation was that you closed ranks and turned a blind eye to anything which might impugn the reputation of the police. Malpractice and corruption went unchecked. The Yard, which saw itself as the elite of the British police, was enmeshed in corruption scandals at the time, and its leadership, in the face of the evidence, indignantly refused to acknowledge the problem, and resented and obstructed investigations. Against this background, it was a major achievement to get the Oluwale case before a jury.

Perkins's sympathy for Oluwale also set him apart. His daughter showed me a letter from Alderman Jowitt, Chairman of the Leeds Watch Committee, to the Commissioner of the Metropolitan Police, in which Oluwale was referred to as 'an individual who has brought considerable opprobrium on the police officers of Leeds.' So why was Perkins, this upright Freemason from the Home Counties, so committed to securing justice for a Nigerian vagrant, when most of his colleagues believed that he'd brought his fate on himself?

It was simply that the bullying of a lone man offended his sense of what a policeman ought to be. Policing, in Perkins's view, wasn't just about thief-taking, protecting property and street-cleaning. I was shown a paper Perkins had written on police/public relations some years before the Oluwale case and in it he described the ideal officer as a 'protector of the weak, shield against the oppressor'. He took that very seriously.

There are also clues from his early life. Just before Christmas 1935, when he was ten, he and his three brothers were sent to the Fegan's Children's Home in Stony Stratford, Buckinghamshire, after his mother left his father; he was there for the remainder of his childhood and joined the navy in 1943. Perkins never talked about these difficult early years, but he displayed no bitterness towards his parents and later in life he made a home for his mother in the annexe to his own house. After his retirement from the police on grounds of ill-health in 1974, he had a part-time job working with Suffolk social services in the areas of fostering and adoption. He was fifty-one when he died from coronary heart disease in 1977.

Further information came to me about Oluwale, though much of it was depressing.

I met Tom Booth after giving a reading in Ilkley. Booth spent almost the entirety of his working life at Menston and High Royds Hospital – he started his training as a seventeen-year old in 1954, retired in 1994 – and got to know Oluwale on the refractory ward.

Menston was a bleak place in the postwar years, Booth admits: staff were identified by white coats and big bunches of keys, patients were decked out in shapeless clothes, all browns and blacks, with the number of their ward stitched inside; baths were taken no more than once a week; food was nutritious but not enticing, a chunk of 'sylum duff was a fixture at dinner times. On Ward 8 (later Hazelwood), meals were eaten with spoons and patients couldn't leave the table until they'd all been handed in.

Some patients assisted staff with menial tasks around the ward. Dominoes, cards and snooker and, from the late 1950s, television, helped pass the time, though some simply curled up at their favourite spots, under the full-sized billiards table, on the window sill or next to the radiators. Patients exercised by walking round an 'airing court', with nurses keeping points duty at the railings. Newspapers provided some contact with the outside world: if the dominant charge nurse was from Bradford it would be the *Telegraph and Argus*, if Leeds the *Evening Post*. Special buses brought in relatives twice a week. 'They came and they went, not taking a great deal of interest. Nobody questioned care or treatments.' Booth doesn't recall anyone visiting Oluwale.

Oluwale was one of those who didn't participate in the activities of the ward, being content to park himself by a radiator with his coat over his head, shutting out the world. 'There was a space around him; people didn't approach him. He drifted through the day, never asked for anything. He would respond to 'Breakfast', 'Lunch', 'Cigarettes, lads'. He was isolated. We didn't know where he came from, we didn't know his background.'

Ward 8 wasn't somewhere for sensitive souls. In this closed, locked environment, fights often broke out. The weak might be bullied out of their cigarettes – the currency – by those at the top of the pecking order. Verbal insults were an accepted part of ward banter. 'One patient had very odd eyes,' Booth recalled, 'and he would get, *come on you marble-eyed bastard.*' In all of Oluwale's time at Menston and High Royds, Booth recalls only three black patients, including a Jamaican swimming champion. In the mid-1950s Oluwale was the only one, Booth thinks. The verbal abuse he received was the trigger for many fights.

Booth remembers the biting incidents involving the nurse Sam Graham, which Eric Dent would refer to in his police statement. (Booth told me that Dent's appearance in the witness box was regarded by staff as a cynical move to ingratiate himself with the police.) Booth witnessed two violent incidents at first-hand. Oluwale was sleeping under his bed when he should have been in the day room, and as a nurse bent down to stir him he grabbed his throat and didn't release his grip until another managed to drag him off. The nurse was 'going blue' and had to be resuscitated. It was an impulsive reaction not a malicious attack, Booth says. The second incident came one mealtime when Oluwale became involved in an argument with a fellow patient, Harry James Fox. Oluwale got a Melaware cup over Fox's nose and mouth and slammed it hard, shattering the cup and taking off a piece of his nose. Oluwale was bundled off to one of the side rooms, the 'traps'. After being let out he would have been put at one of the special tables reserved for patients who needed close watch, the tables referred to as 'Valley Parade' after the Bradford City football ground.

Oluwale's physical condition deteriorated during the long years locked away. Booth can't remember anything of his treatment, but he recalls him 'shuffling instead of walking' towards the end. 'They all deteriorated. We never discharged anyone 'condition treated', they were always discharged 'relieved'.'

Oluwale's death and the trial were the talk of the hospital for a while, Booth recalled. 'He's one of our patients. We expected him back in, and there he is – bottom of the river. *Who's caring for people when we send them into the community? What are we discharging them to?* But then it was a shrug of the shoulders and here comes another, there's a bed going to be filled again. And he was quickly lost.'

* * *

I'd heard much about John 'Slim' Otse from Gayb, and in November 2007 met him at his Birmingham flat. Otse endured a torrid journey to England as a stowaway, and remarkably was only twelve when he landed in 1948, though he was tall and passed for much older. As a younger boy in Lagos he'd supported himself by hustling on the streets, anything from writing letters for the illiterate to fixing sailors up with women, and this resourcefulness would be called on in Leeds. He took up boxing to protect himself on the streets and got the name Battlin' Slim. He wasn't one to be pushed around: if anyone refused him entry to a public place he would give a passionate speech about his brother fighting for King and Country in Burma. None of it was true.

Otse knew Oluwale at his best and his worst. He recalls a quiet man, unhappy with the dirty jobs he was doing, keen to go to night-school and improve his writing. He remembers someone who lived for the weekend. 'Anywhere where there was a party, you must find Oluwale.' Otse remembers him, broad smile, girl by his side, drink in his hand – 'he don't look for trouble'. He was well-dressed and walked with a bit of a swing which made people look twice. He would amuse his friends with his 'Yankee' routine. 'Say man, do you dig it?' he'd say as he strutted around with his thumbs tucked into the back of his trousers.

Otse told me that he didn't know that Oluwale had been sent to Menston. When he re-appeared in Leeds he was a changed man – 'he'd started to disintegrate'; even his English had deteriorated. He tried hard to look decent but struggled to keep himself clean. Otse tried to find Oluwale accommodation and work, without success. He was making a living selling African food door-to-door and Oluwale would sometimes go along for the ride. Most of his old friends didn't want to get involved. 'Oluwale was not that bad. He needed people. When you come out from a place like that you want people to start building your confidence again. You want people to take you around, be with you from time to time, to just say *come on let's go for a walk*. But no.'

In 1971, Otse and a few friends, moved by the plight of their friend, started The Institute for Nigerian Welfare. He showed me the minutes of their second meeting, held two days after the close of the trial, at the Leeds home of one of the group. There were pledges to help destitute and 'unaided' Nigerians by setting up a hostel, commitments to fight against racial discrimination and to provide legal advice to those in trouble. But it was to be a rare moment of solidarity, the sense of urgency soon faded and nothing got off the ground. 'The blame should rest squarely on us as well, because we didn't do what we should have done for him, all living in a foreign country,' Otse says. 'I felt guilty. If we had only got ourselves together we could have been able to save Oluwale's life.'

It's too early to say whether the reawakening of interest in the case in Leeds will inspire any deep civic soul-searching, though some have adopted his cause. A committee was assembled in 2007 by Max Farrar, a sociologist at Leeds Metropolitan University, in the hope of persuading those who control the city's public space to allow a memorial. Farrar says, 'Its ethos is to learn the lessons of the past in order to reconcile the city and help the movement towards racial and social justice'. The campaign is gathering momentum.

St George's Crypt are planning their own memorial, to be sited at Faith Lodge, an annexe of the Crypt where Oluwale lived for a short time. Martin Patterson, the fundraiser, tells me that the memorial will be situated in the garden and that Oluwale's name will appear alongside other homeless and rootless men who died tragically early.

A memorial of a different kind will be the adaptation of this book for the stage. West Yorkshire Playhouse have commissioned the acclaimed British-Nigerian playwright Oladipo Agboluaje, and the play is planned to open in 2009, forty years on from Oluwale's death. West Yorkshire Playhouse occupies the large site where Quarry Hill Flats once was, little more than a two minute walk from where the old Millgarth station stood.

Soon after the book was first published, Ian Duhig wrote the poem 'God Comes Home', and he has kindly allowed me to include it here –

'God Comes Home'

This poem was written in the context of Leeds's celebrations of the 800th anniversary of the granting of its charter, and sought to reflect that by evoking Medieval Latin and old terms for mendicants. The 'Via Negativa' is one of the mystical roads to God, as the name implies, through what and where He is not. The Christian items found on Oluwale's body seemed to imply religion was still important to him, and the title of the second part, 'Least of Brethren', is an obvious Biblical reference although 'Jericho' in English isn't, where it means somewhere indeterminately remote – '. . . a place far distant and out of the way' (OED) – like Leeds, which was attempting to remedy this during Oluwale's time with major road-building projects, destroying much of itself in the process.

I Via Negativa

'The Middle Latin 'wargus' – i.e. 'expulsus' or 'stranger' – is also the same as 'wolf'; and thus the two conceptions – that of the wild beast to be hunted down and that of the man to be treated as a wild beast – are intimately associated.' Hamilton Grierson, *The Silent Trade*

> Not circumcellion, gyrovague or beggar
> but Lagos Christian College graduate.
> Not abbey-lubber but job-seeker.

> Not City of God but Motorway City.
> Not office career but slaughterhouse shifts.
> Not faint heart but weak stomach.

> Not taken fighting the good fight
> but in a brawl over food.
> Not Ave Maria but Black Maria.

Not penance of a decade of the rosary
but gaol then a decade in asylums.
Not Church Latin but medical Latin.

Not demonic visions but psychotic episodes.
Not Catechism but questionnaires.
Not Pentecost tongues but echolalia.

Not the African Fathers,
but 'the African Mind'.
Not the Divine Spark but ECT.

Not the sleep of the just or the mystic
but Insulin Coma Therapy.
Not Cloud of Unknowing but Largactil fog.

Not absolution with a blessing
but discharge, condition untreatable.
Not halfway house or hostel but the streets.

Not confessional boxes but cardboard boxes.
Not the Holy Eucharist
but the cold host of a Leeds moon.

II Least of Brethren

'The first and most constant problem with the City of Leeds is to find it. There never was a more faceless city or a more deceptive one. It hasn't a face because it has too many faces, all of them different.' Patrick Nuttgens, *Leeds: The Back to front, Inside out, Upside down City*

For hostel work, by chance I found
this back to front, inside out,
upside down contrary place –

its name alone's an argument:
Urbs Leodensis Mystica,
as lost as 'Jericho' in English.

A blind man, Metcalf, made the road
from my house now to a city centre
you'd guess blind men were redesigning;

old graffiti on a Chapeltown wall,
long since knocked down, still hangs in the air:
REMEMBER OLUWALE. A Yoruba name,

'God Comes Home' – to God's Own County,
which garbled it on forms and notes;
'Ally', 'Ussywale', 'Allowalo', 'Olly' –

we argued about it, got it wrong,
inside out, back to front:
he should've been at home in Leeds.

Then two policemen – old school Law –
showed him a stranger face of town,
one shopping tourists never see;

they turned his whole world upside down
then into the River Aire, his pockets
leaking rosary beads like oxygen . . .

but stranger still, a copper shopped them;
lodge brothers shunned them; they went down
and Leeds Kop songs remembered David Oluwale

SOURCES AND ACKNOWLEDGEMENTS

This book is based on a combination of archival research and interviews with those close to events. Information about the assaults on David Oluwale was derived exclusively from contemporary police statements. Police officers who assisted me in my research, in response to an advertisement in *The Beat* and also direct correspondence, spoke mainly in general terms about the impact of the Oluwale case on force morale, and in most cases did not (because they could not) provide any new information on the assaults or the allegation of manslaughter. The main purpose of these interviews was to give me a better understanding of policing, and in particular what it was like to have been a Leeds City Police officer in the 1950s and 60s ('The Old Law' chapter is derived mainly from these interviews).

Material in the National Archives in the copyright of the Metropolitan Police is reproduced by kind permission of the Metropolitan Police Authority.

PRIMARY SOURCES

I Manuscript Sources

Government and official papers
National Archives, Kew, London
'The Death of David Oluwale', case papers: MEPO 26/55; MEPO 26/56; MEPO 26/57; MEPO 26/61; DPP 2/4910; DPP 2/4911; DPP 2/4912; DPP 2/4766; ASSI 45/1057; ASSI 45/1058

Immigration/Race Relations: 'Working Party on Coloured People seeking Employment in the United Kingdom, 1953', CO 1028/22; 'Public Attitude to Immigrants and the Race Relations Act 1968', HO 376/147; 'The Police and Coloured Communities: comments on the replies to the Home Office circular of 31 July 1969', HO 242/75

Menston/High Royds: hospital inspectors' reports, BN 37/88

Repatriation: AST 7/1928; CO 876/226; CO 1028/42; T 227/2460; T 227/3381

Stowaways, Colonial: HO 344/101; HO 344/35; AST 7/1183; FO 369/4364–6; CO 1028/22

West Yorkshire Archive Service, Wakefield
Leeds City Police:
Annual Reports on the Policing of the City of Leeds
Occurrence Books (1953): WYP/LE/A90/211-15
'Report of a Working Party on Unit Beat Policing and Related Matters in Leeds' (October 1969): WYP/LE/A137/251

Menston Asylum:
Register of Patients: C488 7/93

Private papers
Church Mission Society, Waterloo Road, London
Report of the Senior Education Officer for Lagos (1942)

Hatfield Court, Leominster, Herefordshire
Jeremy Sandford papers (private collection)
Correspondence between Mrs Dorothy Ellerker and Martin Wright, Director of The Howard League for Penal Reform
Prison welfare and probation reports of David Oluwale

II Audio-Visual

Film/video

Injustice (2001), directed by Ken Fero

Mental Health Testimony Archive at the British Library, particularly video C905/48/01-04

Photographs

p. 120: exposed pauper coffin, 9 December 1970, Killingbeck Cemetery, Leeds

p. 157: Bridal House from The Headrow, city centre of Leeds

p. 161: Bridal House doorway

p. 171: John Peters' furniture shop, front and entrance, Lands Lane, city centre of Leeds, where, on the night of 17/18 April 1969, David Oluwale was last positively sighted alive

p. 187: River Aire at Knostrop, near Leeds, showing the weir and, a little further downstream, the bend at which point David Oluwale's body was recovered on 4 May 1969

p. 236: nameplate on coffin lid – David Oluwale

Reproduced by kind permission of the Metropolitan Police Authority

Taped interviews and conversations

Africans in Leeds and Yorkshire

Gabriel (Gayb) Adams, 6 June 2005, 29 November 2005; Vincent Enyori, 27 May 2005; Joe Okogba, 9 June 2005; Daniel Okpovie, telephone conversation, 5 June 2005.

Albert Johanneson and Leeds United

Freddy Apfel, 29 November 2005; Peter Lorimer, 29 November 2005.

David Oluwale, local impact of

Bernard Atha, 2 June 2005; Maureen Baker, 10 August 2004, 22 October 2004; Tony Harney, 14 October 2004, 23 February 2006; Tony Stanley (Leeds Racial Equality Council), 27 July 2004.

David Oluwale, criminal investigation and trial

Judge Peter Fingret, 12 August 2004, 13 August 2004, 27 October

2004; Gilbert Gray QC, 20 May 2005; Basil Haddrell, 3 and 7 February 2006; Judge Donald Herrod QC, 5 June 2005; Judge Arthur Myerson QC, 7 June 2005; Ronnie Teeman, 23 April 2004, 7 May 2004; Bill Wheatley, 23 August 2006.

Homeless in Leeds

Don Blackmore, telephone conversation, 7 October 2004; Bill Kilgallon, 12 September 2005; Martin Patterson, 6 October 2004.

Leeds City Police

Chris Abbott, 18 October 2004; Frank Atkinson, 11 November 2004; Maurice Brayson, 10 November 2004, 27 May 2005; Mel Bunting, 28 January 2005; Steve Hall and Albert Sedman, 27 January 2005; Arthur Hawkesworth, 13 October 2004; Chris Helme, 5 August 2004; Ronnie Holliday, 15 October 2004; Brian Lonsdale, 11 October 2004 and (with Charlie Mawson) 2 November 2004; Terry MacLean, 29 April 2004; David Ogle, 20 October 2004; Roy Pledger, 4 August 2004; Harold Robinson, 22 October 2004; Dave Sowden, 21 October 2004; Dave Stanton, 29 December 2005.

Legal Leeds

Freddy Apfel, 31 May 2005; Judge Barrington Black, 26 October 2004; Wifred Hoyle (aftercare officer), telephone conversation, 3 May 2006; Judge Vivian Hurwitz, 2 June 2005; Judge Alan Simpson, 29 May 2005.

Political Leeds

Owen Hartley (University of Leeds political scientist), 16 November 2005; Michael Meadowcroft (former Leeds Liberal MP), 27 June 2006; Alison Ravetz (Leeds Metropolitan University), 29 November 2005; Cllr Keith Wakefield, 27 June 2006.

III Printed Primary Sources

Butterworth, E., *Immigrants in West Yorkshire* (London, 1967)

Carothers, J. C., *The African Mind in Health and Disease: A Study in Ethnopsychiatry* (Geneva, 1953)

City of Leeds, 'First Review of City Development Programme', Draft Report of Survey (August 1967)

City of Leeds, *Planning Tomorrow's Leeds* (1973)

City of Leeds, *Project Leeds* (Cheltenham, 1972)

Heap, A., and Brears, P., *Leeds Describ'd: Eye Witness Accounts of Leeds 1534–1905* (Derby, 1993)

Humphry, D., 'Was it a tragedy of errors at Leeds?', *Sunday Times*, 3 August 1969

Humphry, D., 'The Oluwale Mystery', *New Statesman*, 15 December 1972

Humphry, D., and John, G., *Because They're Black* (Harmondsworth, 1971)

Kila, A. A., *Òwe Yoruba in Proverbs* (London, 2003)

Lambo, Adeoye, 'A Report on the Study of Social and Health Problems of Nigerian Students in Britain and Ireland' (London, n/d *c.*1960)

Leeds Civic Trust, *Let's Put Leeds-Upon-Aire* (Leeds, 1973)

Nuttgens, P., *Leeds: The Back to front Inside out Upside down City* (Otley, 1979)

Owomoyela, Oyekan, *A Kì í: Yorùbá Proscriptive and Prescriptive Proverbs* (Lanham, 1988)

Pevsner, N., *Yorkshire, The West Riding* (Harmondsworth, 1967 revised edn)

Phillips, R., 'The Death of One Lame Darkie', *Race Today* (January 1972)

Rolph, C. H., 'The Man Nobody Wanted', *Times Literary Supplement*, 8 August 1975

Sandford, J., *Smiling David: The Story of David Oluwale* (London, 1974)

Thompson, B., *Portrait of Leeds* (Leeds, 1971)

Thompson, Ces, *Born on the Wrong Side* (Durham, 1995)

Wade, D., *Yorkshire Survey: A Report on Community Relations in Yorkshire* (Leeds, 1971)

SELECT SECONDARY SOURCES

Bagchi, R., and Rogerson, P., *The Unforgiven: The Story of Don Revie's Leeds United* (London, 2003 edn)

Baker, P., *Urbanization and Political Change: The Politics of Lagos, 1917–1967* (Berkeley and Los Angeles, California, and London, 1974)

Bannister, A., *In Splendid Isolation: A Short History of High Royds Hospital, the former West Riding Pauper Lunatic Asylum at Menston* (Leeds, 2005)

Bennett, A., *Untold Stories* (London, 2005)

Briggs, A., *Victorian Cities* (London, 1963)

Clay, E. W. (ed.), *The Leeds Police 1836–1974* (Leeds, 1974)

Cohen, S., *States of Denial: Knowing about Atrocities and Suffering* (Cambridge, 2001 edn)

Douglas, M., *How Institutions Think* (London, 1987 edn)

Douglas, M., *Purity and Danger: An analysis of concept of pollution and taboo* (London, 2004 edn)

Foucault, M., *Madness and Civilisation: A History of Insanity in the Age of Reason* (London and New York, 2005 edn)

Fraser, D. (ed.), *A History of Modern Leeds* (Manchester, 1980) [in particular, the essays by Gordon Forster and Owen Hartley]

Hansen, R., *Citizenship and Immigration in Post-War Britain* (Oxford, 2000)

Hunt, T., *Building Jerusalem: The Rise and Fall of the Victorian City* (London, 2004)

Loader, I., and Mulcahy, A., *Policing and the Condition of England: Memory, Politics, and Culture* (Oxford, 2003)

McCulloch, J., *Colonial Psychiatry and the African Mind* (Cambridge, 1995)

Peace, D., *The Damned Utd* (London, 2006)

Peil, M., *Lagos: The City and the People* (London, 1991)

Phillips, M., and Phillips, T., *Windrush, The Irresistible Rise of Multi-Racial Britain* (London, 1999 edn)

Reiner, R., *The Blue-Coated Workers: A sociological study of police unionism* (Cambridge, 1978)

Sadowsky, J., *Imperial Bedlam: Institutions of Madness in Colonial Southwest Nigeria* (Berkeley and Los Angeles, California, 1999)

Sandbrook, D., *White Heat: A History of Britain in the Swinging Sixties* (London, 2006)

Sumner, C. (ed.), *Censure, Politics and Criminal Justice* (Milton Keynes and Philadelphia, 1990)

Vasili, P., 'The Right Kind of Fellows: Nigerian Football Tourists as Agents of Europeanization', *International Journal of the History of Sport*, 11, 2 (August 1994)

Vasili, P., 'Colonialism and Football: The First Nigerian Tour to Britain', *Race and Class*, 36, 4 (1995)

Winder, R., *Bloody Foreigners: The Story of Immigration to Britain* (London, 2004)

Young, J., *The Exclusive Society: Social Exclusion, Crime and Difference in Late Modernity* (London, 1999)

The author is grateful for permission to use lines from the following: 'Still I Rise', copyright © 1978 by Maya Angelou, from *And Still I Rise* by Maya Angelou. Used by permission of Random House, Inc.

Every effort has been made to obtain necessary permissions with reference to copyright material. The publishers apologise if inadvertently any sources remain unacknowledged.

Special thanks to Robin Robertson for commissioning this book and for wise and inspired editing.

For believing that the story of David Oluwale ought to be told and for his creative input, I would like to thank my agent Peter Straus.

A very special thanks to Keith Hayward for his friendship over the years, as well as for the many helpful criminological suggestions and insights given during my research.

David Peace has inspired and encouraged me all the way and helped me to look at Leeds in a different way.

To all at Jonathan Cape, particularly Chlöe Johnson-Hill, Alex Bowler and Matt Broughton. Thanks to the staff at Rogers, Coleridge and White literary agency, especially Rowan Routh for advice on early drafts.

I would like to thank all those who were interviewed in the course of the research. I am deeply grateful to Gabriel ('Gayb') Adams, Peter Fingret, Basil Haddrell, Tony Harney and Ronnie Teeman, without whom the book couldn't have been written.

Thanks to the staff of the Leeds Local Studies Library, Sheffield Local Studies Library, the West Yorkshire Archive Service at Wakefield, and to Sue King of the National Police Library, Bramshill.

I am grateful to 'Dice' George for unearthing the Jeremy Sandford papers and making them available. I am grateful to West Yorkshire Police for allowing me to quote from Leeds City Police sources lodged at Wakefield.

For the map of Leeds, I am very grateful to Alan Campbell and Marcus Aspden.

For research assistance during my years away from the UK, I am very grateful to Joy Collier and James Tall. Thanks also to John Barraclough, Peter Bond, Michael Brown, Joyce Callaghan, Fr Martin Carroll, Paul Chatterton, Carol Doyle, Edwin and Roger from the Engine pub, Robert Endeacott, Max Farrar, Paul Fletcher, Gordon Forster, Arthur France, Murray Freedman, Carl Galvin, Julie Geaney, Abosede George, James Henderson, Brian Higgins, Alicia Johanneson, Lisa Lindsay, William Miller, Denise Mina, David Mosley, Russell Murray, Clara Odamo, Tom Palmer, Caryl Phillips, Leroy Phillips, John Quayle, Sasha Roseneil, Amanda Telfer, Glyn Wide, Colin Wilson and my former 'History of Crime' students. Katrina Honeyman shared her expertise on the Leeds clothing industry. The late Maurice Beresford taught me much about Leeds.

Thanks to Kerry and Warren Barner, Elaine Conroy, Eleanor Crisp, Jo Ede, John Leigh, Calum Murray, Andy Savage, Dom Stankiewicz, Jenny Williams, Jim and Lucia, Daniel and Deborah, Frank and Cassie, Marcello and Jane and Alex, the Rainsford family, friends from Moscow and Istanbul, and all my old friends (reunited) from the Bar Convent, York.

Thanks to all my family, Lancashire and Yorkshire sides (and London-Italian), especially to Marcus and Adele for their support over the years, and to Maureen Greenwood. To Ellie and Chris Anderson, thanks for your belief in the book, for your close reading of the typescript, and for all your moral and practical support along the way. To Dad, I owe so much.

This book is for Sarah.

www.vintage-books.co.uk